DELAWARE BIBLE RECORDS

Volume 4

Donald M. Hehir

HERITAGE BOOKS
2011

HERITAGE BOOKS
AN IMPRINT OF HERITAGE BOOKS, INC.

Books, CDs, and more—Worldwide

For our listing of thousands of titles see our website
at
www.HeritageBooks.com

Published 2011 by
HERITAGE BOOKS, INC.
Publishing Division
100 Railroad Ave. #104
Westminster, Maryland 21157

Copyright © 1994 Donald M. Hehir

Other Heritage Books by Donald M. Hehir:

Carolina Families: A Bibliography of Books about North and South Carolina Families

CD: Delaware Bible Records, Volumes 1-4
Donald O. Virdin and Donald M. Hehir

Delaware Bible Records, Volume 4
[The previous three volumes of this series were compiled by Donald O. Virdin.]

Georgia Families: A Bibliographic Listing of Books about Georgia Families

Kentucky Families: A Bibliographic Listing of Books about Kentucky Families

Missouri Family Histories and Genealogies: A Bibliography

Ohio Families: A Bibliographic Listing of Books about Ohio Families

Tennessee Families: A Bibliography of Books about Tennessee Families

All rights reserved. No part of this book may be reproduced or transmitted in any form or by any means, electronic or mechanical, including photocopying, recording or by any information storage and retrieval system without written permission from the author, except for the inclusion of brief quotations in a review.

International Standard Book Numbers
Paperbound: 978-0-7884-0134-3
Clothbound: 978-0-7884-8694-4

PREFACE

This book, Delaware Bible Records Volume 4, is dedicated to those members of the Delaware Chapters of the Daughters of the American Revolution who, over a period of thirty-one years (1943-1974), located, copied, typed and bound into thirteen volumes the most complete collection of Delaware Bible Records ever assembled. As a result of their devotion to this task, it has been possible to print these books.

When the first of the Bible records were prepared for publication, I secured the approval of the head of the DAR in Delaware, Ms. Elizabeth Hancock. She was delighted that some honor would be given to the ladies who did this work and she was glad to see the material published.

It might be noted (insofar as I know) that there are only three sets of the original DAR Bible Records available to the public. All are typed sets. One is in the DAR Library in Washington, D. C. Another is in the Delaware State Archives Library in Dover, Delaware. The third set is in the Historical Society of Delaware Library in Wilmington, Delaware.

The original thirteen volume set of DAR Bible Records includes not only Bible records that have been located by DAR members, but also some narrative family histories, which were written by members of the family or others. Some of the Bible records were gathered originally from the adjacent States of Pennsylvania and Maryland with a very few from other States. For various reasons, the selections published were not made in any chronological or alphabetical order. They were originally selected because they were clear, concise, and understandable. Some records have charts with only names and no dates. Information like that, although it might be helpful, was not generally included in the Heritage Books published because it was believed that it might mislead or confuse the reader.

The book, Delaware Bible Records Volume 4, as the reader will note is being compiled by another author, Donald M. Hehir. Several of his books have been published by Heritage Books, Inc. and they all show the scholarship, knowledge, skill and dedication that he brings to the task.

July 1994   Donald O. Virdin

TABLE OF CONTENTS

JOHN BEARD FAMILY BIBLE RECORDS	4
EPHRAIM BLACKWELL & MARY ANN WOOLSEY BIBLE RECORDS	9
THEODORE JEFFERSON BLACKWELL FAMILY BIBLE RECORDS	10
BOULDEN FAMILY BIBLE RECORDS	12
BRAINARD-GILMORE BIBLE RECORDS	14
BROOKS 1810 BIBLE RECORDS	14
BROOKS 1850 BIBLE RECORDS	15
BROOKS 1829 BIBLE RECORDS	16
CHARLES BRYAN FAMILY BIBLE RECORDS	17
THOMAS CAZIER FAMILY BIBLE RECORDS	18
ROBERT CHAMBERLAIN FAMILY BIBLE RECORDS	20
SIDNEY and TERESA PRICE CHANDLEE BIBLE RECORDS	23
JOSHUA CLAYTON FAMILY BIBLE RECORDS	25
WILLIAM CLINGEN & DR. WARWICK MILLER FAMILY BIBLE RECORDS	27
COLLINS, McALLEN & HOLLOWAY FAMILY BIBLE RECORDS	28
CORNOG FAMILY BIBLE RECORDS	30
CROOKS FAMILY BIBLE RECORDS	32
CURTIS CRUMPTON FAMILY BIBLE RECORDS	35
DeHAVEN FAMILY RECORDS	38
DICKEY FAMILY BIBLE RECORDS	40
DIXON FAMILY BIBLE RECORDS	42
DORSEY FAMILY BIBLE RECORDS	43
ERNEST FAMILY BIBLE RECORDS	46
DR. JOHN EVANS FAMILY BIBLE RECORD	47
ROBERT EVANS FAMILY BIBLE RECORD	48
EVANS - SPRINGER BIBLE RECORDS	52
FOULK FAMILY BIBLE RECORD	54
FRAZIER - CUBBAGE FAMILY BIBLE RECORD	56
FRAZIER - EMORY FAMILY BIBLE RECORD	59
AGNES FRAZIER REDGRAVE FAMILY BIBLE RECORD	61
GALLAHER FAMILY BIBLE RECORD	62
JOHN EVANS GALLAHER-ANNIE CHANDLEE FAMILY BIBLE	63
ROBERT GALLAHER FAMILY BIBLE RECORD	64
WILLIAM M. GAMBLE FAMILY BIBLE RECORD	65
GARRETT FAMILY BIBLE RECORD	66
REV. GEORGE GILLISPIE FAMILY BIBLE RECORD	68
GOTTIER - BOOTH - ALDRICH FAMILY BIBLE RECORD	76
HANSON FAMILY BIBLE RECORD	79
ANDREW & LYDIA (McCAULEY) HARVEY FAMILY BIBLE	83
JOHN HAYES FAMILY BIBLE RECORD	84

HENKEL FAMILY BIBLE RECORDS	87
JOHN HERDMAN FAMILY BIBLE RECORDS	92
EMLEY HOLOCOMBE FAMILY BIBLE RECORDS	93
JAMES HOOPES FAMILY BIBLE RECORDS	96
HULL FAMILY BIBLE RECORDS	97
JAMES JACOBUS FAMILY BIBLE RECORDS	98
JONES - PATTEN FAMILY BIBLE RECORDS	98
JONES - GILLISPY FAMILY BIBLE RECORDS	102
CHARLES LEAK FAMILY BIBLE RECORDS	103
JAMES LINDSAY FAMILY BIBLE RECORDS	105
THOMAS AND MARY MACKEY FAMILY BIBLE RECORDS	105
DANIEL McCAULEY FAMILY BIBLE RECORDS	106
JAMES AND SARAH ANN McCAULEY FAMILY BIBLE RECORDS	108
[McCAULEY] - BAKER FAMILY BIBLE RECORDS	109
ALEXANDER McDONALD FAMILY BIBLE RECORDS	113
ROBERT MONTGOMERY FAMILY BIBLE RECORDS	114
DANIEL McKINLEY & MARY S. ERWIN FAMILY BIBLE RECORDS	115
JOHN McINTIRE FAMILY BIBLE RECORDS	116
JAMES McKEAN FAMILY BIBLE RECORDS	117
THE PRICE-BLACKWELL FAMILY BIBLE RECORDS	119
THE JOHN PRICE FAMILY BIBLE RECORDS	120
THE JACOB PRICE FAMILY BIBLE RECORDS	121
THE RAWLINGS FAMILY BIBLE RECORDS	122
REED-SIPPLE FAMILY BIBLE RECORDS	123
JAMES REYNOLDS FAMILY RECORDS	126
REYNOLDS - COLE FAMILY BIBLE RECORDS	127
ANDREW COLE REYNOLDS FAMILY BIBLE RECORDS	128
THOMAS SAWYER & MARGARET LEWDEN FAMILY BIBLE RECORDS	130
THOMAS ALEXANDER SMITH FAMILY BIBLE RECORDS	133
WILLIAM SMITH FAMILY BIBLE RECORDS	135
THOMAS STEEL FAMILY BIBLE RECORDS	139
SAMUEL VAIL FAMILY BIBLE RECORDS	143
ALEXANDER WILSON FAMILY BIBLE RECORDS	143
STEPHEN WILSON FAMILY BIBLE RECORDS	144
JOHN WITT FAMILY BIBLE RECORDS	147
THOMAS WOLLASTON FAMILY BIBLE RECORDS	147
WOOD - JENNINGS FAMILY BIBLE RECORDS	149
WOODWARD-LYNAM-JARMON FAMILY BIBLE RECORDS	151
[WOODWARD] - LYNAM FAMILY RECORDS	153
SAMUEL YOUNG DESCENDANTS' RECORDS	158

DELAWARE BIBLE RECORDS

JOHN BEARD FAMILY BIBLE RECORDS

Marriages:

Hans Hamilton married Margaret Morris [in] Belfast.
James Hamilton [son of Hans] married Mary [Maiden Name Not Given].
John Beard married Esther Hamilton.
Hugh Beard, son of John, married Margaret Lawson.
Thomas Hughes married Elizabeth Gatchell.
John Moody, son of James Moody married Elizabeth.
William Moody, son of John Moody, married Jane.
Elisha Hughes, son of Thomas, married Mary [Maiden Name Not Given].
John Beard, son of Hugh, married Elizabeth Moody in 1748.
Joseph Carroll and Mary Hughes were married December 29, 1779 (Cecil County, Maryland Marriage Licenses, P. 3.)
Hugh Beard, son of John and Elizabeth Beard, married Mary Hughes Carroll in July, 1799.

[Children of Hugh Beard & Mary Hughes Carroll:]
    Eliza Beard married Richard Simpers.
    Marion Beard [first name also shown as Marie] married Francis Jervis December 30, 1823 (Cecil County Marriage Licenses, p. 48.
    Margaret Beard married Robert Walmsley.
    Rachel Beard married Daniel McCauley.
    Sarah Beard married James McCauley.
    Jane Ann Beard married Samuel McCullough.
Mary Eliza Jervis, daughter of Francis and Marie Beard Jervis, married Samuel Benoni Wright January 20, 1851, Cecil County Marriages Licenses, p. 48. [sic].

Marriages: (Cont'd).

[Children of Samuel Benoni and Mary Jervis Wright:]
    Samuel John Wright married Isabel Pilling June 29, 1880 in Newark, Del.
    Mary Eliza Wright married Andrew Fischer.
    Hugh Beard Wright married Kate Adel Lewis.
    Catherine Brown Wright married Harry S. Golden
    Caroline Clark Wright married Clarence Short.
[Children of Samuel John Wright and Isabel Pilling:]
    John Pilling Wright married Elizabeth Johnson.
    Norris Nathan Wright married Fleta Robertson.
    Ernest Brinton Wright married Marion Lee Harrington.
    Elizabeth Kelley Wright married Benjamin Franklin Proud.
Ernest Brinton Jr. married Marjory Cowherd June 25, 1936 in Columbia, Virginia.

Births:

John Beard was born in 1621.
Hugh Beard [the immigrant] was born 1676.
John Beard, son of Hugh, was born in 1725.
Elizabeth Moody, his wife, was born in 1739.
Hugh Beard, son of John and Elizabeth Beard, was born in 1770.
Mary Hughes Carrol, his wife, was born in 1782.
Francis Jervis was born March 15, 1797.
[Children of Hugh Beard and Mary Hughes Carroll:]
    Eliza Beard was born in 1800.
    Marion Beard [first name also shown as Marie] was born January 20, 1802.
    Margaret Beard was born in 1804.
    Rachel Beard [No Date Given].
    Sarah Beard [NDG].
    Jane Ann Beard [NDG].
Samuel B. Wright was born July 13, 1826 near Elkton, Md.
[Children of Francis Jervis and Marie Beard:]
    2 Sons [dates of birth not given].
    Mary Eliza Jervis was born January 31, 1828.
John Pilling, father of Isabel, was born March 6, 1830, Atherton, Lancashire, England.
[Children of Samuel B. Wright and Mary Eliza Jervis:]
    Samuel John Wright was born October 29, 1851.
    Mary Eliza Wright [NDG].
    Hugh Beard Wright [NDG].
    Catherine Brown Wright [NDG].
    Caroline Clark Wright [NDG].

Births: (Cont'd).

[Children of Samuel John Wright and Isabel Pilling:]
John Pilling Wright was born May 17, 1881.
His wife, Elizabeth Johnson was born July 2, 1881.
Mary Eliza Wright was born September 13, 1882.
Norris Nathan Wright was born March 29, 1886.
His wife, Fleta Robertson was born March 18, 1892.
Ernest Brinton Wright was born April 2, 1888.
Elizabeth Kelley Wright was born June 16, 1895.
[Children of Norris Nathan Wright and Fleta Robinson:]
Eugenia Isabel Wright was born March 6, 1922.
Martha Wright was born April 12, 1924.
[Children of Ernest Brington Wright and Marion Lee Harrington:]
Ernest Brinton Wright Jr. was born May 26, 1915.
His wife, Marjory Cowherd was born September 4, 1914 in
Harrisonburg, Va.
Samuel John Wright II was born October 28, 1924.
Isabel Wright Proud, daughter of Elizabeth Kelley Wright and Benjamin
Franklin Proud, was born March 6, 1922.
[Children of Ernest Brinton Wright, Jr. and Marjory Cowherd:]
Ernest Brinton Wright III was born June 11, 1838 at Homeopathic
Hospital, Wilmington, Delaware.
Gypsy Prior Wright was born March 30, 1840 at Homeopathic Hospital,
Wilmington, Delaware.

Deaths:

John Beard died in 1729.
Thomas Hughes died 1745, buried East Nottingham Quaker Burying Ground.
Hugh Beard died in 1770, buried in Old Rock Graveyard, Branch of Elk,
Cecil County, Maryland.
Elisha Hughes, son of Thomas Hughes, died in 1771.
Margaret Lawson, wife of Hugh Beard, [NDG], buried in Old Rock
Graveyard, Branch of Elk, Cecil County, Maryland.
John Beard, son of Hugh Beard and Margaret Lawson, died April 1, 1802
in Cecil County, Maryland.
Elizabeth Moody, his wife, died in 1798.
Hugh Beard, son of John Beard and Elizabeth Moody, died March 28,
1820.
Mary Hughes Carroll, wife of Hugh, died March 17, 1815.
Francis Jervis died March 24, 1829, buried Cherry Hill, M.E.
Churchyard, Cecil County, Maryland.
Marie Beard Jervis died January 31, 1867.
John Pilling, father of Isabel Pilling, died November 8, 1900. Buried
Head of Christiana Cemetary, near Newark, Del.

Deaths: (Cont'd).

Samuel Benoni Wright died August 19, 1901, Newark, Del. Buried Old M.E. Cemetary, Newark, Del.
Mary Eliza Jervis, his wife, died April 29, 1906. Buried Old Methodist Cemetary, Newark, Del.
Samuel John Wright died September 18, 1926. Buried Old Methodist Cemetary, Newark, Del.
Isabel Pilling, his wife, died November 7, 1926. Buried Old Methodist Cemetary, Newark, Del.
Ernest Brinton Wright died November 16, 1934.

[Genealogical Note:]

"Esther Hamilton, wife of John Beard, was the daughter of Mary James Hamilton, whose parents were Margaret Morris and Hans Hamilton of Cavanduggan. 'Hamilton Manuscripts' Belfast. Archer and Sons, 10 Wellington Place, Page 158, Genealogical History of Brabazon by H.S. Sharp, Paris, July 1825, Chart III (Proven Line to Charlemagne)."

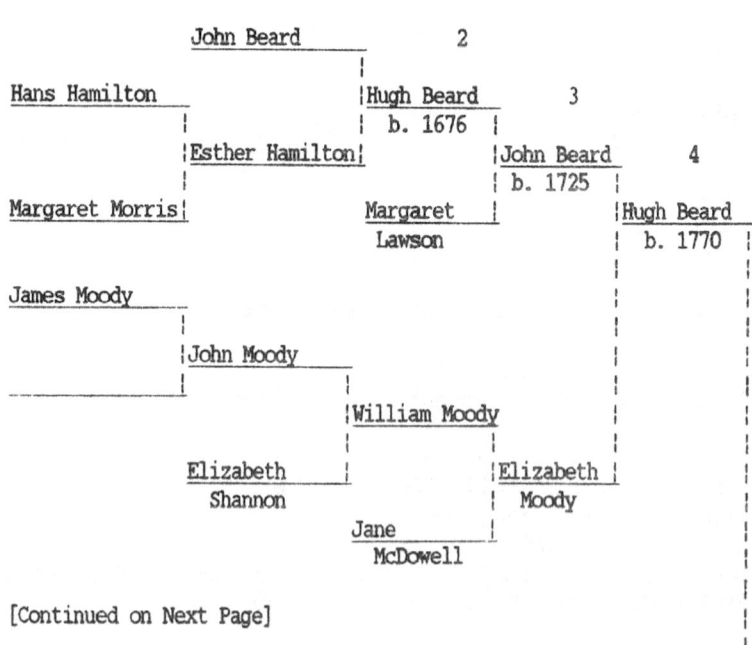

[Continued on Next Page]

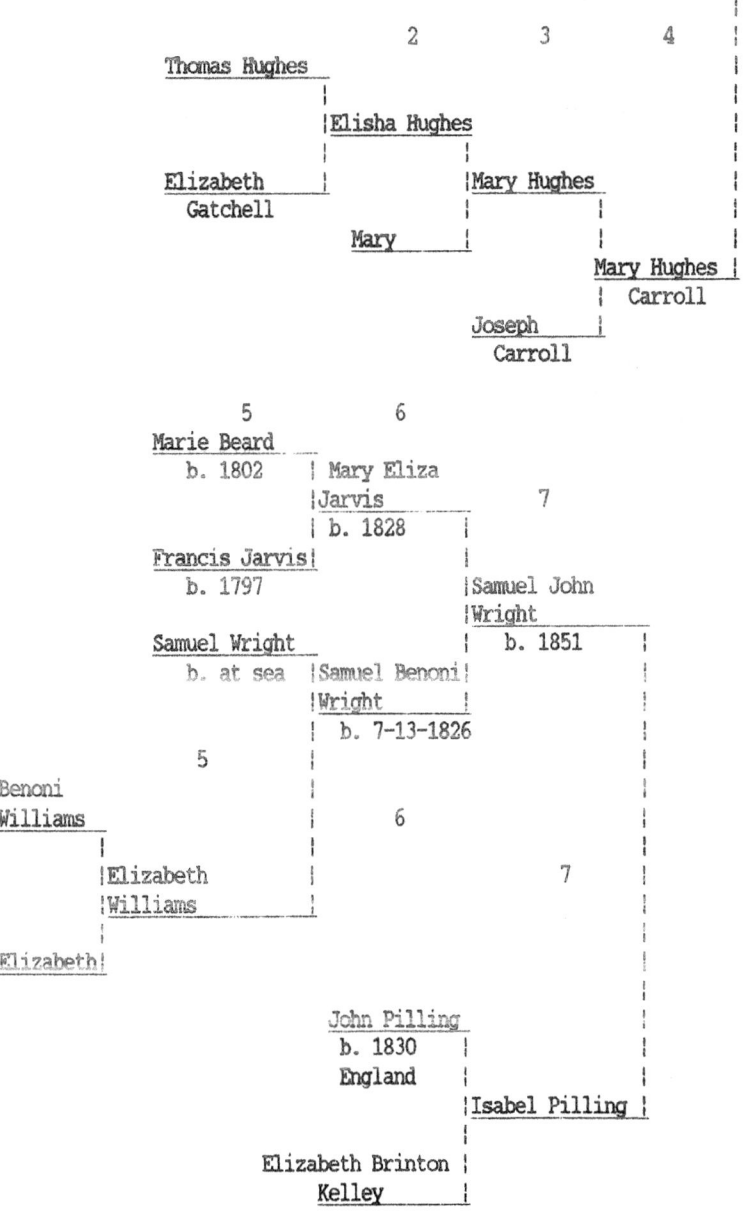

EPHRAIM BLACKWELL & MARY ANN WOOLSEY BIBLE RECORDS

Published by Whilt and Yost, Philadelphia, Pa. Bible has no date.

Marriages:

Phileman Blackwell married Mary Ann Woolsey February 4, 1818.
Jacob Blackwell married Elizabeth Updyke in December, 1858.
James C. Armstrong and Fannie Blackwell were married December 24, 1863.
Ezra Thompson and Lizzie Blackwell were married February 22, 1871.
Theordore J. Blackwell and Elizabeth Thomas were married February 1, 1875. [See Theodore Jefferson Blackwell Records].

Births:

Mary Ann Woolsey was born October 4, 1795.
Phileman Blackwell was born January 4, 1798.
Ephriam W. Blackwell was born November 4, 1818.
Jacob Blackwell was born June 14, 1820.
Sarah Ann Martindell was born December 4, 1821.
Emily Blackwell was born July 3, 1857.
Theodore Blackwell was born July 18, 1853.
Florence Blackwell was born May 22, 1857.
Frank L. Armstrong was born September 5, 1864
Annie S. Armstrong was born October 13, 1872.
Ernest Armstrong was born October 14, 1874.
Mabel Armstrong was born January 9, 1879.

Deaths:

Phileman Blackwell died August 2, 1849.
Fannie Armstrong died February 22, 1874.
Mary Ann Blackwell died August 5, 1882.
Theodore J. Blackwell died August 12, 1889 [?]
Sarah Ann Blackwell died July 24, 1894.
Lizzie Thompson died April 7, 1896.
Ephraim W. Blackwell died August 9, 1888.
Annie C. Armstrong died October 25, 1888.
Emily Blackwell die July 7, 1914.

BLACKWELL-ARMSTRONG LINEAGE CHART

Phileman Blackwell   1. Ephraim W. Blackwell   1. Theodore Blackwel
   b. 1798   b. 11/14/1818   2. Mary Frances
                    m. Sarah Ann Martindell   Blackwell
                                                 3. Lizzie Blackwell
Mary Ann Woolsey

Theodore Blackwell
                 Walter A. Blackwell, Newark, Delaware

Elizabeth Thomas

Mary Frances Blackwell   1. Frank L. Armstrong
                          2. Annie S. Armstrong
                          3. Florie B. Armstrong
                          4. Ernest Armstrong
                          5. Mabel Armstrong
James C. Armstrong   m 1. Draper
                            m 2. Judge Daniel Thompson

Lizzie Blackwell

Ezra Thompson

THEODORE JEFFERSON BLACKWELL FAMILY BIBLE RECORDS

(Published by A. J. Holman and Co. No 930 Arch St.)

Marriages

Richard L. Thomas married Sarah Jones Jackson; married second Ruth Ann McCracken in 1845.

Births

Richard L. Thomas was born June 30, 1809.
Theodore Jefferson Blackwell was born June 14, 1853.
Elizabeth Halwadt Thomas was born November 8, 1853.

Births: (Cont'd).

Walter Armstrong Blackwell was born Nov 4, 1876.
Stella Worrall Blackwell was born March 24, 1878.
Harry Martindale Blackwell was born December 5, 1879.

Deaths

Sarah Jones Jackson died 1838.
Ruth Ann McCracken died 1845.
Richard L. Thomas died June 17, 1888.
E. W. Blackwell died Aug 9, 1888.
Theodore Jefferson Blackwell died Aug 2, 1889

BLACKWELL-WOOLSEY-JEMES [LINEAGE]

Lineage of Walter A. Blackwell, Jr. and Leslie Blackwell Calloway, children of Mr. and Mrs. W. A. Blackwell, West Main St., Newark, Delaware.

1.	2.	3.
Walter A. Blackwell	Theodore J. Blackwell	Ephraim W. Blackwell
(Father)		
Elsie R. McCauley		Sarah Ann Martindell
(Mother)		[See ♦ Next Page]
	Elizabeth Thomas	

4.	5.	
Phileman Blackwell	Jacob Blackwell	
	Elizabeth	
		6.
Mary Ann Woolsey	Ephraim Woolsey	Jeremiah Woolsey
	Ann Johnson	Mary Hart

7.	8.	9.
George Woolsey	Capt. George Woolsey	George Woolsey
	Settled in Hopewell, NJ	Came to Manhattan Island 1635 and lived among the Dutch. Later removed to Jamaica, L.I. 1665.

```
      ↦       3.                    4.            5.
         Sarah Ann Martindell   Phineas Martindell
            b. 12-4-1821        |                 Lt. John Jemes
            d. 7-24-1894        |                 |
                                |                 | b. 11-14-1758
                                | Sarah Whatley Jemes | d. 6-20-1834
                                                  |
                                                  | Sarah Whatley
```

Rev. War Service. Lt. John Jemes enlisted June 26, 1776 for 5 months, served as a private in Cap Joab Hougton's Co. Col Phil Johnston's N.J. Regt. Was in the Battle of Long Island after which the Regt proceeded up North River to Ft. Washington where he assisted until Oct 1776 in the erection of the works there. Was in the battle of White Plains in which he was wounded; was carried to Bethlehem, Pa where he remained in the hospital until March 1777 when he returned home to Trenton. Here he was appointed Foragemaster in which capacity he served until Oct 1778 when he was discharged. He was commissioned Lt. of J.J. Militia and went to Pa to quell an insurrection during the Whiskey insurrection.

THE BOULDEN FAMILY BIBLE RECORDS

Published by the American Bible Society 1837.
Bible belonged to George Boulden, Glasglow, Del. Later in possession of Miss Agnes Boulden, Grandaughter.

Births

Louisa Biddle, daughter of Spencer Biddle and Ann, his wife, was born February 21, 1813.
George Boulden, son of Jesse and Hannah Griffith Boulden of Newark, Del. was born February 11, 1811.
Mary Matilda, daughter of George and Louisa Boulden was born September 14, 1835.
Edward, son of George and Louisa Boulden, was born April 4, 1837.
Francina, daughter of George and Louisa Boulden, was born June 12, 1838.
David, son of George and Louisa Boulden, was born November 17, 1839.
Annie F. daughter of George and Louisa Boulden, was born April 14, 1841.
Hannah, daughter of George and Louisa Boulden, was born February 11, 1843.

Births: (Cont'd).

Olivia, daughter of George and Louisa Boulden, was born August 19, 1844.
Amelia J., daughter of George and Louisa Boulden, was born April 10, 1846.
Martha, daughter of George and Louisa Boulden, was born July 5, 1848.
George, son of George and Louisa Boulden, was born February 18, 1850.
Fanny, daughter of George and Louisa Boulden, was born August 31, 1851.
Louisa, daughter of George and Louisa Boulden, was born March 21, 1860.

Deaths

Francina, daughter of George and Louisa Boulden, died July 29, 1839.
Amelia J. Boulden, wife of Samuel Alrich, died July 4, 1873.
Edward Boulden died Dec 19, 1893.
Hannah Boulden, wife of Robert Barr, died December 10, 1906.
Mary M. Boulden, wife of James McMullin, died June 4, 1907.
Annie F. Boulden, wife of Samuel Frazer, died May 8, 1912.
Martha Boulden, wife of William H. Frazer, died September 30, 1917.
Louisa Boulden, wife of George Boulden, died February 23, 1873.
George Boulden died December 3, 1885, in his seventy fifth year.
Fannie Boulden, wife of Frank Eliason, died Dec 29, 1923.
David Boulden died December 11, 1928.
Olivia Boulden, wife of T. A. Cann, died December 12, 1936.
George Boulden, Jr. died February 10, 1939.
Louisa Boulden, wife of William S. Ellison, died December 20, 1939.

Additional record:

James Boulden Sr
will 2-17-1784

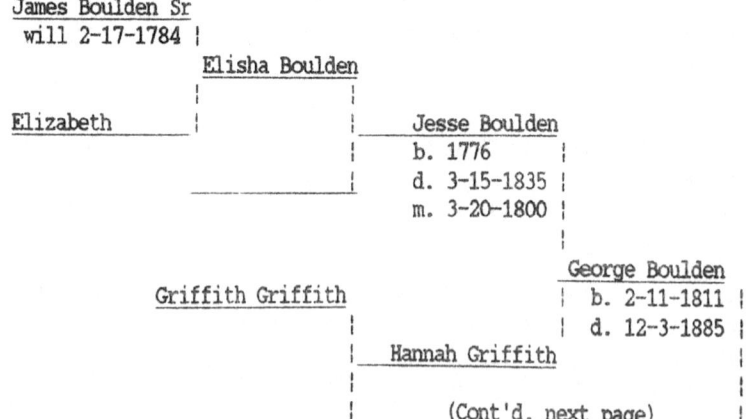

(Cont'd. next page)

Spencer Biddle

Ann Foard

Louise Biddle
b. 12-1-1813
d. 2-23-1873

BRAINARD-GILMORE BIBLE RECORDS

Last recorded in possession of: Mrs. Leon W. Gilmore, Newark, Deleware.

Marriages

Nathaniel Brainard and Emily Edmunds, September 3, 1839.
Samuel B. Wells and Aurelia Root, December 24, 1840.
Jay Brainard and Melissa M. Wells, December 21, 1871.
Elmer Elliott and Perces Emily Brainard, May 14, 1902.
Leon Weeks and Cora Aurelia Brainard, July 24, 1908.

Births

Nathaniel Brainard, August 12, 1809.
Emily Edmunds, January 24, 1819.
Samuel B. Wells, December 1, 1805.
Aurelia Root, July 30, 1822.
Jay Brainard, October 18. 1842.
Melissa M. Wells, April 15. 1851.
Willis O. Brainard (adopted) August 2, 1873.
Perces E. Brainard, October 8, 1882.
Cora A. Brainard, August 18, 1886.
Marion Clarabel Gilmore, April 3, 1914.
Wanda Maria Gilmore, January 29, 1925.

Deaths

Nathaniel Brainard, January 26, 1851.
Emily Edmunds, April 12, 1850.
Samuel B. Wells, August 28, 1866.
Aurelia Root, December 9, 1898.
Jay Brainard, February 18, 1927.
Melissa M. Wells, February 12, 1921.

BROOKS 1810 BIBLE RECORDS

Holy Bible printed by Matthus Carey, Philadelphia 1810.
Inside fly leaf is this record "This Bible is the property of John Trumann, bought Aug the 4th 1812."

Marriages

William W. Brooks and Mary S. Coverdill was married July 15, 1829.

Births

Eliza ann (sic) Trumman, daughter of John and Hester Trumman was born Aug the 5th A.D. 1811.
Sarah Ann Brooks, the daughter of William W. Brooks and Mary Brooks, his wife, was Bornd in the year of our Lord one thousand and eight hundred and thirty two. June 21st 1832.
Joseph W. Brooks, the son of William W. Brooks and ????? bornd March twelveth one thousand and eight hundred and thirty four. March 12th 1834.
William Brooks, the son of William W. Brooks and Mary Brooks, his wife, was borned in the year of our Lord one thousand and eight hundred and thirty six. September 2nd 1836.
Theodore C. Brooks, the son of William W. Brooks and Mary Brooks, his wife, was borned in the year of our Lord one thousand and eight hundred and thirty nine.
Rachel Jane, the daughter of William W. Brooks and Mary S. Brooks, his wife, was born January twenty first in the year of our Lord one thousand eight hundred and forty-one. January 21st 1941.
James Thomas, the son of William W. Brooks and Mary Brooks, his wife, was borned in the year of our Lord one thousand and eight hundred and forty two. November 26th 1842.
Henry L. Brooks, the son of William W. Brooks and Mary Brooks, his wife, was borned in the year of our Lord one thousand and eight hundred and forty five. August 21, 1845.

Deaths:

Theodore C. Brooks died December 9th 1842 about ten oclock in the morning.

[Genealogical Notes]

Rachel Jane Brooks m Robert Armstrong and was the mother of Mrs. Elsie Armstrong No 299457 D.A.R.
James Thomas Brooks is the father of Mrs. Angie Perkins.

BROOKS 1850 BIBLE RECORDS

RECORD FROM BIBLE Published in Philadelphia by John Ball, 1850.

Births

J. Armstrong Brooks was born August Monday 15th 1859 at 7:50 in the morning.
William Kean Brooks, born July 15th 1861.
Mary Julia Brooks, born December 17, 1863.
Robert Lewis Brooks, born February 4th, 1968.

Incomplete

BROOKS 1829 BIBLE RECORDS

Bible Record from Bible at one time in the possession of Mrs. Angie Perkins. Original Owner Joseph M. Brooks. Published in 1829 by T. Kinnersley, Junction of Broadway and Bowery, New York. Explanatory Notes, Evangelical Reflections by Rev. John Brown, minister of Gospel at Haddington.

Deaths

Mary Paulson (Armstrong) Brooks departed this life December 31, 1903, 67 years.
Joseph Armstrong Brooks departed this life February 1904. 46 years.
Joseph W. Brooks departed this life August 5, 1906.
Mary Julia Brooks departed this life August 20, 1920, 7:40 A.M.
William Kean Brooks departed this life Dec 8th 1922.

Additional Related Family Records - Sent to Deleware DAR by Ida J. Brooks, Media, Pa.

Births - Children of James C. and Rachel Hays Brooks:
William Webb Brooks, born Jan 16, 1801.
James Brooks, born April 21, 1803.
Josiah Brooks, born Sept 28, 1805.
Jacob Brooks, born Jan 22, 1808.
Wensruer Brooks, born Feb 15, 1811.
Eliza Brooks, born Oct 29, 1813.
Elizabeth Brooks, born July 18, 1815.
Thomas Brooks, born Nov 23, 1817.
John Heralon Brooks, born Aug 8, 1820.

Marriages -
    Eliza Brooks m. Gray.
    Elizabeth Brooks m. James Wilson.

Deaths -
    James C. Brooks husband of Rachel Hays Brooks died 1829 of smallpox.
    James Brooks died 1842.

Additional Records taken from Family Register -

(Not Recorded in the Brooks Bible.)

Births -
    Smith R. Brooks, born Sept 15th, 1847.
    Alfred G. Brooks, born Jan 6th, 1849.
    Francis C. Brooks, born October 26, 1852.
    Mary G. I. Brooks, born Jan 1st 1855.

Marriages -
    Alfred G. Brooks, married Feb. 3, 1875.

Deaths -
    Smith R. Brooks, d. June 12, 1848.

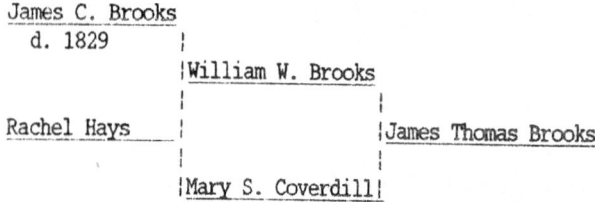

James C. Brooks
    d. 1829
               William W. Brooks

Rachel Hays
                                James Thomas Brooks

                Mary S. Coverdill

CHARLES BRYAN FAMILY BIBLE RECORDS

The Charles Bryan Bible was published by John B. Perry, 198 Market St. Philadelphia 1852. Bible given to Estella G. Bryan by her parents was published 1870 by J. R. Jones in the office of the Library of Congress, Washington, D. C.

Marriages:

Father and mother, Charles A. Bryan and Anna M. Bennett was married by the Rev. F. A. Femley, March 22 in the year 1852.

Marriages: (Cont'd).

Benjamin Campbell and Estella G. Bryan were married March 3, 1881 by Elder F. A. Chick.
Charles A. Bryan Jr and Nora M. Lunt were married April 9, 1891 by Rev. W. I. Cambrona.
Richard R. Maxwell and Anna E. Bryan were married February 1, 1893 by Rev. M. H. Miller.
William G. Bryan and Mary D. Gibson married April 24, 1893 by Rev. Howard E. Thompson.
J. Edwin Steel and Florence B. Bryan married Dec. 26, 1895 by Rev. N. H. Miller.

Births:

Father & Mother:

Charles A. Bryan was born November 4, 1822.
Anna M. Bennett Bryan was born April 12, 1831.

Their Children:

The eldest, Estella Grace Bryan, daughter of Charles and Anna M. Bryan was born June 11, 1857.
Jesse Bennet Bryan, second daughter, was born August 16, 1859.
William Guy Bryan was born November 8, 1861.
Charles A. Bryan, Jr. was born December 18, 1863.
Annie E. Bryan, daughter of Charles and Anna M. Bryan, was born August 31, 1866.
Florence Bennett Bryan was born February 28, 1869.
Carrie Watkins Bryan was born November 10, 1871.

Children of Benjamin and Estell Campbell:

Freddie B. Campbell, born February 2, 1882, died when 7 mos. old.
Ellie May Campbell, born January 20, 1884.

Deaths:

Jessie B. Bryan, died August 31, 1862. 3 years old.
Charles A. Bryan Senior died June 1st 1886, age 62.
Anna M. Bryan Senior died March 16, 1904, age 72.
Charles A. Bryan, Jr. died December 13, 1924, age 61.
Nora W. Bryan, his wife, died September 16, 1941, age 72.
William Guy Bryan died August 10, 1925, age 62.
Mary Gibson Bryan, his wife, died in 1924.
Benjamin Campbell, husband of Estella Bryan Campbell, died in 1913, age 61.
Estella Campbell died June 18, 1927, age 70.

Deaths: (Cont'd).

Annie Bryan Maxwell died August 15, 1929, age 61.
Her husband, Richard R. Maxwell, died 1923.

THOMAS CAZIER FAMILY BIBLE RECORDS

Family Bible Record of Thomas Cazier and Cornelia Foard Cazier, Cecil County, Maryland. Published by John Grigg, No. 9 No. Fourty Street. I. Ashmead & Co., Printers 1829.

Marriages:

Thomas Cazier and Cornelia Foard, daughter of John Foard and Millicent Hyland, were married 1797.
William Simco and Rebecca Cazier were married.
John McCracken and Martha J. Cazier were married February 17, 1829.
Thomas C. Cazier and Maria Louisa Ward were married August 3, 1837.
Thomas Moffitt and Araminta Cazier were married.
David White and Millicent Cazier were married.
Thomas C. McCracken and Martha E. Brown were married February 13, 1867.
Wm. S. McCracken and Anna B. Hayes were married January 17, 1874.

Births:

Thomas Cazier, son of Abraham Cazier and Rebecca, his wife, was born February 27, 1773.
[Children of Thomas Cazier and Cornelia Foard:]
 Rebecca Cazier was born July 23, 1798.
 John C. Cazier was born July 27, 1800.
 Araminta Cazier was born June 18, 1804.
 Martha Jane Cazier was born August 29, 1808.
 Thomas Coke Cazier was born October 14, 1811.
 Millicent Cazier was born May 18, 1813.
Charles Evans Cazier, son of Thomas C. Cazier and M. L. Cazier, his wife, was born October 29, 1838.
Anna B. McCracken, wife of W. S. McCracken, was born August 1, 1852.
[Children of W. S. and Annie B. McCracken:]
 James Henry McCracken was born April 6, 1875 at Perth Amboy, N. J.
 Kate Rebecka McCracken was born June 4, 1882 at North East, Md.

Deaths:

Thomas Cazier died June 26, 1821, Aged 48 years, three months and twenty-nine days after a protracted illness of five months and six days, which he bore with utmost resignation leaving behind him an affectionate wife and six children.
Lucy Ann Ward, wife of Joseph Ward, died June 16, 1835.
Joseph Ward died in July, 1837.
Caleb Ward died February 2, 1838. Aged 22 years.
Maria Louisa Cazier, wife of Thomas C. Cazier died on Sunday, June 9, 1839.
Charles Evans Cazier, son of Thomas C. and M. L. Cazier died [NDG].
Thomas C. Cazier, son of Thomas and Cornelia Cazier, died April 23, 1862 in the 52nd year of his life.
Martha T. McCracken, daughter of John and Martha McCracken, died March 16, 1875, aged 20 years 11 months and 8 days.
Anna B. McCracken, wife of W.S. [McCracken] died Jan 7, 1889 at North East, Md.

CAZIER FAMILY LINEAGE CHART

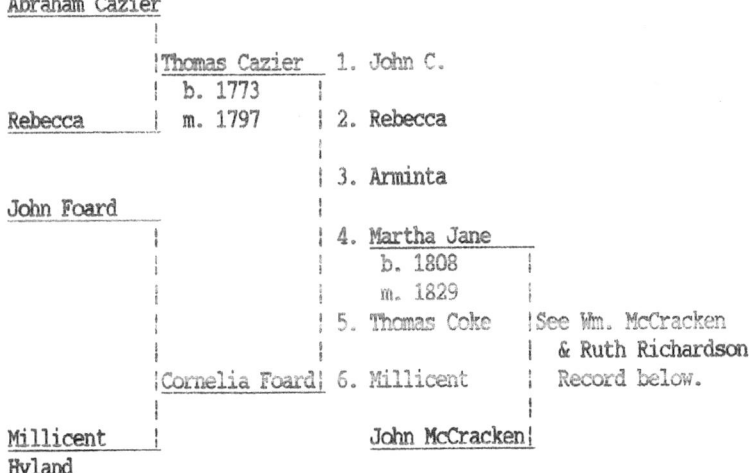

ROBERT CHAMBERLAIN FAMILY BIBLE RECORDS

Marriages:

Robert Chamberlain was married in England. Wife's name not given.
Joseph Chamberlain (2) married Suzanna Sharpless.

Marriages: (Cont'd).

John Chamberlain (3) married Lettice Ray.
Mary Chamberlain (4) married David
Robert Chamberlain (5), son of Robert, married 1st Sarah Woodward
    [NDG]. Married 2nd Cecily Hall [NDG].
Robert Chamberlain (6), son of Robert Chamberlain (5), married Ann
    Paynter [NDG].
Joseph Chamberlain (7), their son, married Martha Palmer.
[Children of Joseph Chamberlain and Martha Palmer:]
    Dr. Joseph Chamberlain (8) married Elizabeth Thomson, daughter of
        John and Hannah Evans Thomson.
    Margaret Chamberlain (9) married James Johnson.
    Anna Chamberlain (10) married a Mr. Meteer.
    Rev. Pierce Chamberlain (11) married Christine Whitehall.
    Dr. Palmer Chamberlain (12) married Grace Ricketts.
[Children of Dr. Joseph Chamberlain and Elizabeth Thomson:]
    Charles T. Chamberlain (15) married Pamelia.
    Martha Chamberlain (16) married Charles Long.
    Annie Chaberlain (19) married Rev. Albert Barnes.
    Mary Chamberlain (20) married George Earle.
    George Chamberlain (29) son of Rev. Pierce Chamberlain married Mary
        [Chamberlain] [No maiden name given].
[Children of Dr. Palmer Chamberlain and Grace Ricketts Thomson:]
    Kate Chamberlain married [a Mr.] McNiell.
    Clara Chamberlain married [a Mr.] Kerr [NDG].

Births:

[Children of Robert Chamberalin - the immigrant (1686):]
    John Pyle Chamberlain (1)
    Joseph Chamberlain (2)
    John Chamberlain (3)
    Mary Chamberlain (4)
    Robert Chamberlain (5)
    Robert Chamberlain (6), son of Robert Chamberlain (5)
    Joseph Chamberlain (7), son of Robert Chamberlain (6) and Ann
        Paynter.
[Children of Joseph Chamberlain (7) and Martha Palmer:}
    Dr. Joseph Chamberlain (8)
    Margaret Chamberlain Johnson (9)
    Anna Chamberlain Meteer (10)
    Rev. Pierce Chamberlain (11)
    Dr. Palmer Chamberlain (12)
[Children of Dr. Joseph Chamberlain (8) and Elizabeth Thomson:]
    Dr. Joseph Chamberlain (13)
    Samuel Chamberlain (14)

Births: (Cont'd).

Charles T. Chamberlain (15)
Martha Chamberlain (16)
Josephine Chamberlain (17)
Elizabeth Chamberlain (18)
Annie Chamberlain (19)
Mary Chamberlain (20)
[Children of Margaret Chamberlain and James Johnson:]
Joseph Johnson (21)
Churchman [sic] (22)
Margaretta (23)
Edward (24)
[Children of Rev. Pierce Chamberlain [11] and Christine Whitehall:]
Elizabeth Chamberlain (25)
Martha Chamberlain (26)
Mary Chamberlain (27)
James Chamberlain (28)
[Children of Dr. Palmer Chamberlain (12) and Grace Ricketts Thomson:]
Kate Chamberlain [who married a McNiell] (30)
Hannah (31)
Joseph Chamberlain (32)
Mary Emma Chamberlain (33)
Martha (34)
Clara Chamberlain [who married a Kerr] (35) was born in 1840.

Deaths:

Clara Chamberlain died in 1921.

LINEAGE CHART OF THE CHAMBERLAIN FAMILY

```
        1
Robert Chamberlain      2
         |
         |Robert Chamberlain       3
         |
                       |Robert Chamberlain     4
                       |
         Sarah Woodward |                      |Joseph
                                               | Chamberlain
                            Ann Paynter        |
                                               |
                                               Martha
(Continued on Next Page)                       Palmer
```

20

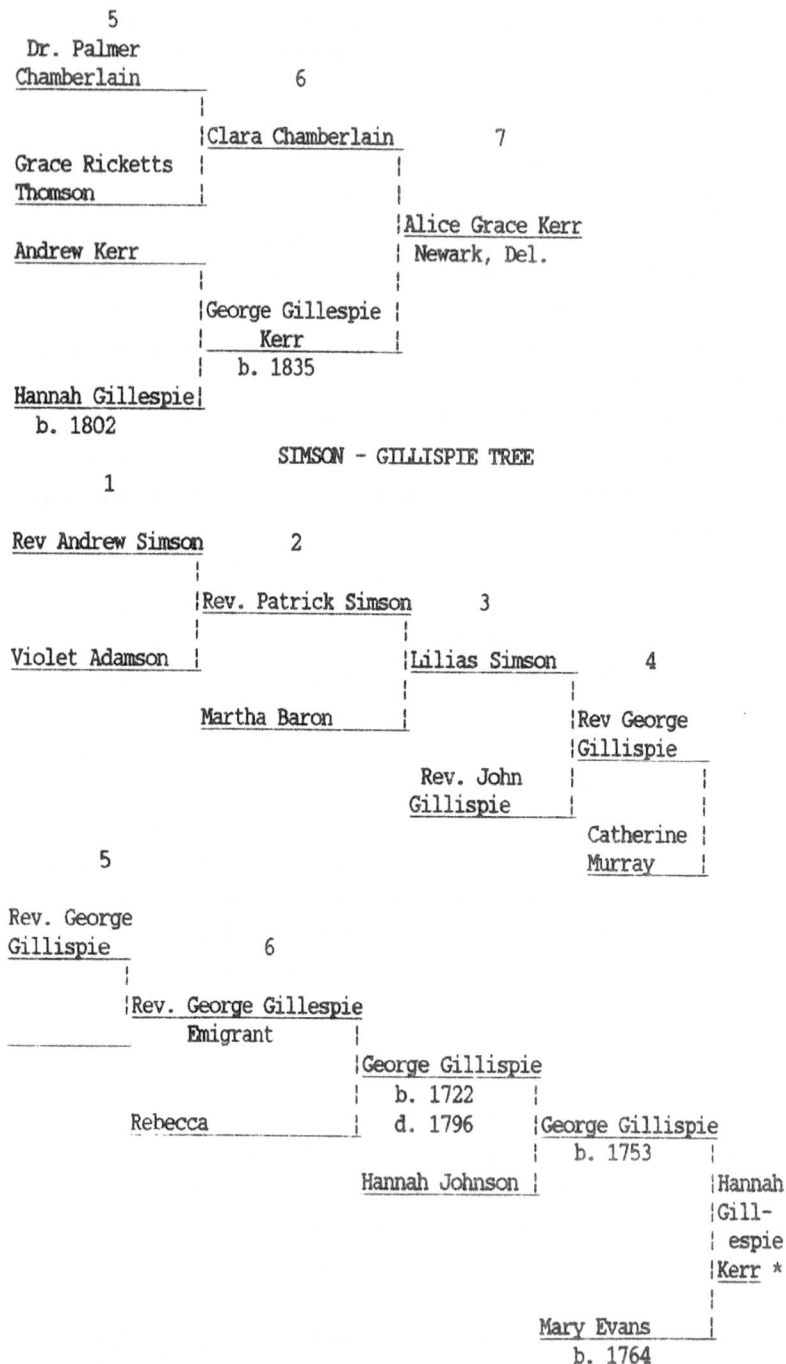

```
       5
  Dr. Palmer
  Chamberlain          6
                       |
                       |Clara Chamberlain        7
  Grace Ricketts       |
  Thomson              |
                       |Alice Grace Kerr
  Andrew Kerr          | Newark, Del.
                       |
                       |George Gillespie |
                       |     Kerr        |
                       |    b. 1835
  Hannah Gillespie|
     b. 1802
                        SIMSON - GILLISPIE TREE
       1
  Rev Andrew Simson        2
                           |
                           |Rev. Patrick Simson       3
                           |                          |
  Violet Adamson           |                          |Lilias Simson        4
                                                      |                     |
                    Martha Baron       |              |Rev George
                                                      |Gillispie
                                   Rev. John          |
                                   Gillispie          |
                                                          Catherine
       5                                                  Murray
  Rev. George
  Gillispie           6
                      |
                      |Rev. George Gillespie
                      |        Emigrant          |
                                                 |George Gillispie
                                                 |   b. 1722
                    Rebecca                      |   d. 1796     |George Gillispie
                                                 |               |  b. 1753
                                             Hannah Johnson                    |Hannah
                                                                               |Gill-
                                                                               | espie
                                                                               |Kerr *

                                                          Mary Evans
                                                            b. 1764
```

Historical Note:

Robert Chamberlain [the immigrant] came to America with his wife in 1686 and settled near Philadelphia.

SIDNEY and TERESA PRICE CHANDLEE BIBLE RECORDS

Marriages:

Sidney W. Chandlee and Teresa T. Chandlee, his wife, were married November 1, 1821.

Births:

Sidney W. Chandlee, son of Ellis Chandlee and Elizabeth G. Chandlee was born July 6, 1798.
Teresa T. Price, daughter of Jacob Price and Millicent R. Price, was born May 20, 1802.
George W. Chandlee, son of Sidney W. Chandlee and Teresa T. Chandlee, was born June 14, 1823.
Jacob Edwin Chandlee, son of Sidney W. Chandlee and Teresa T. Chandlee, was born August 28, 1824.
Veazey John Chandlee, son of Sidney W. Chandlee and Teresa T. Chandlee, was born January 25, 1827.
Henry Peters Chandlee, son of Sidney W. Chandlee and Teresa T. Chandlee, was born September 28, 1828.
Ann Elizabeth Chandlee, daughter of S. W. Chandlee and Teresa T. Chandlee, was born December 28th 1830.
William Ellis Chandlee, son of S. W. Chandlee and Teresa T. Chandlee, was born April 2, 1883.
Millicent Rebecca Chandlee, daughter of Sidney W. and Teresa T. Chandlee, was born February 5, 1836.
Teresa Maria Chandlee, daughter of Sidney W. Chandlee and Teresa, his wife, was born July 31, 1838.
Sydnianne Chandlee, daughter of S. W. Chandlee and Teresa T. Chandlee, his wife, was born December 23, 1840.

Deaths:

George W., son of Sidney W. Chandlee and Teresa T. Chandlee, departed this life July 8, 1823, aged 24 days.
Veavey John Chandlee, son of Sidney W. Chandlee and Teresa T. Chandlee, departed this life September 6, 1827, aged 7 months and eleven days.

Deaths: (Cont'd.)

Sidney W. Chandlee departed this life November 27, 1840, aged 41 years, 4 months, and 21 days.

Teresa T. Chandlee departed this life May 21, 1845, aged 43 years, 1 day.

Note on Chandlee Family from the Delaware Bible Records:

Eli Terry of Connecticut is usually hailed as the father of the Clock Industry in America, but Chandlee and Son of Nottingham, Maryland were just going out of business was Terry was beginning.

According to Johnston's History of Cecil Co. Md. the concern of Chandlee and Sons, makers of Scientific and Mathematical instruments was not surpassed in its work by any other concern in America. The business of making Grandfather Clocks of Hall clocks was started by Benjamin Chandlee about 1710 and continued under the management of his son, Benjamin Jr. Benjamin died 1794 leaving the growing concern to his sons, Isaac and Ellis Chandlee. Isaac's death occurred in 1813. Water power was used to turn its lathes and do the heavy work.

A very interesting and finely illustrated book has recently been published by the Pennsylvania Historical Society and distributed by David McKay Co., Washington Square, Philadelphia. It is written by Edward E. Chandlee, a descendant of Benjamin Chandlee, who has gathered his data over a long period, and his very fine photographs of some 70 odd clocks and other scientific instruments makes a worthwhile addition to Historical lore.

The Great great grandfather of Mrs. W.A. Blackwell, John Price owned one of the Chandlee grandfather clocks, also a compass with a brass face and other surveying instruments. The Compass and Clock are in possession of Mrs. Blackwell's brother John Hays McCauley, Leeds, Cecil Co., Md. This clock came to him thru Millicent Price McCauley, his grandmother and has been in its present location for 100 years.

JOSHUA CLAYTON FAMILY BIBLE RECORDS

Publisher - Leavith & Allen, 379 Broadway, New York; Owner - Joshua Clayton, Bohemia Manor, Delaware, October 20, 1857. Last known owner - Mrs. Dorsey W. Lewis, 217 N. Broad St. Middletown, Delaware.

Marriages:

Thomas Clayton, Esquire [father of Joshua] married Jeanette [NDG].
Joshua Clayton and Lydia A. Clayton were married March 8, 1833.
Joshua Clayton and Martha E. Lockwood were married February 21, 1850.
[Children of Joshua and Lydia A. Clayton:]
   Thomas Clayton married Emma Purner [NDG].
   Henry Clayton married Margaret Lockwood (sister of Martha) [NDG].
   Richard Clayton married married Clara Cann [NDG].
[Children of Joshua and Martha E. Clayton:]
   Adelaide Young Clayton married Charles S. Ellison [NDG].
   Macomb Clayton married Porter Laws [NDG].
   Mary Wilson Clayton married J. Fletcher Price [NDG].
   Joshua Clayton married Estelle Pennington [NDG].
   Margaret Elizabeth Clayton married first ___ Lewis and second Dr.
      Thomas Williams of New York City [NDG].
   Eugene Clayton married Jessie Wilson [NDG].
   Fannie (or Francis) L. Clayton married Nathaniel J. Williams on
      April 28, 1886 at Middletown, Delaware.
Mary Clayton Williams, their daughter, was married to Dr. Dorsey W.
   Lewis on December 15, 1904 at Forest Presbyterian Church in
   Middletown, Del by Rev. Francis H. Moore.

Births:

[Children of Joshua and Lydia A. Clayton:]
   Thomas Clayton was born December 6, 1833.
   Henry Clayton was born January 3, 1839.
   Richard Clayton was born September 13, 1842.
[Children of Joshua and Martha E. Clayton:]
   Adelaide Young Clayton was born November 25, 1850.
   Macomb Clayton was born June 21, 1852.
   Edgar Lockwood Clayton was born September 4, 1853.
   Mary Wilson Clayton was born April 20, 1855.
   Joshua Clayton was born July 28, 1856.
   Margaret Elizabeth Clayton was born July 6, 1868.
   Eugene Clayton was born February 2 [22?], 1860.
   Fannie (or Francis) L. Clayton was born April 19, 1865 at 5:45
      o'clock P.M.
Mary Clayton Williams, her daughter was born May 2, 1887 in
   Middleton, Delaware.

Deaths:

Thomas Clayton, Esquire, Father of Joshua Clayton died at New Castle,
   August 21, 1854 in his 77th year and was buried in Presbyterian
   Cemetary beside his wife Jeanette.

Deaths: (Cont'd).

Lydia A. Clayton, (1st) wife of Joshua Clayton, died January 26, 1849 at 9 o'clock P.M. in the 33rd year of her age.

Edgar Lockwood Clayton, son of Joshua and Martha E. Lockwood Clayton, died June 11, 1864 about daylight in the morning in the 11th year of his age.

Martha (E.) Lockwood Clayton wife of (second wife of) Joshua Clayton [son] (of Thos.) died 3/ /87 and was buried at St. Annes Cemetary, Middletown, Delaware.

Joshua Clayton [son] (of Thos.) husband of Martha (E.) Lockwood Clayton died 2/13/88 and was buried beside her at St. Annes Cemetery near Middletown, Delaware.

Fannie, or Frances, Clayton Williams, wife of Nathaniel J. Williams died in Atlantic City, N.J. Hospital on February 26, 1930 and was buried in St. Annes Cemetery near Middletown, Delaware.

CLAYTON-LOCKWOOD-WILLIAMS-LEWIS LINEAGE CHART

```
Thomas Clayton
    d. 1854
                   |Joshua Clayton      1. Thomas Clayton
                   |   m. 1833      |          b. 1835
Jeannette          |                |          m. Edna [Emma?] Purdner
                                    |      2. Henry Clayton
                                    |          b. 1839
                                    |          m. Margaret Lockwood
                                    |      3. Richard Clayton
                                    |          b. 1842
                   Lydia A.          |          m. Clara Cann

                   m. 1850
                   Martha E. Lockwood|  4. Adelaide, b. 1850
                                    |  5. Macomb, b. 1852
                                    |  6. Edgar, b. 1853
                                    |  7. Mary Wilson, b. 1855
                                    |  8. Joshua, b. 1856
                                    |  9. Martha, b. 1858
                                    | 10. Eugene, b. 1860
                                    | 11. Frances Clayton
                                             b. 1865    |
                                             m. 1886   |Mary Clayton
                                                       |Williams
                                          Nathaniel J. |
                                          Williams     |
                                                        Dr. Dorsey W.|
                                                        Lewis        |
```

WILLIAM CLINGEN & DR. WARWICK MILLER FAMILY BIBLE RECORDS

Fly leaf of Wm. C. Miller's Bible. 1843. Presented by his affectionate mother. Martha B. Clingen's book presented by her dearly beloved mother, J. Clingen on Sept. 10, 1820.

Marriages:

William Clingen, Esq. married Jane [Clingen] [NDG].
Dr. Warrick Miller and Martha B. Clingen were married November 15, 1820 by the Rev. Dr. Broadhead.
William C. Miller and and Martha E. Black were married May 13, 1852 by the Rev. Dr. Richard Newton of St. Paul's Church, Philadelphia.
William C. Miller and Rebecca J. Ferguson were married May 2, 1859.
Martha Black Clingen married [second Dr.(?)] Murphy [NDG].

Births:

William Clingen, Esq. was born in 1756.
[His wife] Jane was born in 1765.
[Their Children:]
    Frances Clingen [was born c. 1793].
    William Clingen, Jr. [was born 1791 or 1792].
    Jane Clingen [NDG].
    Martha Black Clingen [was born c. 1796].
[Children of Martha Black Clingen and Dr. Warrick Miller:]
    William C. Miller was born April 30, 1822.
    James Edwin [Miller] was born December 23, 1823.
    Martha E. Beach [relationship not shown] was born August 5, 1822.

Deaths:

Jane Clingen, wife of William Clingen, Esq., departed this life August 3, 1822 at 6 o'clock A.M., aged 57 years 11 months, and 17 days. On the day following her remains were interred in Faggs Manor where an appropriate ciscourse was delivered by the Rev. Dr. White.
William Clingen, Jr. departed this life October 27, 1825, aged 33 years, 10 months & 16 days.
William Clingen, Esq. departed this life December 26, 1826 at 12 o'clock noon aged 70 years & on Monday 18, his remains were interred in Fagg's Manor after an appropriate discourse by Rev. R. White and Rev. J. Latta.
Frances [Clingen], daughter of William and Jane Clingen, departed this life May 19, 1822, aged 29 years, one month.
Jane P. Israel [their daughter?] departed this life Feb 15, 1843.

Deaths: (Cont'd).

Martha B. Murphy departed this life January 13, 1844, aged 48 years. Her remains were interred at Fagg's Manor but afterward removed to Octorara where a monument was erected to here memory by Dr. Murphy, Wm. C. & J. E. Miller.

LINEAGE CHART OF CLINGEN FAMILY

```
William Clingen, Esq.   1. Frances d. 1822
   b. 1756; d. 1826     2. Wm. Clingen, Jr.
                              d. 1825
                        3. Jane
Jane                    4. Martha Black
   b. 1765; d. 1822        Clingen            1. Wm. C. Miller
                           m. Dr. Warrick >>>>    b. 1822
                           Miller 1820     2. James Edwin
                                                  b. 1823

                           m. Murphy 2nd
```

COLLINS, McALLEN & HOLLOWAY FAMILY BIBLE RECORDS

Marriages:

John Collins married Mary Hammond of Queponco, Worcester Co., Md. [NDG].
James Collins married Mary Predux [NDG] and moved to Adams Co., Ohio.
Parker Collins married Kitty Duncan [NDG].
Charles Parker Collins married married Roseanna Jane Rogers of Northampton Co., Virginia April 25, 1854.
Annie Snow Collins married William A. McAllen at Snow Hill, Md., October 31, 1883.
Jane Eldred McAllen married John Laws Holloway December 28, 1909 in Snow Hill, Md.
John Laws Holloway, Jr. married Nell Elizabeth Everett of Chestertown, Maryland September 12, 1934.

Births:

John Collins born in Aryeshire, Scotland in 1749. Came to this country and settled on Eastern Shore of Maryland in Worcester Co., in 1770.

Births: (Cont'd).

[Children of John Collins and Mary Hammond:]

James [No date of birth given].
Joseph Collins [NDG].
Parker Collins was born March 1, 1782.

Children of Parker Collins and Kitty Duncan:

Charlotte [NDG].
William [NDG].
Mary [NDG].
Charles Parker Collins was born in 1823.
Roseanna Jane Rogers, his wife, was born August 14, 1820.

Children of Charles & Roseann Jane Colllins:

Charles Robert was born August 2, 1855.
Annie Snow Collins was born June 8, 1857.

William A. McAllen, husband of Anie Snow Collins, was born at Snow Hill, Md. October 31, 1883.
Jane Eldred McAllen, daughter of William A. and Annie McAllen, was born November 17, 1887.
John Laws Holloway, her husband, was born June 5, 1851.

Children of John & Jane Holloway:

John Laws Holloway, Jr. was born December 2, 1910.
William D. Holloway was born February 15, 1915.
John Laws Holloway III, son of John Laws Holloway, Jr., was born April 29, 1937.

Deaths:

Parker Collins died January 18, 1826.
Charles Robert Collins died January 19, 1856.
Kitty Duncan died September 13, 1868.
Charles Parker Collins died August 27, 1894.
Roseanna Jane Rogers died December 24, 1894.
William A. McAllen died July 2, 1928.
Annie Snow Collins died September 29, 1937.

COLLINS LINEAGE

```
1
John Collins      2
  b. 1749       |
   Scotland   |Parker Collins      3
              |  b. 1782         |
Mary Hammond|   d. 1826        |Charles Parker Collins    4
                               |  b. 1823               |
                 Kitty Duncan |   d. 1894              |Annie Snow Collins
                                                       |
                                 Roseanna Jane Rogers |
                                   b. 1820            |
                                   d. 1894            Wm. A. McAllen
                                   m. 1854

5
Jane Eldred McAllen       6
                         |
                         |John Laws Holloway, Jr.      7
                         |  b. 1910                  |
John Laws Holloway|                                  |John Laws Holloway 3rd
  b. 1881                                            |  b. 1937
  m. 1909        Nell Elizabeth Everett|
```

CORNOG FAMILY BIBLE RECORDS

Harding's medium edition, William W. Harding, 1862.

Marriages

Catharine L. Cornog married William Stitler.
Isabella C. L. Cornog married James Weaver.
Anna Maria Cornog married James B. Street.
Harry Cornog married Alice Lynam.
Ulysis Cornog married Bertha George.
Stephen Love Cornog married Alice Lutton.
Abram Ethelbert Cornog married Amanda Manuel.
Blanche Elma Street married William P. Compton
Mary Irene Street married Henry Newell Reed.
Anna Gertrude Street married George E. Knauss.
Ella Naomi Street married Oscar Knauss.

Births

Abraham Cornog was born September 5, 1846.
Isabelle Love Cornog, his wife, was born August 22, 1824.
Catharine L. Cornog, daughter of Abraham and Isabella Love Cornog, was born June 7, 1846.
Abner Cornog, son of Abraham and Isabella Love Cornog, was born January 27, 1848.
Eliza L. Cornog, daughter of Abraham and Isabella Love Cornog, was born February 11, 1848.
Sarah T. Cornog, daughter of Abraham and Isabella Love Cornog, was born August 25, 1850.
Abraham Cornog, son of Abraham and Isabella Love Cornog, was born October 28, 1851.
Harriet C. Cornog, daughter of Abraham and Isabella Love Cornog, was born July 11, 1853.
Isabella C. L. Cornog, daughter of Abraham and Isabella Love Cornog, was born September 15, 1856.
Margaret W. Cornog, daughter of Abraham and Isabella Love Cornog, was born July 18, 1858.
Anna Maria Cornog, daughter of Abraham and Isabella Love Cornog, was born August 22, 1860.
Harry Cornog, son of Abraham and Isabella Love Cornog, was born June 3, 1862.
Ulysis Cornog, son of Abraham and Isabella Love Cornog, was born June 2, 1864.
Stephen Love Cornog, son of Abraham and Isabella Love Cornog, was born July 8, 1867.
Franklin H. Cornog, son of Abraham and Isabella Love Cornog, was born May 6, 1855.
Blanche Elma Street, daughter of James B. Street and Anna Maria Cornog.
Mary Irene Street, daughter of James B. Street and Anna Maria Cornog.
Anna Gertrude Street, daughter of James B. Street and Anna Maria Cornog.
Ella Naomi, daughter of James B. Street and Anna Maria Cornog.
Anna Mary Compton, daughter of Blanche Elma Street and William P. Compton.
James Clifford Compton, son of Blanche Elma Street and William P. Compton.
George Edwin Knauss, Jr. son of Anna Gertrude Street and George E. Knauss.
Donald Lee Knauss, son of Ella Naomi Street and Oscar Knauss.

CROOKS FAMILY BIBLE RECORDS

OLD CROOKS BIBLE:

This data was copied from a small family bible, published 1868 by the American Bible Society. It was used by James David Crooks until the death of his wife, December 15, 1901. It was given to his son, E. B. Crooks, August 1902, and was last known to be in the possession of his wife, Mary Lasher Crooks.

Marriages:

Usual Crooks married a Miss Crooks.
Robert Franklin Crooks married Doke Breckenridge, [c1843].
James D. Crooks and Mary E. Brigg, March 28, 1872.
Amos A. Crooks and Salome Mathis, April 1901.
Ezra Crooks and Mary E. Groves, September 10, 1902.
 *** Mary died in Sao Paulo Brazil, May 5, 1906. ***
Ezra Crooks married Mary Lasher, Ashland, Va. September 8, 1909.

Births:

Robert Franklin Crooks was born March 27, 1817 in E. Kentucky.
Doke Breckenridge was born about 1819, Mt. Starling, Kentucky.
John William Crooks was born 1844. [Son of Robert Franklin Crooks and Doak Breckenridge].
Margaret Crooks was born 1846. [Daughter of Robert Franklin Crooks and Doak Breckenridge].
James D. Crooks was born February 20, 1849. [Son of Robert Franklin Crooks and Doak Breckenridge].
Robert Turpin Crooks. [Son of Robert Franklin Crooks and Doak Breckenridge].
Benjamin Harrison Crooks. [Son of Robert Franklin Crooks and Doak Breckenridge].
Mary Clementine Crooks. [Daughter of Robert Franklin Crooks and Doak Breckenridge].
Ezra Breckenridge Crooks was born October 6, 1874. [Son of James David Crooks and Mary Elizabeth Brigg].
Mary E. Crooks was born January 25, 1878.
Amos Alexander Crooks was born January 25, 1878. [Son of James David Crooks and Mary Elizabeth Brigg].
Anna Elizabeth Crooks born Piracicaba, Brazil September 1, 1904.
David Groves Crooks born Sao Paulo, Brazil, April 16, 1906.
James Lasher Crooks was born October 1, 1911.

Deaths:

Usual Crooks died c1920.
Miss Crooks died c1920.
Mother (Mary E. Crooks, wife of James D.) died December 15, 1901 of
Typhoid Fever at Patoka, Illinois.
Father (James D. Crooks) died at brother's home, Peoria, Illinois
April 16, 1922; buried beside mother 19th.

Family of Ezra B. Crooks:

First wife, Mary Ellizabeth Groves, born Macon, Mo., September 26,
1876.
Second wife, Mary Lasher born Mariaville, N.Y. February 13, 1866.
Anna Elizabeth [Crooks] born Piracicaba, Brazil September 1, 1904.
David Groves [Crooks] born Sao Paulo, Brazil, April 16, 1906.
James Lasher Crooks born October 1, 1911.

Family Tree of Crooks Family: "Entered March 12, 1902."

Usual Crooks married a Miss Crooks; lived in East Kentucky (Bath
Co.?). Both died about 1820.
Children:
    William   Robert Franklin
    Harrison   Eliza
    Alfred   Fannie

Robert Franklin Crooks married Doke Breckenridge
b. 3-27-1917   b. abt. 1819, Mt. Sterling, Ky.
d. September, 1900   d. August, 1861.
Both died in Graves Co. [Kentucky].
Moved to Graves Co. about 1843 (marriage).
Children:
    John William b. 1844; d. 1863.
    Margaret b. 1846; d. infancy.
    Jas. David (see below)
    Robert Turpin
    Benjamin Harrison - Mary Clementine

James David Crooks married March 28, 1872 to Mary Elizabeth Brigg,
b. 1/22/1851 in Hickman Co. Ky. d. at Patoka, Ill.
12/15/1901. James was born February 20, 1849 Graves Co. Ky;
settled in Graves Co.; moved to Hickman Co. 1874; to Illinois
1880 (died Peoria, Ill, April 16, 1922).
Children:
    Ezra Breckenridge b. 1874 9/6 [or 10/6]?
    Amos Alexander b. 1878 1/15 in Hickman Co. [KY].

CROOKS NEW BIBLE:

Published 1897. Prof. E. B. Crooks, University of Delaware, d. March 8, 1941; buried near New Castle, Del.

FAMILY TREE INSERT:

"Inserted in the bible is a leaf copied from the Family Tree Page in the older Bible with additional data about the Breckinridge [sic] line as follows:"

1. <u>Alexander Breckenridge</u> (died 1741?) came from Scotland (via Ireland) to Philadelphia 1728. Settled in Orange Co., Va. about 1739. Married Jane ___. He was the founder of the Breckenridge Family in U.S.A.

2. <u>George Breckenridge</u>, his son, b. about 1714; d. 1790; married Ann Doak, daughter of Samuel Doak and Jane Mitchell.

3. <u>Robert Breckenridge</u>, their son d. 1814. m. Mary Doak.

4. <u>John Doak Breckenridge</u>, their son b. December 4, 1796; d. March 12, 1825; m. Jane Peebles (b. July 5, 1798; d. May 9, 1846).

5. <u>Mary Doke Breckenridge</u>, their daughter b. 1819; d. August, 1861; m. Robert Franklin Crooks who was b. March 27, 1817; d. September 1900. He went to south west Kentucky where their son

6. <u>James David Crooks</u> was born February 20, 1849.

> Note: Doke in our records is Doak in Virginia Records. Usual Crooks in our records is Usal Crooks in Virginia Records.

Marriages:

"This certifies that Rev. E. B. Crooks of Manchester, Mo. and Miss Mary E. Groves of Fayette, Mo. were joined by me in the Bonds of Holy Matrimony, Fayette, Mo. on the 10th day of September, in the year of our Lord 1902 in the presence of N. V. Bratton, Stella Somes, C. W. Webdell, C. R. Duncan - Hiram D. Groves, Minister."

Ezra Breckenridge Crooks and Mary Lasher, September 8, 1909 at Ashland Va.
Robert Bingham Downs and Anna Elizabeth Crooks, August 17, 1929, Newark, Delaware.
James Lasher and Virginia Scott, August 8, 1941, Ft. Thomas, Ky.

Births:

Ezra Breckenride Crooks was born October 6, 1874, Hickman Co., Kentucky, U.S.A.
Mary Elizabeth Crooks nee Groves was born September 26, 1876, Macon, Missouri, U.S.A.
Anna Elizabeth Crooks was born September 1, 1904; 5:45 P.M. Piracicaba, Brazil.
David Groves Crooks was born April 16, 1906; 5:30 A.M. Sao Paulo, Brazil.
NOTE: Both children registered as U.S.A. citizens at birth.

Mary Lasher Crooks was born in Mariaville, N.Y. February 13, 1866.
James Lasher Crooks was born October 1, 1911, 2:30 P.M. Ashland, Virginia.
Robert Bingham Downs was born May 25, 1903.
Virginia Scott was born July 9, 1915.
Clara Breckenridge Downs was born Durham, N.C. August 22, 1934.
Mary Roberta Downs was born June 14, 1938, Durham, N.C.
Scott Breckenridge Crooks, son of James Lasher Crooks and Virginia Scott, was born March 9, 1943.

Deaths:

Mary Elizabeth Groves Crooks died in Samaritan Hospital, Sao Paulo, Brazil May 5, 1906. 12:40 A.M.
David Groves Crooks died at Fayette, Mo. October 12, 1906.
Ezra Breckenridge Crooks died March 8, 1941 at Newark, Del.

CURTIS CRUMPTON FAMILY BIBLE RECORDS

Printed by Mark Baskett, Printer to the King's most Excellent Majesty: and by the assigns of Robert Baskett MDCCLXVII (1768). Copied by Tillie W. Harrington (Mrs. H. Ridgely Harrington, Dover. Presented by Col Haslet Chapter, Dover, Delaware. [Copiest's note indicates Tillie Harrington had "lots of Gum - Long records tracing back to the Crusades".]

Marriages:

Curtis Crumpton and Jamima Bowman was married [sic] by Parson Nile Aris in 1780.
Margaret Kelley married William Thompson January 2, 1290.
John Crumpton and Nancy Thompson was married by Parson _____ June 17, 1809.

Marriages: (Cont'd).

Sally Crumpton married Manaen Gum September 26, 1836.
Lavina Curtis Gum married Ebe Walter June 19, 1877.
Tillie Crumpton Walter married Henry Ridgely Harrington June 7, 1905.
Ruthaanna Wilson [Harrington] married Thomas L. Frymire April, 11, 1931.
Virginia Walter Harrington married Edward Martin Schoenborn June 18, 1940.

Births:

Curtis Crumpton, son of John Crumpton, was born October 15, 1755.
Elizabeth Crumpton [his sister?] was born September 30, 1756.
Mary Crumpton [his sister?] was born August 2, 1760
____ Crumpton was born July 19, 1762.
____ Crumpton was born November 1, 1764.
____ Crumpton was born February 14, 1767.
____ Crumpton was born March 3, 1770.
Margaret Kelley, mother of Nancy Thompson, was born January 2, 1790.
Children of Curtis Crumpton and Jamima Bowman:
  Mesia Crumpton was born May 11, 1782.
  Mary Crumpton was born March 8, 1784.
  John Crumpton was born January 4, 1787.
  Susanna Crumpton was born September 17, 1792.
  Thomas Crumpton was born February 4, 1794.
Children of John Crumpton and Nancy Thompson:
  ____ Crumpton was born June 20, 1810.
  Sally Crumpton was born March 18, 1812.
  ____ Crumpton was born January 30, 1815.
  Margaret Ann Crumpton was born May 18, 1818.
  John Crumpton was born October 13, 1820.
  Clarey Crumpton was born October 30, 1822.
  Leasbeth Crumpton was born January 29, 1825.
Lavina Curtis Gum, daughter of Sallie Crumpton & Manaen Gun was born July 16, 1849.
Ebe Walter was born October 14, 1850.
Tillie Crumpton Walter was born April 13, 1878.
Henry Ridgely Harrington was born March 11, 1873.
Thomas L. Frymire was born June 30, 1903.
Children of Tillie Crumpton Walter and Henry Ridgely Harrington:
  Ruthanna Wilson [Harrington] was born January 13, 1907.
  Henry Ridgely Harrington, [Jr.?] was born October 27, 1910.
  Virginia Walter Harrington was born September 13, 1914.
Ruth Anna Frymire, daughter of Ruthanna Harrington Frymire, was born May 17, 1935.

Births: (Cont'd).

Edward Martin Schoenborn III, son of Virginia Walter Harrington, was born November 17, 1942.

Deaths:

Jamima Crumpton departed this life February 25, 1811.
Manaen Gum died June 21, 1886.
Lavina Curtis Gum died July 16, 1926.
Ebe Walter died May 6, 1931.
Ruthanna Wilson died August 14, 1945.

CURTIS FAMILY TO MRS. H. RIDGELEY HARRINGTON

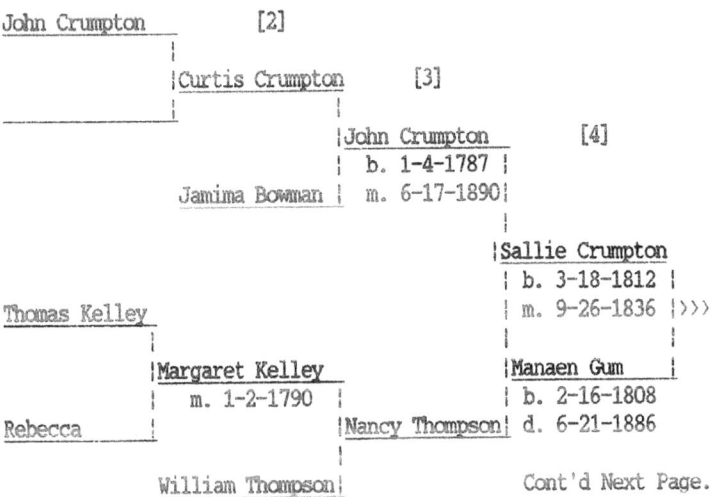

[1]

John Crumpton   [2]
    |Curtis Crumpton   [3]
                    |John Crumpton   [4]
                    | b. 1-4-1787 |
        Jamima Bowman | m. 6-17-1890|
                            |Sallie Crumpton
                            | b. 3-18-1812 |
Thomas Kelley | m. 9-26-1836 |>>>
        |Margaret Kelley |Manaen Gum
        | m. 1-2-1790 | | b. 2-16-1808
Rebecca |Nancy Thompson| d. 6-21-1886
        William Thompson| Cont'd Next Page.

[5]

Lavina Curtis Gum   [6]
  b. 11-28-1849 |(Mrs. H. Ridgely Harrington)
  d. 7-16-1926 |Tillie Crumpton Walter
  m. 6-19-1877 | b. 4-13-1878
               | m. 6- 7-1905
Ebe Walter |
  b. 10-14-1850
  d. 5 -6-1931 Henry Ridgely Harrington|
                    b. 3-11-1873

Genealogical Notes:

According to Delaware Wills Orphan Court D 455, Curtis Crumpton was the son of John Crumpton who left 900 acres in Murderkill [hundred] to some Curtis February 15, 1785.

Notes by Tillie W. Harrington, Jemima Bowman traces back to Hunn and Kitchen to 1672 in Delaware - back to 1635 in Massachusetts. The same line includes the Rodney, Bowers, Jenkins and other Quaker lines.

Thomas Kelley [appears in] Del. Archives Vol 1. p. 52 Sgt at arms 1-23-1776 enlisted at Dover under Capt. Nath. Adam, Col. Haslett's Regiment.

THE DeHAVEN FAMILY RECORDS

[Note: While the following appears in the 1st volume of the Delaware Bible Records, it appears to be a genealogical history of the family rather than a Bible Record].

Marriages:

William DeHaven married Hannah Cramber].
Samuel DeHaven, their son, married Catherine [Maiden Name not Given].
Jesse DeHaven, son of Samuel and Catherine DeHaven, married Mary
  Madeline Pluck in 1800.
Mary DeHaven, daughter of Jesse DeHaven and Mary Madeline Pluck,
  married William H. Smith in 1821.
Catherine DeHaven, daughter of Jesse and Mary DeHaven, married James
  Kennedy.

Births:

William DeHaven was born in 1714.
Birth date not given for his son Samuel.
Jesse DeHaven, son of Samuel, was born in 1773.
Mary Madeline Pluck, wife of Jesse DeHaven, was born in 1774.
James Kennedy, husband of Catherine DeHaven, was born in 1785.
Catherine DeHaven, daughter of Jesse DeHaven and Mary Madeline Pluck,
  was born in 1793.
William H. Smith, husband of Mary DeHaven, was born in 1797.
Mary DeHaven, daughter of Jesse DeHaven and Mary Madeline Pluck, was
  born in 1803.

Deaths:

William DeHaven died in 1784.
Samuel DeHaven died in 1815.
Jesse DeHaven died in 1835.
Mary Madeline Pluck DeHaven died in 1838.
James Kennedy died in 1860.
William H. Smith died in 1862.
Mary DeHaven Smith died in 1882.
Catherine DeHaven Kennedy died in 1883.

Genealogy of the DeHaven Family:

The DeHavens, Jacob, Samuel, Edward and Peter emigrated to America from the borders of France between 1750-1760. They were well to do for those days. During the long dreary winter 1777-1778, Washington's troops at Valley Forge were perishing with want adn were suffering almost indescribable hardships. Congress had no supplies nor money. Washington turned to the Citizens of Pennsylvania entreating aid. Jacob DeHaven among others was appealed to for help. He responded by advancing the Continental Congress $450,000 thru Robert Morris, the financier of the Revolution. Sameul DeHaven gave $17,000 as well as supplies to the army.

The following members of Cooch's Bridge Chapter, D.A.R. are Descendants of Peter DeHaven, the emigrant:

Mrs. Ernest Frazer   Mrs. Elizabeth Garrett
Mrs. Agnes Jones   Mrs. Mary Rebecca Garrett
Miss Anna Frazer   Miss Mary Bomann Smith
Mrs. Ola Cann

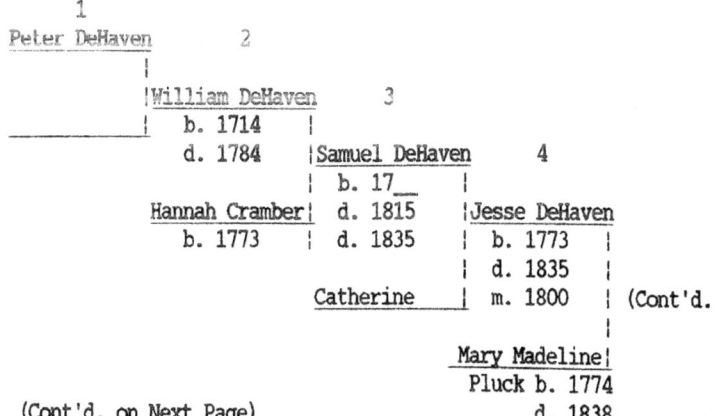

(Cont'd. on Next Page)

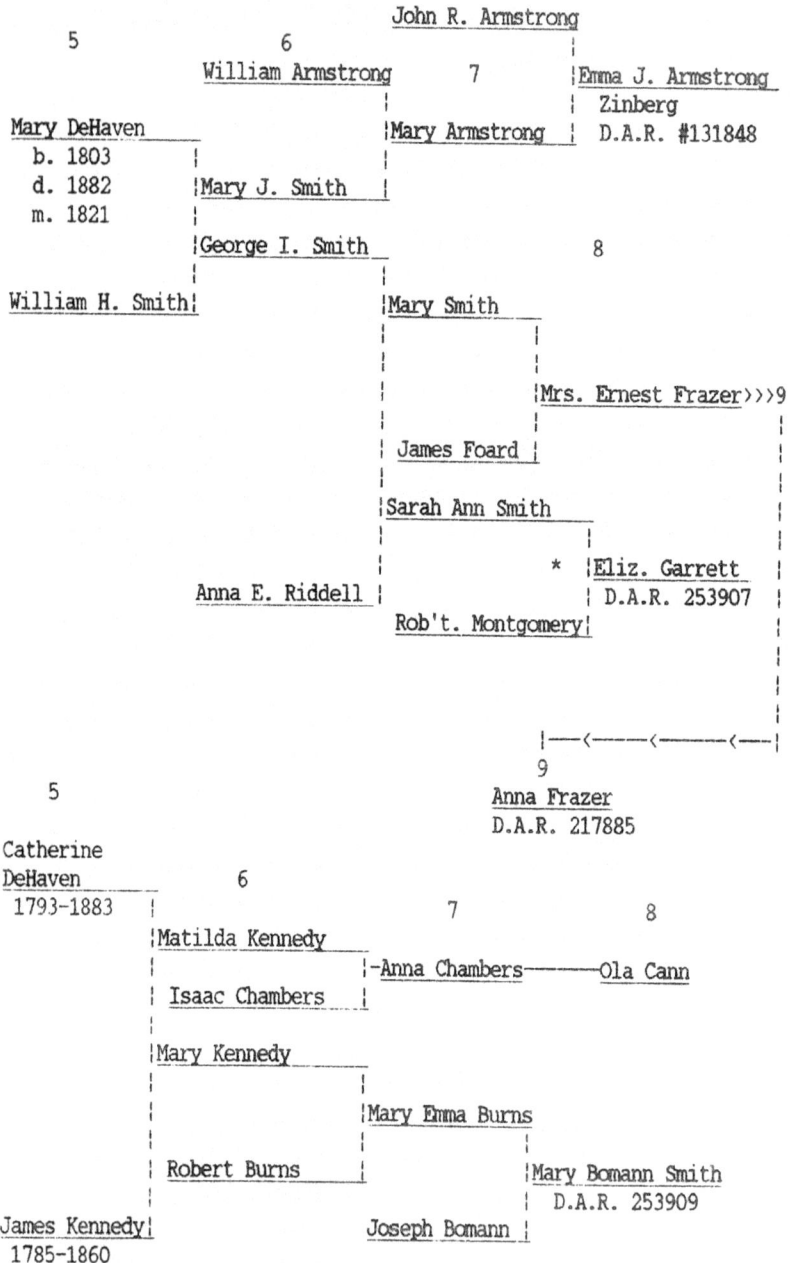

* It is not fully clear from the original lineage chart whether Eliz. Garrett is the daughter of Sarah Ann Smith or Mary Smith.

DICKEY FAMILY BIBLE RECORDS

1789 BIBLE:
Once owned by Miss M. Edna Chambers, 196 S. College Avenue, Newark, Delaware. Printed Edinburgh [Scotland] by Mark & Charles Kerr, His Majesty's Printers, MDCCLXXXIX 1789.

Births:

Children of Benjamin Dickey and A. Elizabeth as of 1812:
Joseph Dickey was born August 26, 1794.
Benjamin Dickey was born July 26, 1797.
Thomas Dickey was born August 31, 1800.
Margret Dickey was born September 10, 1803.

Charles Hays Dickey was born October 27, 1832.
Hester Jane Andreson [sic] was born July 5, 1840.

Later BIBLE: Once owned by Mrs. Harry B. Wollaston, Elsmere, Delaware. Published by Edward W. Miller, 1102 and 1104 Sansom Street, Philadelphia, Pa.

Marriages:

Nathan Guest and Lydia Mendenhall were married August, 1828.
Charles A. Dickey and Elizabeth A. Guest were married December 9, 1856.

Births:

Nathan Guest was born 1805.
Lydia Mendenhall was born March 15, 1805.
Charles H. Dickey was born October 23, 1833.
Elizabeth Dickey was born July 18, 1833.
Amor C. Dickey was born April 4, 1859.
C. Parmer Dickey was born March 30, 1861.
Lydia J. Dickey was born December 25, 1864.
Eliza D. Dickey was born July 25, 1866.
Hettie Dickey was born April 11, 1869.
Benjamin Lewis Dickey was born December 28, 1872.
Elizabeth B. Dickey was born October 17, 1873.

Deaths

Nathan Guest died March 21, 1845.
Amor C. Dickey departed this life March 10, 1863.

Deaths: (Cont'd).

Eliza D. Dickey departed this life July 28, 1866.
Lydia Mendenhall departed this life March 4, 1890.
Elizabeth Dickey departed this life November 11, 1900.

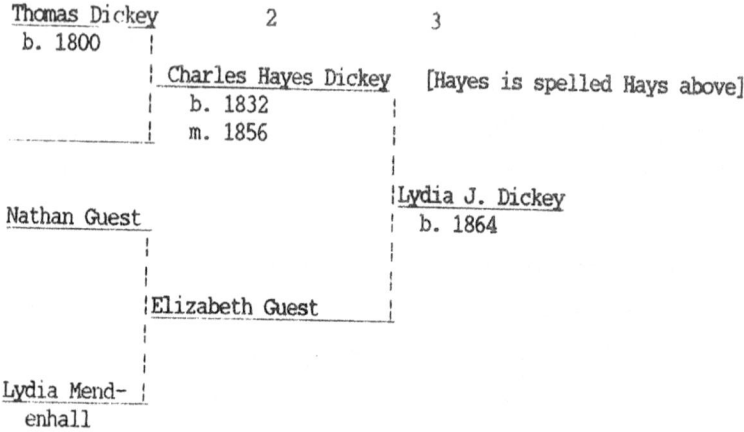

DIXON FAMILY BIBLE RECORDS

Bible last known to be in the possession of Miss Anna Dixon, Kennett Square, Pennsylvania.

Marriages:

Jehu Dixon married Mary Taylor.
Martha Dixon married Amos Sharpless.
Samuel P. Dixon married Mary.
Mary Dixon married Marshall P. Yeatmen.

Births:

Jehu Dixon, son of Isaac and Ann Dixon, was born June 21, 1760.
Mary Taylor, daughter of George and Hannah Taylor was born March 13, 1765.
[Children of Jehu & Mary Taylor:]
   John Dixon was born February 9, 1791.
   Hannah Dixon was born November 25, 1792.
   Ann Dixon was born January 25, 1795.
   Phebe Dixon was born November 17, 1796.

Births: (Cont'd).

Martha Dixon was born November 9, 1798.
Samuel P. Dixon was born October 27, 1800.
Mary Dixon was born December 25, 1802.
Sarah Dixon was born February 23m, 1805.
James Dixon was born September 21, 1813.
John D. Veale was born March 28, 1816 [parents not indicated].

Deaths:

John Dixon died in May 1792.
Jehu Dixon died September 17, 1807.
Sarah Dixon died September 21, 1808.
Mary Dixon [wife of Marshall Yeatman] died December 30, 1829.
John D. Veale died April 20, 1840.
Ann Dixon died September 27, 1851.
James Dixon died September 15, 1864
Phebe Dixon died November 17, 1878.

Ref.: Chandler & Lamborn Families - Vol. III of this series.

DORSEY FAMILY BIBLE RECORDS

Bible was once owned by Mrs. John Pilling Wright, Newark, Delaware. Kimber and Sharpless Edition, Holy Bible - Stereotyped by E. White, New York. Published and sold by Kimber and Sharpless, at their Store, No. 8 South Fourth Street, Philadelphia, Pa.

Note: Items marked * are written in the back of the Bible, those marked # are apparently written in the front of the Bible. No mark is given if the information appears in both locations or in chart form in either bible.

Marriages:

Edward Dorsey married Ann Worthington [date not given].
Joshua Dorsey married Sarah Richardson [date not given].
Colonel John Dorsey married Comfort Stimson, August 22, 1712, Anne Arundel County, Md. *
Joshua Dorsey married Flora Fitzsimmons, November 3, 1734. *
Joshua Dorsey [their son] married Margaret Watkins March 9, 1787.*
Nicholas Dorsey married Elizabeth Straughan May 22, 1810 Caroline County, Md.

Marriages: (Cont'd).

William Nicholas W. Dorsey married Elizabeth Bradley Cropper, January 2, 1833. *
Elizabeth Ellen Dorsey married Alexander Johnson, February 26, 1868.
Henrietta Straughan married 1st John, 2nd George Holmes.
Elizabeth Johnson married John Pilling Wright, September 9, 1908, P.E. Church of the Transfiguration, New York, N.Y.

Births:

Edward Dorsey was born 16__, in England. *
Joshua Dorsey [his son] was born in Virginia. *
Colonel John Dorsey [his son] was born in Anne Arundel Co., Maryland.*
Joshua Dorsey [his son] was born 1711, [apparently in Anne Arundel Co., Md.]. *
Joshua Dorsey, son of Joshua Dorsey (son of Colonel John Dorsey and his wife Comfort Stimson) and Flora Fitzsimmons, his wife, was born March 3, 1745# or 1746*. St. Margaret's Westminster Parish, Anne Arundel County, Maryland.
Nicholas Dorsey, son of Joshua and Margaret Watkins Dorsey, was born November 7, 1789.
Elizabeth Straughan, daughter of Samuel and Henrietta, his wife, was born July 9* (7#), 1788.
William Nicholas W. Dorsey, son of Nicholas and Elizabeth Straughan Dorsey, was born March 18, 1811.
William Nicholas Dorsey, son of William N. W. Dorsey and Elizabeth, his wife, was born September 27, 1834. #
Charles Henry Dorsey, son of William N. W. Dorsey and Elizabeth Dorsey, was born March 20, 1838. #
Elizabeth Ellen Dorsey, daughter of William Nicholas W. Dorsey and his wife, Elizabeth Bradley Cropper Dorsey, was born September 12, 1840, Milford, Kent County, Delaware.
Henrietta Straughan Dorsey, daughter of William N. W. Dorsey and his wife, Elizabeth, was born April 25, 1843. #
Crucinda Dorsey, daughter of William N. W. Dorsey and Elizabeth, was born June 12, 1852. #
Charles Anna Dorsey, daughter of William N. W. Dorsey and wife, Elizabeth, was born February 12, 1859. #
William Nicholas Dorsey, son of William N. W. Dorsey and Elizabeth, was born February 15, 1847. #
Elizabeth Johnson, daughter of Alexander Johnson and his wife, Elizabeth Ellen Dorsey, was born July 2, 1881, "Coon Den" near Farmington, Kent County, Delaware.

Deaths:

Joshua Dorsey [husband of Sarah] died in Anne Arundel County, Md. *
Joshua Dorsey [husband of Margaret Watkins] died in 1791. *
Nicholas Dorsey died June 8, 1812. *
Elizabeth Straughan, his wife, died in 1824. *
Charles Henry Dorsey, died 1840, aged 1 year, 10 months, 4 days. #
William Nicholas Dorsey, died 1840, aged 5 years, 5 months, 15 days. #
Elizabeth Bradley Cropper [wife of Wm. Nicholas W. Dorsey] died
March 26, 1872. Buried Old M.E. Cemetery, Milford, Del. *
Wm. Nicholas W. Dorsey died April 17, 1883, buried Odd Fellows
Cemetary, Milford, Delaware. *
Alexander Johnson died March 9, 1896, buried Christ P. E.
Churchyard, Dover, De. *
Elizabeth Ellen Dorsey, his wife, died September 19, 1902, buried
Christ P. E. Churchyard, Dover, De. *

Revolutionary War Service: #

Joseph Watkins signed the oath of Allegiance and Fidelity in Maryland.
Josuha Dorsey took the oath of Allegiance and Fidelity in Maryland.
He served in U.S. Army and received a discharge. Archives of
Maryland Vol. 18, p. 103.

Colonial Service: #

John Watkins III [great grandfather of Margaret Watkins Dorsey] fought
    in war with Nanticoke Indians. Archives of Md Vol 7, p. 96.
Captain Thomas Beeson [great great great grandfather of Margaret
    Watkins Dorsey] was military officer, Province of Maryland,
    1661. Archives of Md. Vol 2, p. 9, 63; Vol 3, p. 444.
Col. Nicholas Gassaway [great great grandfather of Margaret Watkins
    Dorsey] Re 1630-1691 Anne Arundel Co., Md. Member of Quorum 1691.
    Held commission as Capt., Maj., and Col. Ref. Soc. of Col Wars
    "Index of Ancestors and Honor Roll" 1922, p. 1922. Also Founder
    of Anne Arundel and Howard Counties, Maryland by Warfield, pages 40
    and 70.
Ens. Levin Cropper [great grandfather of Elizabeth Cropper Dorsey]
    1705-1775, Milford, Sussex Co. Del. Rep. Sussex Co. 1760-1773.
    Ensign, Colonial Militia 1756-58. Ref. Publication of Genealogical
    Society of Pa. Vol 5, p. 254-257. Del archives Vol 1 p. 13-15
William Manlove [great great great maternal grandfather of Alexander
    Johnson] 1653-1694, Kent Co. Del. Member of the General Assembly
    under Penn 1689, 92, 93. Province of Penna. Provincial Offficer
    of the three lower counties. Ref. 41 - IX Penna Archives page 660.
Col. John Dorsey   -1726 Anne Arundel Co. and Caroline Co. Md.
    Member of the Md. Assembly, Baltimore Co. 1721-22. Served as Maj.

and Col. in Md State Militia. Archives of Maryland; Maryland Historical Society Records.

Maj. Edward Bowman [great great great great great maternal grandfather of Elizabeth Cropper Dorsey] 1625-1691 Accomack Co. Va. Captain of Va. Militia 1665. Maj. 1674.

The Johnson family migrated from Annandale, County Dumfries, Scotland to Kent Co. Del.

The Cropper family migrated from Scotland to Sussex Co. Del. by way of Somerset Co., Md.

The Manlove family migrated from Staffordshire, England to Northampton Co. Virginia and Kent Co. Del.

The Hayes family [maternal line of Alexander Johnson] migrated from Exeter, Devon England to Sussex Co. Del.

The Watkins family migrated from Brecknock, Wales to Lower Norfolk Co., Virginia.

The Gassaway and Beeson families settled in Anne Arundel Co. Maryland.

ERNEST FAMILY BIBLE RECORDS

The following names are taken from the Ernest family Bible [last known to be] in the possession of John R. Ernest, Newark, Delaware.

Marriages:

Fagan Ernest and Martha Ann Mitchell were married September 20, 1836.
Charles R. Ernest and Laura Stelzer were married [no date given].
Joseph Delaine and Mary E. Ernest were married January 11, 1870.
Martha V. Ernest and J. Z. Staats were married January 15, 1872.
James M. Ernest and Ella W. Brice were married October 15, 1874.
George W. Ernest and Annie J. Brice were married March 21, 1876.
John F. Ernest and Annie Elmer Ellsworth Reynolds were married December 4, 1879.
May Ernest and Michael J. Taggart were married October 29, 1903.
Mary Natalie Ernest and B. Howard Craddock were married June 19, 1905.
James Mitchell Ernest and Mabel E. Spicer were married June 12, 1912.
John R. Ernest and Mildred K. Brown were married May 14, 1915 at Chestertown, Md. by Dr. Martin.
Douglas Ellsworth Ernest and Anna Margaret Price were married June 14, 1917 at their home. Middle Neck, Md.

Births:

Oliver Mitchell was born October 10, 1780.
Abby F. Mitchell was born May 3, 1794.

Births: (Cont'd).

Fagan Ernest was born September 11, 1807.
Martha Ann Ernest was born March 13, 1816.
George W. Ernest was born Mary 23, 1838.
Charles L. Ernest was born September 20, 1841.
Elijah C. Ernest was born September 8, 1843.
Mary E. Ernest was born February 19, 1846.
James M. Ernest was born November 2, 1848.
John F. Ernest was born November 21, 1850.
Martha V. Ernest was born September 19, 1853.
Ernest M. Delaine was born June 14, 1871.
Lena V. Staats was born August 14, 1872.
Julie L. Staats was born September 21, 1875.
Josephine Staats was born December 31, 1877.
Willie B. Dulaney was born March 24, 1877.
Lillian Ernest was born May 27, 1875.
May Ernest was born May 12, 1877.
Mary Natalie Ernest was born February 12, 1879.
James Mitchell Ernest, Jr. was born December 23, 1885.
Annie Elmer Ellsworth Reynolds was born April 23, 1862.
Charles Randolph Ernest was born December 19, 1876.
Nellie Grant Ernest was born February 8, 1878.
Gladys Ernest was born February 6, 1888.
John Reynolds Ernest was born July 28, 1890.
Douglas Ellsworth Ernest was born July 11, 1893.
James Mitchell Ernest, Jr. was born September 7, 1913.
Rosalynd Jane Ernest was born May 11, 1916.
Douglas Ellsworth Ernest, Jr. was born September 30, 1918.
Jacqueline Ernest was born August 15, 1920.

Deaths

Charles R. Ernest died September 27, 1842.
Abby F. Mitchell died August 1, 1865.
Oliver Mitchell died December 1, 1867.
Nellie B. Dulaney died July 7, 1877.
Mary Ellen Dulaney died March 28, 1880 in her 35th year.
Fagan Ernest died February February 2, 1883 in his 76th year.
Elijah C. Ernest died December 11, 1885 in his 43rd year.
Gladys Ernest died February 6, 1888.
James M. Ernest died April 22, 1890 in his 42nd year.
George W. Ernest died November 14, 1890 in his 52nd year.
Martha Ann Ernest died March 14, 1893 in her 77th year.
John F. Ernest died March 8, 1916 at 1 a.m. in his 66th year, 3 mo. &
    16 days.
Martha V. Staats died 1936 at Philadelphia, Pa.

DR. JOHN EVANS FAMILY BIBLE RECORD

Butler's Edition, The Holy Bible, Containing the Old and New Testamants. Translated out of the original tongues and with the Former Translations Diligently compared and Revised with References and Various Readings. Together with the Apocrypha.

Philadelphia: Published by E. H. Butler & Co. 1853. Once Family Bible of Mrs. Henry S. Young, 106 Bridge Street, Elkton, Md.

Marriages:

Dr. John Evans was married to Rebecca N. Sappington (daughter of Dr. John R. Sappington) at Blenheim, Harford Co., Maryland on Tuesday, June 6, 1854 by the Rev. Wm. Finley.

Births:

John Evans, son of Robert and Isabella Evans, was born April 25, 1810.
Rebecca N. Evans was born June 6, 1833.

[Their Children:]
Frank Sappington Evans was born May 5, 1855 at 2:30 p.m.
Helen was born Wednesday, November 5, 1856 at 3:15 [sic].
Isabel Creigh was born Saturday, February 13, 1858 at about 10:30 p.m.
Roberta was born Monday, November 14, 1859 about 6:30 p.m.
William Rowland Evans was born Friday, September 19, 1861 at 7:00 a.m.
Josephine Rebecca was born Tuesday, June 6, 1865 at 12 o'clock noon.
Jennie Evans was born October 21, 1867 at 7:30 a.m.
John Alexander was born Sunday, March 27, 1870 at 2:30 a.m.

Deaths:

Isabel Creigh Died December 5, 1863 in Havre de Grace [Md.], aged 5 years, 10 months & 8 days.
Frank S. Evans died at his home, Bel Air, Harford Co., Maryland, May 3, 1889.
W. Rowland Evans died at the home of his brother, Bel Air, Maryland, September 1, 1906.
Roberta Evans died March 21, 1908.
Dr. John Evans died at his home at Locust Grove, Cecil County, Maryland June 18, 1878.
Jennie B. Evans died October 12, 1884.
Rebecca N. Evans died June 25, 1917.

ROBERT EVANS FAMILY BIBLE RECORD

Belonged to H. E. Vinsinger, Newark, Delaware. [See Genealogical Note].

Marriages:

John Evans married Jean Moore.
Robert Evans married Margaret Kirkpatrick.
John Evans married Mary Alexander of New Munster on February 20, 1782.
Jean Evans married Col. Henry Hollingsworth (Rev. Service).
Hannah Evans married Rev. James Finley.
Mary Evans married Zebulon Hollingsworth.
Isabella Evans married William Montgomery.
Margaret Evans married James Black.
Eleanor Evans married Amos Alexander of New Munster.
Robert Gallaher and Sarah Evans married December 19, 1812.
Margaret Jane Gallaher and Joseph Steele married July 23, 1840.
Mary Gallaher and John Lowry married April 12, 1842.
Martha Ann Gallaher and William Price Strickland married October 21, 1845.
Robert Hamilton Gallaher and Ann Jane Adams married December 23, 1847.
Sarah Amelia Gallaher and George Fisler Harlan married September 30, 1852.
John Evans Gallaher married Annie E. Chandlee May 26, 1853.
Cornelia Rayburn Strickland married Henry Vinsinger at Elkton [MD? - no date given].
William T. Vinsinger and Carried [sic] Gray married [no date given].
Henry E. Vinsinger and Ruth Elizabeth Rupp of Washington, DC married at New York City July 9, 1907.
Ruth Elizabeth Vinsinger and Theo R. Dantz married of Newark, Delaware October 20, 1928.
Ruth Elizabeth Dantz married Ryron[sic] G. Rawson of Northeast Maryland in New York City on March 7, 1832.
Margaret S. Vinsinger married Bernard L. Greer of Jenkins Kentucky, at Newark, Delaware on February 3, 1937.

Births:

John Evans, about 1680 [in Wales?].
Robert Evans, 1710-11.
Children of Robert Evans & Margaret Kirkpatrick:
 Robert Evans [Jr.] was born January 4, 1756.
 John Evans was born May 8, 1760
 Jean Evans.
 Hannah Evans.
 Mary Evans.

Births: (Cont'd).

Isabella Evans.
Margaret Evans.
Eleanor Evans.

Children of John Evans and Mary Alexander:
Margaret Evans was born December Tuesday morning, 1783.
Amos A. Evans was born November 26, 1785.
Sarah Evans was born January 1, 1788.
Robert Evans was born January 5, 1789, Tuesday ten o'clock PM.
John Evans was born November 14, 1791.
James Evans was born February 3, 1794, Monday morning at 7 o'clock.
Levi H. Evans (Judge Evans) was born March 15, 1799, Thursday at 3 o'clock in the afternoon.
George Evans was born August 12, 1800, Tuesday morning at 4 o'clock.
William Evans was born January 26, 1803, Wednesday night at 9 o'clock.
Mark Evans was born January 24, 1806, Tuesday night.

Children of Robert Gallaher and Sarah Evans:
Margaret Jean Gallaher was born March 25, 1821.
Mary Gallaher was born May 19, 1815.
Robert Hamilton Gallaher was born October 6, 1818.
John Evans Gallaher was born April 17, 1823.
Martha Ann Gallaher was born June 7, 1826.
Sarah Amelia Gallaher was born March 21, 1830.
Isabella Gallaher was born February 6, 1832.

Children of William Price Strickland and Martha Ann Galaher:
Cordelia Royborn [Elsewhere given as Rayburn] Strickland.
David Taylor Strickland.
Sarah Rebecca Strickland.
Mary Scott Strickland.
Isabella Strickland.
Margaret E. Strickland.
Robert Evans Strickland.

Children of Cordellia Rayburn [Elsewhere = Royburn] Strickland and Henry Vinsinger:
William T. Vinsinger was born October 8, 1872 at Elkton, Md.
Henry Edward Vinsinger was born October 21, 1874 at Elkton, Md.

Children of Henry E. Vinsinger and Ruth Elizabeth Rupp:
Ruth Elizabeth Vinsinger was born May 27, 1908 at Elkton, Md.
Margaret Strickland Vinsinger was born May 28, 1909 at Newark, Delaware.
Henry Edwin Visinger, Jr. was born May 5, 1923 at Newark, Delaware.

Children of Margaret S. Visinger and Bernard L. Greer:
Ann Greer was born at Jenkins, Kentucky.
Bernard Lewis Greer was born September 11, 1940 at Knoxville, Tenn.

Deaths:

John Evans died June 1738.
Will filed at West Chester, Pa.
Jean Moore died 1751.
Robert Evans died November 1775.
Will dated October 20, 1775.
Probated December 22, 1775.
Robert Evans, Jr. Commissioned Lt. in Rev. War; killed by fall from a horse before he entered army.
Margaret Evans died 1781.
Mark Evans died Saturday, October 2, 1815, aged nine years, nine months.
Mary Evans [wife of John Evans] died Friday, September 1, 1820 about 7 o'clock in the evening.
James Evans died February 25, 1822.
John Evans (son of Robert) died March 3, 1823, aged 63 years.
Sarah Gallaher died September 16, 1853, aged 65 years.
Isabella Strickland died September 19, 1856, aged 1 years lacking 8 days.
William Price Strickland died April 5, 1864, aged 53 years.
Mary Lowry died July 20, 1872, aged 56 years.
Isabella Gallaher died September 21, 1874, aged 41 years.
Robert Gallaher died December 24, 1877, aged 87 years.
Martha A. Strickland died November 26, 1880, aged 53 years.
David Taylor Strickland died November 16, 1881, aged 32 years.
Robert E. Strickland died May 11, 1907, aged 44 years.
Cordelia R. Vinsinger died March 20, 1915, aged 68 years.
Margaret E. Strickland died May 31, 1920, aged 62 years.
Henry Vinsinger died October 1, 1925 at Elkton, Md.
Theo R. Dantz died March 12, 1929 at New York City.
Sarah Rebecca Strickland died May 11, 1931 at Elkton, Md, aged 79.
Mary Scott Strickland died March 30, 1933 at Elkton, Md. aged 80.
Ruth Elizabeth Vinsinger, wife of Henry E. Vinsinger, died February 6, 1937 AT Jenkins, Kentucky; buried Oak Hill Cemetary, Washington, D.C., February 10th.

Genealogical Notes:

"This book I with my money bought. Therfore to keep it sure I ought. And after I am dead and gone, I leave this book unto my son, Robert Evans".

Colonial War Service:

Robert Evans [b. 1710] was a member of Capt. Zebulon Hollingsworth [Sr.] Co. 1740 Ref. Md. Hist Mag. Vol 6 Pg. 48.

Revolutionary War Service:

Amos Alexander fought in the Revolution.
Robert Evans, Jr. was commissioned officer in Rev. War. killed by
fall from horse while home on furlough. [This taken from
related EVANS-KILPATRICK BIBLE, which otherwise duplicates some,
but not all of the material in this Bible record.]

In Memory:

They [Robert & Margaret Evans] lived together in love and comfort
Died in a good and humble hope
And their mingled dust here awaits
The last trumpets Joyful sound

They longed to leave this mournful place
This music dull where none
But heavy notes have grace
And mirth accents the moan

Farwel dear friends a short farwel
Til we shall meet above
Where Jeasus lives with happy souls
The family of love.

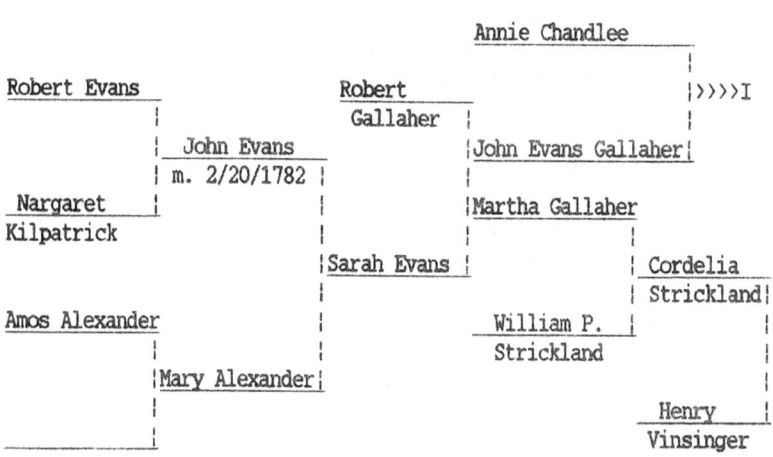

>>>>I —R. S. Gallaher

EVANS - SPRINGER BIBLE RECORDS

These records copied from Bible printed in Trneton M D C C X C I [1791]. Bible printed and sold by Isaac Collins. Bible last known to be in possession of Mrs. Elizabeth A. Evans, 651 Nth 63rd St. Philadelphia, Pa.

Marriages:

[Thomas Moore married Sarah _____.]
[Thomas Evans married Elizabeth Moore].
Joseph W. Springer, son of Joseph and Sarah Springer, married Rachel Armstrong.
Robert L. A. Springer, their son, married Mary Bockus.

Births:

Thomas Evans, son of David Evans, was born April 5, 1743.
[Mary Evans married James Plumly].
Elizabeth Evans, daughter of Thomas Moore and Sarah, his wife, was born April 28, 1746.
Children of Thomas and Elizabeth Evans:
  John Evans was born April 5, 1768.
  Eli Evans was born December 1, 1769
  David Evans was born March 12, 1771.
  Rees Evans was born February 7, 1772.
  Jesse Evans was born March 2, 1774.
  Mary Evans was born September 26, 1776.
  Thomas Evans [Jr.?] was born December 25, 1781.
  Sarah Evans was born May 1, 1785.
  Ruth Evans was born December 21, 1788.
Joseph Springer, son of Levi Springer and Rebecka[Sp?] his wife, was born October 31, 1789.
[Children of Joseph Springer and Sarah, his wife:
  Thomas Evans Springer was born February 28, 1821.
  Levi Springer was born December 16, 1822.
  Joseph W. Springer was born April 16, 1827.
Thomas Stewart [parents not indicated] was born December 29, 1829.
Robert Louis Springer, son of Joseph W. and Rachel Armstrong, his wife, was born November 9, 1856.

Deaths:

Rees Evans departed this life January 11, 1772, aged 11 months.
Thomas Evans, [Jr.?] departed this life August 30, 1793, aged 11 years 8 months and 5 days.

Deaths: (Cont'd).

Jesse Evans departed this life March, 1807, aged 33 years.
David Evans departed this life February 9, 1810, aged 30 years, 11 months.
Elizabeth Evans, wife of Thomas Evans and daughter of Thomas Moore, departed this life August 25, 1820, aged 74 years, 4 months, 5 days.
Thomas Evans departed this life January 19, 1826.
Joseph Springer, son of Levi Springer and Rebecka, his wife, departed this life August 3, 1827.
Thomas Evans Springer, son of Joseph Springer and Sarah, his wife, departed this life December 9, 1842, aged 21 years.
Eli Evans diedMarch 20, 1861, aged 92 years.
Sarah Springer, wife of Joseph Springer died August 12, 1863, aged 77 years.
Mary [Evans?] Plumly, wife of James Plumly, died February, 1863, aged 87 years.

FOULK FAMILY BIBLE RECORD

Last owned by Henry Wilson, Hockessin, Delaware. Printed by Mathew Carey, No. 118 Market St., Philadelphia, Pa., Oct. 28, 1802.

Marriages:

William Foulk, son of John Foulk and Hannah Sharpley were married on January 28, 1779 by Rev. George Craig according to the Constitution of the Church of England.
[John Foulk, son of William Foulk, married Candace Foulk (maiden name and date not given].

Births:

Hannah Foulk, daughter of William Sharpley was born February 4, 1755, which is the wife of William
William Foulk, son of John Foulk was born September 15, 1757 "in whom is the Right of this Book."
John Foulk was born June 24, 1780.
Susanna Foulk was born September 8, 1781.
Sarah Foulk was born May 24, 1783.
Hannah Foulk was born October 7, 1784.
Naomi Foulk was born September 8, 1786.
Aquila Foulk was born May 17, 1788.
William Sharpley Foulk was born October 24, 1789.

Births: (Cont'd).

Esther Foulk was born July 28, 1791.
Jacob Foulk was born November 25, 1793.
Elizabeth Foulk was born July 5, 1796.
Stephen Foulk was born February 18, 1799.

Children of John and Candace Foulk:

Susan Foulk was born August 22, 1808.
Hannah Foulk was born April 27, 1810.
Sarah Foulk was born June 17, 1811.
Maria Foulk was born September 21, 1812.
Esther Foulk was born December 20, 1814.
William Foulk was born June 18, 1817.
Candace Foulk was born January 20, 1822.
John Foulk Jr. was born December 24, 1823.

Deaths:

Naomi Foulk departed this life October 22, 1794, aged 8 years, 1 month, and 14 days and buried in Christiana Church Yard.
Hannah Foulk departed this life March 24, 1799, aged 14 years, 5 months, and 17 days and buried in Christiana Church Yard.
Aquila Foulk departed this life September 28, 1815, aged 27 years, 4 months and 11 days and buried in Christiana Church Yard.
William Foulk, husband of Hannah Foulk, departed this life September 18, 1818 and was buried September 20th in Christiana Church Yard.
Hannah Foulk, wife of William Foulk departed this life December 21, 1827 and was intered in the Christiana Church Yard.
John Foulk, son of William and Hannah Foulk departed this life June 28, 1850.
William Foulk, son of John and Candace Foulk, departed this life February 6, 1856 and was interred in the Brandywine Cemetary.
Candace Foulk departed this life April 13, 1864 and was interred in Brandywine Cemetary, April 18, 1864.
John F. Rowland, son of Isaac and Sarah Rowland, departed this life March 10, 1856 and was interred in Brandywine Cemetary.
John Foulk, son of John and Candace Foulk, departed this life March 27, 1877, Greeley, Colorado.
Esther F. Burgoyne died March 18, 1897 in her 84th year [sic].

Funerals:

James Crossan, July 25, 1906, from his late residence, Hockessin, Del. Interment at Union Hill.

Funerals: (Cont'd).

Esther F. Burgoyne from the residence of her husband, Cyrus F. Burgoyne, 843 Madison St., Wilmington, Del. Monday, March 22, 1897. Interment at Brandywine Cemetary.

Henry Clark from his late residence near the Brandywine Springs on Tuesday, December 15, 1885. Interment at Red Clay Creek Cemetary.

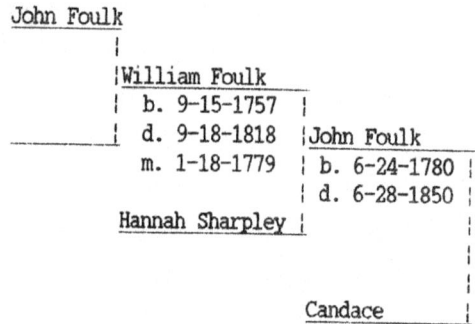

John Foulk
|
|William Foulk
| b. 9-15-1757
| d. 9-18-1818 |John Foulk
m. 1-18-1779 | b. 6-24-1780
| d. 6-28-1850
Hannah Sharpley |

Candace

FRAZIER - CUBBAGE FAMILY BIBLE RECORD

Published by J. B. Lippincott & Company, 1859. Bible last in the possession of Mrs. Wm. E. Holton, Newark, Del.

Marriages:

Thomas Emery Frazier married Rebecca Ruth Meredith December 22, 1823.
Job B. Frazier and Catharine Ann Campbell were married December 11, 1856.
Samuel M. Frazier and Frances Elizabeth Dalton were married October 27. 1886.
John E. Frazier and Annie H. Smith were married June 8, 1887.
Ephraim R. Frazier and Amanda R. Gray were married July 18, 1888.
Calvin Cubbage and Alice J. Frazier were married March 13, 1889.
Ephraim R. Frazier and Martha Dean were married December, 1896.
Benjamin C. Frazier and Ada V. Hall were married June 16, 1897.
William Edward Frazier and Laura Martin were married November 1897.

Births:

Thomas Emery Frazier, son of Lt. James Frazier and Rebecca Emery, was born in 1801.

Births: (Cont'd).

Joseph Meredith was born in 1740.
Rebecca Ruth Meredith, wife of Thomas Frazier. was born about 1805.
Job B. Frazier, their son, was born August 25, 1829.
Catharine Ann Campbell was born December 23, 1828.

Children of Job B. Frazier and Catherine Ann Campbell:
John Emery Frazier was born December 11, 1858.
Samuel Frazier was born November 8, 1860.
Fanny C. Frazier was born November 28, 1862.
Alice Jane Frazier was born August 10, 1864.
William Edward Frazier was born May 5, 1866.
Ephraim Rittenhouse Frazier was born April 25, 1868.
Mary Campbell Frazier was born September 19, 1869.
Benjamin Campbell Frazier was born August 19, 1874[?]

Children of Calvin and Alice J. Cubbage:
Helen Catharine Cubbage was born June 11, 1890.
Calvin Cubbage was born November 27, 1892.
Benjamin C. Cubbage was born October 1, 1895.
Milton Frazier Cubbage was born August 30, 1898.
Calvin Job Frazier, son of Ephraim R. and Amanda Frazier was born March 23, 1889.
Samuel D. Frazier, son of Samuel W. and Frances Elizabeth Frazier was born January 24, 1891.
George Emerson Frazier, son of Samuel W. and Frances Elizabeth Frazier was born September 1, 1894.
Alice J. Frazier, daughter of Benjamin and Ada Frazier was born March 9, 1899.

Deaths:

Joseph Meredit died in 1795.
Rebecca Ruth Meredith Frazier died in 1833.
Fanny C. Frazier died June 7, 1863.
Clarence J. Frazier died May 11, 1889.
Thomas Emery Frazier died in 1891.
Calvin Cubbage, son of Calvin and Alice J. Cubbage, died November 28, 1892.
Minnie R. Frazier, wife of Ephraim R. Frazier, died May 1, 1894.
Catharine A. Frazier, wife of Job M. Frazier, died August 12, 1897.
Job M. Frazier died July 24, 1899.
William Edward Frazier died [no date given].
Alice Jane Frazier Cubbage died February 14, 1904.

Additional Notes by Mrs. W. E. Holton [Somewhat Re-organized].

[Lineage and Relatives of Catharine Campbell Frazier]:

[Children of John Campbell and Jane (Jackson) Campbell - 2d. wife:]

1. Frank Campbell - Son Paul by 1st wife.
    - Married Flossie _____. Child: Tracy.
2. John and Lillie (Illegible) [Campbell]: Their Children:
    Charles [Campbell]
    Jack [Campbell]
    Nell who married McSlater and has one daughter, one grandaughter.
3. William and Julia [Campbell]:
    William [their son] married Sarah [maiden name not given - Had two sons.
    George [Campbell] married Sarah Dean and had these children:
        Margaret m. Irvin Reynolds - dau. Helen [Reynolds].
        Beulah m. Alfred Davis - no children.
        Gilbert [Campbell] - not married.
    Harry [Campbell] married Jennie Stayton, their children:
        Ethel Campbell and Marian Campbell
        Marian Campbell m. Clarence Keyes, their child:
            Clarence Keyes, Jr.
    Samuel [Campbell] married Corrie [sister of Flossie (1. above)]. They had one child Margaret who married and has one child.
    Laura [Campbell] - not married.
4. David [Campbell] m. [wife not given], their child:
    Florence [Campbell] m. Mr. Churchill, they had one son and one daughter.
5. Samuel Campbell m. Artie [maiden name not given]: Their children:
    Olive [Campbell] m. William Johnson, whose children were:
        Ethel [Campbell] m. Herbert Hitchens, their children:
            Robert and Charles Hitchens; Daughter - drowned.
    Johnson[?] [Campbell] m. twice - no children.
    Charles [Campbell] m. [wife's name not given] - several children.
6. Benjamin [Campbell] married Stella - one daughter Elsie [Campbell].
7. Mary [Campbell] - unmarried.
8. Margaret [Campbell] - unmarried.
9. Emma [Campbell] - unmarried.
10. Sarah [Campbell] - unmarried.
11. Elizabeth [Campbell] m. Mr. Finley - no children.
12. Catherine [Campbell] m. Job M. Frazier: - [Their descendants]:
    a. John [Frazier] m. Annie Smith - no children.
    b. Samuel [M. Frazier] m. Frances Dalton, their children:

Marriages: (Cont'd).
1. Samuel [D. Frazier] married and had two daughters.
2. George [Frazier] married Blaine - no children.
3. Edward [Frazier] married Laura Martin:
   Daughter: Margaret [Frazier].
4. Alice [Frazier] married Calvin Cubbage, their children:
   Milton [Cubbage] married Dorothy Smith - no children.
   Helen [Cubbage] married Wm. Holton, their child: Dorothy C. Holton
   Benjamin [Cubbage] married Frances Bernitz, their child: Benjamin Jr.
5. Ephraim [Frazier] married Martha Dean, their children:
   a. not given.
   b. not given.
   c. Irvin [Frazier].
   d. Ernest [Frazier].
6. Henry [Frazier] married Eva [maiden name not given] No children.
7. Benjamin [Frazier] married Ada Hall, their children:
   Alice [Frazier].
   Albert [Frazier].
   Ruth [Frazier].
   Catharine [Frazier].

Colonial and Revolutionary War Service:

Joseph Meridith served as a Private in Capt. John Caton's Co., Kent Co., Del. Militia, French and Indian War, 1757.
Lt. James Frazier served in Col. Neill's Del. Regt. during the Revolution.

FRAZIER - EMORY FAMILY BIBLE RECORD

This is an exact copy of the Family record of James Frashier. The will of this man is given under the name of James Frazor. William Frashier, the son of Thomas E. Frashier spelled his name Frazier and my mother Agnes Frazier Redgrave spelled hers the same, of course. In the Delaware Archives it is spelled er and zier. It is one and the same family, however, and even today various members spell it differently. I am copy these records page for page as given in the old Bible and Mrs. John W. Redgrave (Alzayda Frazier Redgrave) will attest to the correctness of the above statements and the Family record.   Signed Mildred Redgrave Gibbs (deceased)
                D.A.R. No. 23380, Suddlersville, Maryland.

Marriages:

James Frashier and Deborah Emory was married, February 22, 1779 A.D.
Deborah [Frashier] daughter to James and Deborah Frazier, was married to William Colgan, January 15, 1807, A.D.
Isabella [Frashier] daughter to James and Deborah Frazier, was married to Daniel Smith, December 17, 1807, A.D.
William [Frashier] son to James and Deborah Frazier, was married to Ann Cook January 1814 A.D.
James [Frashier] son to James and Deborah Frazier, was married to Rachell Carter December 1814 A.D.
Alexander [Frashier] son to James and Deborah Frazier, was married to Catherine Cooper April 9, 1819 A.D.
Thomas E. Frashier, son to James and Deborah Frazier, was married to Rebecca Meredith, December 22, 1825 A.D.
Elizabeth [Frashier] the daughter of Thomas E. Frashier and Rebecca was married to Benjamin L. Cohes (Coles?) February 19, 1850.
Alexander [Frashier], son of Thomas E. Frashier and Rebecca, his wife, was married to Sary A. Cooper, December 18, 1851 A.D.

Births:

William, son to James and Deborah Frashier, was born January 24, 1784.
Deborah, daughter to James and Deborah Frashier, was born June 22, 1786.
James, son to James and Deborah Frashier, was born December 22, 1782 A.D. ["(?) 1788" written in later].
Isabella, daughter to James and Deborah Frashier, was born February 22, 1791 A.D.
Alexander, son to James and Deborah Frashier, was born December 29, 1796 A.D.
Thomas Emory [FRASHIER], son to James and Deborah Frashier, was born May 23, 1801.
James T. F. Colgan, son of William Colgan and Deborah, his wife, was born October 26, 1807.
Joseph and Mary [COLGAN], son and daughter of William Colgan and Deborah, his wife, were born December 8, 1808 A.D.
Isabella, daughter of William Colgan and Deborah, his wife, was born October 25, 1810 A.D.
Elizabeth Frashier, daughter of Thomas E. Frashier and Rebecca his wife was born September 23, 1826 A.D.
Alexander Frashier, son of Thomas E. Frashier and Rebecca his wife was born February 17, 1828 A.D.
Job Meredith Frashier son of Thomas E. Frashier and Rebecca his wife was born August 25, 1829 A.D.

Births: (Cont'd).

Whiteley H. Frashier son of Thomas E. Frashier and Rebecca his wife was born October 9, 1831 A.D.
William Frashier son of Thomas E. Frashier and Rebecca his wife was born March 9, 1833 A.D.
Mary Ann Frashier daughter of Thomas E. Frashier and Rebecca his wife was born January 10, 1835 A.D.
James Frashier son of Thomas E. Frashier and Rebecca his wife was born November 26, 1836 A.D.
Deborah Ann Frashier daughter of Thomas E. Frashier and Rebecca his wife was born November 16, 1837 A.D.
Rebecca Ann Frashier daughter of Thomas E. Frashier and Rebecca his wife was born October 22, 1839 A.D.
Sarah Frashier daughter of Thomas E. Frashier and Rebecca his wife was born October 29, 1841 A.D.
Thomas E. Frashier, Jr. son of Thomas E. Frashier and Rebecca his wife was born February 19, 1844 A.D.
Catherine Meria daughter of Thomas E. Frashier and Rebecca his wife was born March 16, [184?].
Margaret Jane daughter of Thomas E. Frashier and Rebecca his wife was born August 17, 1848 A.D.

Deaths:

Isabella Smith, daughter to James and Deborah Frashier departed this life March 24, 1809 A.D.
James Frashier, husband to Deborah Frashier, departed this life November 6, 1818 A.D.
Deborah Frashier, wife of James Frashier, departed this life October 6, 1838 A.D.
Deborah Colgan, daughter to James and Deborah Frashier departed this life February [??], 1832 A.D.
James Frashier, son of Thomas E. Frashier and Rebecca his wife, died January 19, 1837.
Whiteley H. Frashier son of Thomas E. Frashier and Rebecca his wife, died August 16, 1837 A.D.
Deborah Ann Frashier daughter of Thomas E. Frashier and Rebecca his wife, died June 12, 1838 A.D.
Margaret Jane Frashier daughter of Thomas E. Frashier and Rebecca his wife, died November 23, 1853 A.D.

AGNES FRAZIER REDGRAVE FAMILY BIBLE RECORD

The following records are taken from the Bible of Agnes Frazier Redgrave.

Marriages:

William M. Frazier and Lucinda Roe was married February 12, 1862.
James Redgrave and Agnes Frazier was married March 12, 1895.
Joseph C. Gibbs and Mildred Redgrave was married November 29, 1919.

Births:

William M. Frazier was born March 9, 1833 A.D. [See William M. Frashier in Bible record just above].
Lucinda Roe was born January 28, 1837.
Agnes Frazier, daughter of William M. and Lucinda Frazier was born November 26, 1865 A.D.
Bedford R. Frazier, son of William M. and Lucinda Frazier was born June 6, 1870 A.D.
James Redgrave son of Isaac and Mary Elizabeth Redgrave was born October 8, 1871.
Mildred Redgrave, daughter of James and Agnes Redgrave was born April 28, 1898.

Deaths:

Bedford R. Frazier died September 13, 1880 age 10 years, 3 months and 7 days.
Abner Roe died March 10, 1887 age 42 years.
William M. Frazier died June 2, 1892 age 59 years, 2 months and 14 days.
Lucinda Frazier died October 12, 1898 age 61 years, 8 months and 14 days.

"The above statements written by Mildred Redgrave Gibbs and "the family Bible records" are correct.

     Alzayda Frazier Redgrave seal
     Mrs. John W. Redgrave seal

"Personally came before me, Clarence Weber, a Notary Public the above named deponents, Mrs Alzayda Frazier Redgrave, sometime known also as Mrs. John W. Redgrave, who first being duly sworn to law did depose and swear that the above statements are true and correct to the best of her knowledge and belief - Clarence P. Weber Notary Public".

 Will of James Frazor is in Kent Co. Court House, Dover, Del. Folio 160.

GALLAHER FAMILY BIBLE RECORD

Published by Sharpless and Kimber, Philadelphia, [Pa.] 1860. John Gallaher bought this Bible for his daughter, Martha, and wrote records for her.

Marriages:

John Gallaher married Mary Allen, March 1797.
John Gallaher married Martha McNight, November 9, 1802.

[Marriages of their children:]
Jane married September 23, 1830.
Elizabeth married January 15, 1831.
Moses married April 10, 1834.
John T. married October 2, 1838.
Martha married October 1, 1839.
Stewart married July 6, 1841.
Anna married August 10, 1841.
Robinson married December 26, 1843.
William married June 27, 1844.

Births:

Margaret Gallaher was born August 4, 1803.
Robinson Gallaher was born November 27, 1804.
Jane Gallaher was born July 14, 1806.
Elizabeth Gallaher was born July 31, 1808.
Moses Gallaher was born March 14, 1810.
Isabella Gallaher was born February 22, 1812.
John Thomas Gallaher was born September 27, 1813.
Stewart Gallaher was born July 11, 1815.
Martha Gallaher was born May 16, 1817.
William Jackson Gallaher |
Anna Maria Gallaher | Twins born April 28, 1821.
Fanny Gallaher was born May 18, 1823.
Robert Henry Gallaher was born March 11, 1866.
Mary Amelia Gallaher was born February 27, 1872.

Children of the above; [last two]
   Leon Henry Gallaher was born July 25, 1894.
   Elmer Hanna Gallaher was born July 21, 1897.
   Frederick Stanley Gallaher was born October 7, 1899.
   Ethel Viola Gallaher was born September 4, 1904.

Deaths:

Mary Allen, otherwise Mary Gallaher [1st wife of John Gallaher] departed this life and was buried at sea August 27, 1797.
John Gallaher departed this life May 22, 1841 age 61 years.
Martha McNight Gallaher died May 9, 1860, age 82 years.
[The Children of John & Martha McNight Gallaher]:
Margaret Gallaher died July 18, 1807.
Isabella Gallaher died October 23, 1813.
Fanny Gallaher Grant died August 9, 1853.
Robinson Gallaher died April 10, 1855.
Anna M. McKaig died June 5, 1866.
William J. Gallaher departed this life February 3, 1897, age 76 years.

JOHN EVANS GALLAHER-ANNIE CHANDLEE FAMILY BIBLE

Record last known to be in the possession of Mrs. Harry Covington, Richardson Park, Delaware. September 1941.

Births:

Sara Terressa Gallaher, daughter of John and Annie E. Gallaher born January 24, 1855.
Annie Maggie Gallaher, daughter of John and Annie E. Gallaher born July 21, 1857.
Edwin Henry Gallaher, son of John and Annie E. Gallaher born January 23, 1860.
Emma Bell Gallaher, daughter of John and Annie E. Gallaher born June 24, 1862.
Mary Ellis Gallaher, daughter of John and Annie E. Gallaher born September 16, 1867.
Martha Rebecca Gallaher, daughter of John and Annie E. Gallaher born August 21, 1870.
Robert Sidney Gallaher, son of John and Annie E. Gallaher born December 29, 1872.
John Evans Gallaher, son of Robert and Sarah born April 17, 1823.
Annie Elizabeth Chandlee, daughter of Sidney and Teressa F. Chandlee born December 28, 1830.

[LINEAGE CHART]

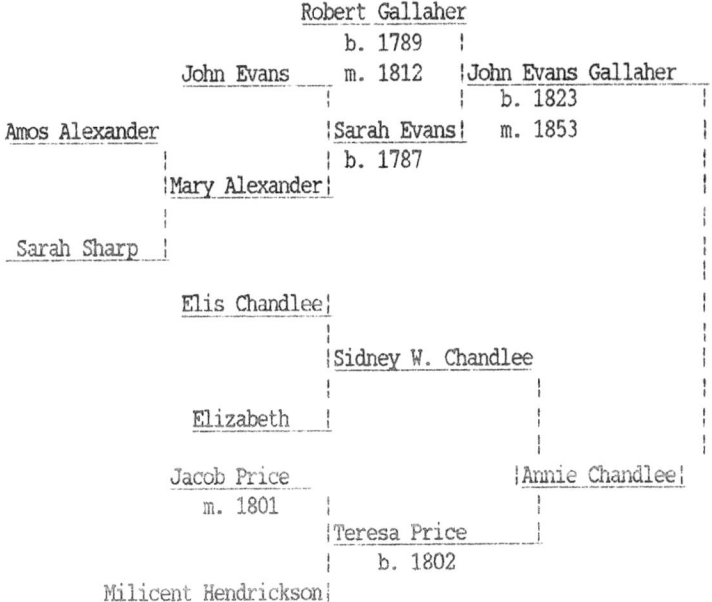

ROBERT GALLAHER FAMILY BIBLE RECORD

Robert Gallaher's book, he being born in the year of our Lord 1790.

Marriages:

Robert and Sarah Gallaher married December 11, 1812.
Margaret Jean Steel, [their daughter], married July 23, 1840 to Joseph Steel.
Mary Lowry, [their daughter], married April 12, 1842 to John Lowry.
Martha Ann Strickland, [their daughter], married October 25, 1845 to Wm. Price Strickalnd.
Robert Hamilton Gallaher married December 23, 1848 to Amyane Adams.
Sarah Amelia Harlan married September 30, 1852.
John E. Gallaher married Mary 26, 1853 to Annie G. Chandlee.

Births:

Robert Gallaher was born in 1790.
Sarah Evans was born January 1, 1788.
[Children of Robert Gallaher and Sarah Evans:]
  Mary Gallaher, daughter of Robert and Sarah Gallaher born May 19, 1815.
  Robert Hamilton Gallaher born October 6, 1818.
  Margaret Jane Gallaher born March 25, 1821.
  John Evans Gallaher born April 17, 1823.
  Martha Ann Gallaher born June 7, 1826.
  Sarah Amelia Gallaher born March 21, 1830.
  Isabella Gallaher born February 6, 1832.

Deaths:

Sarah Gallaher, wife of Robert Gallaher departed this life September 16, 1853 age 65.
Mary Lowry died July 21, 1872.
Isabella Gallaher died September 21, 1874.

WILLIAM M. GAMBLE FAMILY BIBLE RECORD

Marriage:

William M. Gamble and Susanne Pritchard were married July 28, 1870.

Births:

Their Children:
Bertha Gamble, Newark, Delaware
Harlow Gamble, deceased.
Harry Gamble, Muncie, Indiana
Allan Gamble, Covington, Indiana

Genealogical & Historical Notes:

   William Gamble, the son of Samuel Gamble was born at Scoots Hill, Maryland. He had a cobbler's shop in Newark [Delaware] until his death.

   Susanne Pritchard Gamble was born at old St. Patrick's Inn owned by Tobias and Mary Pritchard. St. Patrick's Inn was located on the present[?] site of the Deer Park Hotel. The land between Mote's Garage and the B&O Railroad, that is the strip located west of the B&O Railroad near the Deer Park Hotel was the old burying ground of the Pritchard family until it was purchased by the B&O and the bodies and tombstones were removed to the Newark Cemetery about 1900 or later. According to information received, the B&O was forced to make the bend there at the Deer Park Hotel because of the family burying ground which the Pritchard family would not allow to be sold.

GARRETT FAMILY BIBLE RECORD

Record taken from the family Bible purchased by Clinton H. Garrett, later owned by Harry I. Garrett. Published by William W. Harding, Philadelphia Pa. 1863.

Marriages:

Carver Wilkinson and Rachel F. Mackey were married April 4, 1833 by
 Rev. Robert Graham.
Clinton H. Garrett and Hannah J. Wilkinson were married December 16,
 1858.
Evan H. Garrett and Annie P. Mathias were married December 30, 1885 by
 Rev. J. L. Landingham
Harry I. Garrett and Elizabeth K. Montgomery were marred December 29,
 1886 by Rev. C. W. Prettyman.
Leon C. Garrett and Mary Rebecca Smith were married April 19, 1899 by
 Revs. France, Compton and Price.
Leon C. Garrett and Edna Anderson were married June 24, 1933 by Rev.
 McCorkle.
Leon C. Garrett and Mary Ruth Warrall were married June 20, 1936 by
 Rev. McCorkle.
Robert Anson Garrett and Ada Mae Rickey were married December 14, 1922
 by Rev. Christian Fry.
Lucie Isobel Garrett was married to George F. Hamilton.

Births:

Carver Wilkinson was born August 26, 1807.
Rachel F. Mackey born July 28, 1810.
Clinton H. Garrett, son of Evan and Sarah Garrett, born June 23, 1831.
Hannah Jane Wilkinson, daughter of Carver and Rachel Wilkinson, born
 August 29, 1837.
Harry I. Garrett, son of Clinton and Hannah Garrett, born September
 18, 1859.

Births: (Cont'd).

Anna Rebecca Garrett, daughter of Clinton and Hannah Garrett, born January 2, 1861.
Evan H. Garrett, son of Clinton and Hannah Garrett, born September 5, 1862.
Ella R. Garrett, daughter of Clinton and Hannah Garrett, born March 15, 1865.
Leon Clinton, son of Clinton and Hannah Garrett, born January 15, 1869.
Lizzie [Garrett] daughter of Clinton and Hannah Garrett, born May 3, 1871.
Lucie Isobel Garrett, daughter of Evan and Annie Garrett, born December 17, 1886.
Ella J. Garrett, daughter of Evan and Annie Garrett, born February 20, 1891.
Clinton Humphrey Garrett, son of Harry and Elizabeth Garrett, born February 12, 1890.
Robert Anson Garrett, son of Harry and Elizabeth Garrett, born September 20, 1891.

Deaths:

Carver Wilkinson departed this life September 24, 1838.
Rachel F. Wilkinson departed this life December 22, 1838.
Annie R. Garrett, daughter of Clinton and Hannah Garrett, died January 10, 1963.
Ella R. Garrett, daughter of Clinton and Hannah Garrett, departed this life December 18, 1866.
Lizzie, daughter of Clinton and Hannah Garrett, died May 5, 1871.
Ella J. Garrett, daughter of Evan and Annie Garrett, departed this life August, 1891.
Evan H. Garrett son Clinton and Hannah Garrett, departed this life March 10, 1892.
Battalion Sergeant Major Clinton H. Garrett, eldest son of Harry and Elizabeth Garrett died at Langees Haute Marne France of double lobar pneumonia Sunday, February 9, 1919.
Leon C. Garrett son Clinton and Hannah Garrett, departed this life May 8, 1941.
Mary Rebecca, wife of Leon C. Garrett, departed this life May 10, 1932.
Edna Anderson, wife of Leon C. Garrett, departed this life March 1, 1934.

GARRETT LINEAGE CHART

REV. GEORGE GILLESPIE FAMILY BIBLE RECORD

See Related Chart: Page 20 above.

First Generations

Marriages:

Rev. Andrew Simson married Violet Adamson, sister of Patrick,
  Archbishop of St. Andrews [No Date Given].
Rev. Patrick Simson married Martha Baron [NDG].
Alexander Simson married Elis Stewart [NDG].
Rev. John Gillespie married Lilias Simson, daughter of Patrick Simson,
  minister of Stirling.

Births:

Rev. Andrew Simpson was born in 1520.
Violet Adamson was born in 1537.
Their Children:
  Rev. Patrick Simson was born in 1556.
  Archibald [No Date Given]
  Alexander was born in 1564.
  Richard [NDG].
  William [NDG].

Rev. John Gillespie of Alva [NDG].
Lilias Simson, daughter of Rev. Patrick Simson [NDG].
Children of John Gillespie and Lilias Simpson:
  1. Capt John Gillespie [NDG].

Births:

2. Rev. George Gillespie, Chaplain to Viscount Kentmure and Earl Cassilis; Member Westminster Assembly.
3. Rev. Patrick Gillespie, Principal of Glasgow University [NDG].

Deaths:

Rev. Andrew Simson died in 1590.
Violet Adamson died in 1592.
Rev. Patrick Simson died in 1618.
Rev. John Gillispie of Alva died in 1627.
Alexander Simson died in 1628.

Second Generation

Marriages:

2. Rev. George Gillespie married Catherine Murray [NDG].
7. Elizabeth Gillespie married James Oswald [NDG].

Births:

2. Rev. George Gillespie$_1$ (John$_1$) was born in 1613.

Deaths:

2. Rev. George Gillespie died in 1648.

Third Generation

Births:

[Children of [2] Rev. George Gillespie and Catherine Murray:]

4. Robert Gillespie [NDG].
5. Rev. George Gillispie was born about 1644.
6. Archibald [NDG].
7. Elizabeth Gillespie Oswald [NDG].

Deaths:

5. Rev. George Gillespie died in 1724.

Fourth Generation

Marriages:

8. Rev. George Gillespie₄ (John₁, George₂, George₃) **Emigrant Pastor** of Head of Christiana Church, emigrated from Scotland to New England, brought letters to Rev. Cotton Mather; afterward removed to Delaware and ministered to four churches: White Clay Creek, Red Clay Creek, Elk River and Lower Brandywine married Rebecca [maiden name not given].

Births:

8. Rev. George Gillespie, Emigrant Pastor, was born in 1683.

Deaths:

8. Rev. George Gillespie, Emigrant Pastor, died in 1760
Rebecca, his wife, died on January 2, 1760.

Fifth Generation

Marriages:

9. Hannah married Bryan [first/last name?; No Date Given].
11. Agnes married Jos. Steele [NDG].
13. Martha married Samuel Armitage [NDG].
14. Mary married Joseph Wallace [NDG].
15. George Gillispie married Hannah Johnson [NDG]. Signed Oath of Fidelity Vol. 2, p. 998 before Jos. Black.

Births:
[Children of Rev. George Gillespie and Rebecca, his wife:]
9. Hannah [NDG].
10. Elizabeth [NDG].
11. Agnes [NDG].
12. Samuel Gillespie was born in 1718.
13. Martha Gillespie was born in 1731.
14. Mary [NDG].
15. George Gillespie.

Deaths:

10. Elizabeth Gillespie died in 1772 (See N.C. Cal. of Wills p.69).
12. Samuel Gillespie died in 1766 (See N.C. Cal. of Wills p.66).
13. Martha Gillespie Armitage died in 1772.
15. George Gillespie died in 1796.

Sixth Generation

Marriages:

16. Rebecca [Bryan?] married Francis Elliott.
17. Elizabeth [Bryan?] married Blair.
22. George Gillespie married Mary Evans.
23. Margaret Gillespie married Walter Carson.

Births:

[Children of [9] Hannah Gillespie and Bryan[?]:
16. Rebecca [No Date Given].
17. Elizabeth [NDG].
18. George [Bryan?] [NDG].
[Children of [13] Martha Gillespie$_3$ (John$_1$, George$_2$, George$_3$, George$_4$) and Samuel Armitage:]
19. Rebecca Armitage [NDG].
20. Mary Armitage [NDG].
[Children of [14] Mary Gillespie$_3$ and Joseph Wallace
21. George Wallace [NDG].
[Children of [15] George Gillespie$_4$ (John$_1$, George$_2$, George$_3$, George$_4$) and Hannah Johnson:]
22. George Gillespie, Jr. [NDG].
23. Margaret Gillespie was born 1752.

Deaths:

22. George Gillespie, Jr. died in 1831.
23. Margaret Gillespie died in 1774.

Seventh Generation

Marriages:

25. Margaret [Gillespie] married Capt. Joseph Kirkwood.
26. Agnes [Gillespie] married John Evans in 1807.
28. Mary [Gillespie] married William D. Eves.
31. Elizabeth [Gillespie] married Jas. Hodgson.
32. Hannah [Gillespie] married Andrew Kerr.
33. Franklin [Gillespie] married Eliza Eves.
34. Thomas [Gillespie] married Mary Eves.

Births:

John Evans was born in 1781.
[Children of [22] George Gillespie, Jr., (John, George, George, George, George) and Mary Evans:]
24. George Gillespie was born in 1783.
25. Margaret Gillespie was born in 1785.
26. Agnes (Gillespie) Evans was born in 1787..
27. Thomas [NDG].
28. Mary was born in 1791.
29. Hannah was born in 1793.
Andrew Kerr, husband of [32] Hannah Gillespie, was born in 1794.
30. Samuel was born in 1795.
31. Elizabeth was born in 1797.
32. Hannah was born in 1802.
33. Franklin was born in 1805.
34. Thomas J. was born in 1807.

Deaths:

24. George [Gillespie] drowned at sea in a voyage to the West Indies.
26. Agnes [Gillespie] died in 1787.
27. Thomas [Gillespie] died in 1792.
29. Hannah [Gillespie] died in 1797.
30. Samuel [Gillespie] died in 1797.
31. Elizabeth [Gillespie] died in 1845.
32. Hannah [Gillespie] died in 1880.
34. Thomas J. Gillespie died in 1887.

[Eighth Generation]

Marriages:

35. Hannah Maria [Kirkwood] married James McCune.
36. Sarah [Kirkwood] married Joseph Large.
37. Ann [Kirkwood] married David Allen.
38. Adaline [Kirkwood] married Dr. Henry West.
39. Elizabeth [Kirkwood] married Wm. Kennon.
40. Catherine [Kirkwood] married Dr. James McConahey.
41. Margaret [Kirkwood] married Rev. James Alexander.
42. Josephine [Kirkwood] married Vincent Mitchell.
47. Margaret Ann Evans married John W. Evans.
48. George G. Evans married Mary Black.
49. William D. Evans married Mary Jeanne.
52. Mary Kerr married Francis G. Parke June 7, 1859.

Marriages: (Cont'd).

53. George Kerr married Clara Chamberlain.
58. Mary Gillespie married Joseph Seaver -

>   *   -   Jessie m. W. Percy Simpson.
>   Archer W. & Howard E.

>   * Note: Underlined portion, shown as in original record, is not indexed. Not clear if Jessie is a sister or daughter of Mary Gillespie and whether Archer W. & Howard E. should have the surname or Seaver or Simpson.

Births:

[Children of [25] Margaret Gillespie, (John, George, George, George, George, George) and Capt. Joseph Kirkwood, son of Major Robert Kirkwood who commanded the Delaware Regt., during the Revolution [No Dates Given]:

35. Hannah Maria.
36. Sarah.
37. Ann.
38. Adaline.
39. Elizabeth.
40. Catherine.
41. Margaret.
42. Josephine.
43. Mary died in youth.
44. Robert died in youth.

[Children of [26] Agnes Gillespie, and John Evans:
45. Mary Evans was born in 1808.
46. Hannah Evans was born in 1809.
John W. Evans, husband of Margaret Ann Evans, was born in 1810.
47. Margaret Ann [Evans] was born in 1818.
48. George G. Evans [NDG].
49. William D. Evans [NDG].
Mary Jeanne Provost, his wife, was born in 1820.
50. Mary C. Evans was born in 1820.

[Children of [31] Elizabeth Gillespie, and James Hodgson:
   Robert H. Hodgson. [no number assigned in the record].

Births: (Cont'd).

[Children of [32] Hannah Gillespie, and Andrew Kerr:
51. Samuel T. Kerr was born in 1831.
52. Mary Kerr Parke was born in 1833.
53. George G. Kerr was born in 1835.
54. Andrew W. Kerr [NDG].
55. Andrew B. Kerr was born in 1839.
56. James B. Kerr was born in 1839(?).

[Children of [33] Franklin Gillespie and Eliza Eves:
57. Albert Gillespie [No Date Given].
58. Mary [Gillespie] [NDG].
59. John [Gillespie] [NDG].
60. Jennie [Gillespie] [NDG].
61. George [Gillespie] [NDG].

[Children of [34] Thomas J. Gillespie, and Mary Eves:]
61.[sic] George Gillespie [NDG].
62. John [Gillespie] [NDG].
63. Henry [Gillespie] [NDG].
64. & 65. [Left Blank in original records].
66. Franklin [Gillespie] [NDG].
67. William [Gillespie] [NDG].
68. John F. [Gillespie] [NDG].
69. Mary A. [Gillespie] [NDG].
70. Mary A. [?] [Gillespie] [NDG].
71. Susan [Gillespie] [NDG].
72. Emma [Gillespie] [NDG].

Deaths:

[Children of [26] Agnes (Gillespie), and John Evans:]
45. Mary Evans died in 1818.
50. Mary C. Evans died in 1839.
46. Hannah Evans died in 1862.
Mary Jeanne Provost, wife of William D. Evans, died in 1871.
49. William D. Evans died in 1882.
John W. Evans, husband of Margaret Ann Evans died in 1882.
47. Margaret Ann (Evans) Evans died in 1892.

[Children of [32] Hannah and Andrew Kerr:]
51. Samuel T. Kerr died in 1839.
55. Andrew B. Kerr died in 1839.
54. James B. Kerr died in 1853.
52. Mary Kerr Parke died in 1882.
53. George G. Kerr died in 1916.

74

Ninth Generation

Marriages:

[Children of [37] Ann Kirkwood Allen and David Allen:]
73.   Sutia Ann Kerr Allen [No Date Given].
[Children of [39] Elizabeth Kirkwood and Wm. Kenon:]
Elizabeth [Kenon] married Henry Alexander. [no number assigned in the record for this child].
[Children of [47] Margaret Ann (Evans) Evans and John W. Evans:]
[no numbers assigned in the record for these children].
Hannah C. [Evans] married John F. Terry.
Anna B. [Evans] married W. E. Turner.
John L. Evans married H. Brooke.
Fanny Evans married F. Brewer.
[Children of [48] George G. Evans and Mary Black:]
[no numbers assigned in the record for these children].
Anne M. Evans married Dr. H.G.M. Kollock.
Margaret G. Evans married John S.M. Neill of Helena, Montana.
Agnes Armitage Evans married Chas. W. Reed.
Charles B. Evans married Mary Raub.
[Children of [49] William D. Evans and Mary Jeanne Provost:]
Louis P. Evans married Mary McCalla.
Agnes Gillespie Evans married Samuel R. Shipley.

Births:

[Unless shown, no number was assigned in the original record for these births and no date of birth was given:]

[Child of [37] Ann Kirkwood Allen and David Allen:]
73.   Sutia Ann Kerr Allen.
[Child of [39] Elizabeth Kirkwood and Wm. Kenon:]
Jane, Margaret, Newell, Albert, Elizabeth [Kenon].
[Children of [47] Margaret Ann (Evans) Evans and John W. Evans:]
Mary S. [Evans].
Hannah C.
Anna B.
John L. Evans.
Susan W.
Emma M.
Agnes G.
Fanny Evans
Eugenia
Mary W.

Births: (Cont'd).

[Children of [48] George G. Evans and Mary Black:]
Anne M. [Evans].
Harriet N.
Margaret G. Evans
Charles B. Evans
Lena Evans.

[Children of [49] William D. Evans and Mary Jeanne Provost:]
Louis P. Evans was born June 25, 1848.
Agnes Gillespie Evans was born January 8, 1828.
Mary Exton Evans was born November 17, 1855.

Deaths:

Mary S. Evans died in 1840.
Mary W. Evans died in 1863.
Eugenia Evans died in 1864.
Louis P. Evans died August 19, 1896.
Dr. H.G.M. Kollock died in 1928.
Harriet N. Evans died in 1932 unmarried.

Tenth Generation

Births:

Albert D. Rice, son of Sutia Ann Kerr and David Allen [No Date Given].
[Children of Agnes Armitage and Charles W. Reed.:]
Charles E. Reed [NDG].
Emma G. Reed [NDG].
George G. Reed [NDG].
Albert Reed [NDG].

[Children of Agnes Gillespie Evans and Samuel R. Shipley:
Mary [Shipley] was born June 30, 1892.
Agnes [Shipley] was born January 29, 1896.

GOTTIER - BOOTH - ALDRICH FAMILY BIBLE RECORD

This Bible was owned by a member of the Gottier family and is [over] 200 years old. The Gottiers were French Huguenots. They were cabinetmakers and brought some of their productions with them. They settled around Iron Hill, [DE and] Elkton, Maryland.

The Booths settled around Iron Hill and Fell's Point, Harford Co., John Wilkes Booth was a descendant of the Harford Co., Branch.

John Gottier married Elizabeth, daughter of Ebenezer Booth, of Iron Hill Baptist Church and from these the following Bible records have been obtained.

The Gottiers, Booths and Aldridges intermarried.

Marriages:

Francis Gottier, Sr., emigrant from France, married Margaret Furugson.
Ebenezer Booth married Elizabeth Booth.
Margaret, daughter of Francise Gottier, Sr. married John Kean.
John Gottier married Elizabeth, daughter of Ebenezer Booth.
Rev. Fredus Aldridge married Catherine Cosden, widow of Rev. Jeremiah Cosden in 1796.
Francis Booth Gottier, son of John and Elizabeth Booth Gottier, married Rebecca Wingate, daughter of Edward and Margaret Wingate, March 28, 1826.
John Aldridge and Ann Elizabeth Gottier, daughter of John Gottier, were married October 8, 1827.

Births:

Rev. Fredus Aldridge was born in Elk Neck, Cecil Co., Md. May 7, 1771.
[Children of John and Elizabeth Booth Gottier:]
Francis Gottier was born May 1, 1801.
Elizabeth Gottier was born February 12, 1803.
[Children of John and Elizabeth Booth Aldridge:]
John Gottier Aldridge was born January 28, 1829.
Francis Aldridge was born April 28, 1832.
Wm. Spry Aldridge was born June 31 [sic], 1836.
Sophia Cosden Aldridge was born August 6, 1842.

Deaths:

Francis Gottier, Sr. died December 11, 1826 age 76 years. He is buried in the Old Welsh Tract Baptist Meeting House, Iron Hill, Del.
Margaret Ferguson [Furguson? - see above.] wife of Francis Gottier, Sr. died August 31, 1820 age 79 years and is buried in the Old Welsh Tract Baptist Meeting House cemetary, Iron Hill, Delaware. The inscription on her tombstone is as follows 'was respected by the rich and loved by the poor'.
Margaret Gottier [Kean] their daughter, died October 11, 1821.

Deaths: (Cont'd).

John Gottier, their son, died October 6, 1822 age 49 years is buried in the Old Welsh Tract Baptist cemetery.
Rebecca Gottier, wife of Francis Booth Gottier and daughter of Edward and Margaret Wingate died December 30, 1837.
John Stogden (Stockton) Aldridge died April 1, 1875 in the 80th year of his age.
Ann Elizabeth Aldridge died September 3, 1885 in the 83rd year of her age.
William Spry Aldridge died May 22, 1887 and is buried in Hopewell cemetery, Cecil Co., Md.
Francis Booth Gottier died May 27, 1889 age 89. He is buried in the Elkton Cemetery, Cecil Co., Md.
John Gottier Aldridge died at his home in Pasadena, California August 23rd in the 83rd year of his age. He is buried in Rose Hill cemetery, Chicago, Illinois.
Elizabeth Gottier, daughter of Francis and Rebecca Gottier, died June 2, 1907 age 80 years - Buried in Elkton Cemetary.
Sophia Cosden Aldridge Hammond, daughter of Joh and Elizabeth Booth Aldridge, died May 9, 1928.
Elizabeth Booth Aldridge Miller, daughter of John and Elizabeth Booth Aldridge, died September 22, 1928 aged 94 years, 5 months and 16 days. Buried at Galena, Kent Co., Md. cemetery.
Millicent Howell, daughter of Francis and Rebecca Gottier died in Philadelphia, Pa.

Rev. Fredus Aldridge
   b. 5-7-1771

	John Stockton Aldridge
	b. 2-9-1797
Catherine Cosden	d. 4-1-1875
widow of Jeremiah	m. 1827
Cosden b. 1796	
d. 8-2-1812.	

1.

Francis Gottier, Sr.   2.
  d. 12-11-1826
    age 79 |Margaret Gottier   3.
              | m. John Kean
Signed Oath of | d. 10-11-1821
  Fidelity
                (Cont'd. on next Page).

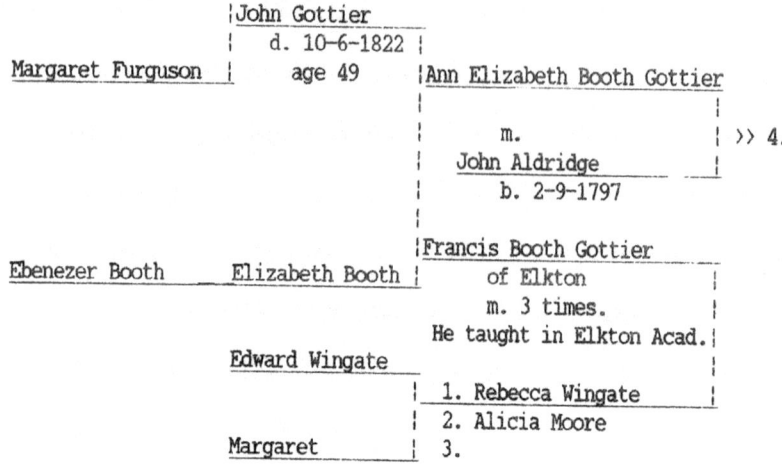

4.

1. John Gottier Aldridge
    b. 1-28-1829
    d. 8-23-1912

2. Francis Aldridge
    b. 4-28-1832

3. Elizabeth Booth Aldridge Miller
    b. 4-28-1832
    d. 9-22-1928

4. William Spry Aldridge
    b. 6-31-1836
    d. 5-22-1887

5. Sophia Cosden Aldridge Hammond
    b. 8 6-1842
    d. 5-9-1928

Revolutionary War Notes:

Francis Gottier, Sr. signed the Oath of Fidelity before Justice Joseph Gilpin. Ebenezer Booth also signed the Oath of Fidelity before Justice Gilpin. Fredus Aldridge signed the Oath of Fidelity at Elkton, Md. before Justice John Ward.

HANSON FAMILY BIBLE RECORD

Genealogy of Dorothy Shonk
Reported by Ella N. Hanson her eldest grand-daughter. - 1915.

Marriages:

Dorothy Shonk married first James Lewis in Plymouth, Del?
Dorothy Shonk married second Jeoffrey Swithenbank in 1851 in West Philadelphia, Pa.
Dorothy Shonk married third John Thorpe, date and place unknown. He was probably from Maryland - no children.

Births:

Jeoffrey Swithenbank was born in England in 1801.
Dorothy Shonk was born in 1821 in Plymouth, Del?
James Lewis, son of James Lewis and Dorothy Shonk.
Henry Lewis, son of James Lewis and Dorothy Shonk. Later adopted by a Mr. Mast and known as Henry Mast, last reported living in Denver, Colorado.
Sarah Elizabeth Swithenbank born 1852, West Philadelphia, Pa.

Deaths:

Dorothy Shonk died in Wilmington, Del. in 1902
Jeoffrey Swithenbank died in Wilmington, Del. in 1861.

Marriages:

Sarah Elizabeth Swithenbank married William Henry Hanson in 1873 in Chester, Pa.
Martha Miller Hanson married [first] Philip McAvaney in 1900 in Wilmington, Del.
Martha Miller Hanson married [second] John Townsend [probably in Wilmington, Del.] Date unknown. No Children.
George F. Hanson married Ruth A. Pyle in 1908 in Wilmington, Del.
Dorothy May Hanson married W. Harry Dawson in 1910 in Wilmington, Del.
James L. Hanson married Myrtle Spencer in 1911 in Camden, N.J.
Philip D. McAvaney married Helen G. Buterbaugh in 1925 in Wilmington Del.
Warren McAvaney married Catherine Ann Schunder, 1927 in Wilmington, Del.

Marriages: (Cont'd).

Sarah Elizabeth McAvaney married Henry E. Barlow, Jr., 1928 in Wilmington, Del.
Ella Pyle Hanson married Thomas Pyle Gebhart, February 18, 1933 in New Castle, Del.
George Hamlin Dawson married Marguerite Dorothy Bedwell, May 10, 1941 in Baltimore, Md.
William Harry Dawson, Jr. married Norma Jane Jarmon, July 3, 1941 in Newark, Del.
Dorothy May Dawson married Harvey Lewis Baldwin, June 20, 1942 in Newark, Del.
Emma Spencer Hanson married Stanley Vail Howell, November 5, 1942 in Wilmington, Del.
John Edgar Dawson married Margaretha Ruth Anderson, June 28, 1943 in Newark, Del.

Births:

William Henry Hanson born 1852 in West Philadelphia, Pa.
Philip McAvaney born 1879 in Wilmington, Del.
Ruth A. Pyle born 1885 in Wilmington, Del.
W. Harry Dawson born 1888 in Wilmington, Del.
Myrtle Spencer born 1892 in New London, Pa.
Helen G. Buterbaugh born 1903 in McConnellsburg, Pa.
Stanley Vail Howell born September 29, 1906 [Wilmington, Del?]
Henry E. Barlow, Jr. born 1908 in Wilmington, Del.
Thomas Pyle Gebhart born June 6, 1909 [New Castle, Del?].
Harvey Lewis born Feruary 16, 1917 in Corner Ketch, Del.
Margaretha Ruth Anderson was born July 22, 1917 in Los Angeles, California.
Norma Jane Jarmon born April 16, 1918 in Newark, Del.
Marguerite Dorothy Bedwell born June 27, 1918.

<u>Children of Sarah Elizabeth Swithenbank and William Henry Hanson:</u>
Ida Jane Hanson born 1874 in Wilmington, Del.
Ella N. Hanson born 1875 in Wilmington, Del.
Susan C. Hanson born 1878 in Wilmington, Del.
Martha M. Hanson born 1880 in Wilmington, Del.
George F. Hanson born 1882 in Wilmington, Del.
James L. Hanson born 1885 in Wilmington, Del.
William H. Hanson born 1887 in Wilmington, Del.
Joseph C. Hanson born 1888 in Wilmington, Del.
Dorothy May Hanson born 1889 in Wilmington, Del.
Joseph C. Hanson born 1893 in Wilmington, Del.
Helen C. Hanson born 1896 in Wilmington, Del.

Births: (Cont'd).

Children of Martha Miller Hanson and Philip McAvaney:
Warren McAvaney born Wilmington, Del. 1901.
Philip McAvaney [Jr?] born Wilmington, Del. 1903.
Sarah Elizabeth McAveney born Wilmington, Del. 1908.

Children of George Foote Hanson and Ruth Pyle:
Ella Pyle Hanson, born 1909, Wilmington, Del.
Ruth Anna Hanson, born June 25, 1915, Wilmington, Del.
Arnold Hanson, born April 5, 1920, Wilmington, Del.

Children of James F. Hanson and Myrtle Spencer:
Emma Spencer Hanson, born Wilmington, Del. 1912.
Dorothy Shonk Hanson, born May 21, 1913, Wilmington, Del.
Robert Lewis Hanson, born February 8, 1926, Wilmington, Del.

Children of Dorothy May and William Harry Dawson:
Willa Virginia Dawson, born Wilmington Del., 1911.
George Hamlin Dawson, born Wilmington, Del., 1912.
Dorothy May Dawson, born November 12, 1915, Wilmington, Del.
William Harry Dawson, Jr., born May 10, 1917, Wilmington, Del.
John Edgar Dawson born September 29, 1919, Wilmington, Del.
Martha Dawson, [no date] premature, lived 10 days.

Later Births:

Catharine Ann McAvaney born to Warren McAvaney & Catherein Ann
   November 14, 1929.
Phillip D. McAvaney [Jr.] born to Philip D. McAvaney & Helen G.
   Buterbaugh November 12, 1930.
Karen Ruth Gebhart born to Ella Pyle Hanson & Thomas Pyle Gebhart
   October 23, 1942 in Wilmington, Del.

Children of Sarah Elizabeth McAvaney & Henry E. Barlow, Jr.:
Phyllis L. Barlow born September 5, 1929 in Wilmington, Del.
Henry E. Barlow III born March 5, 1932 in Wilmington, Del.
Sarah Elizabeth Barlow born August 15, 1935 in Wilmington, Del.
John L. Barlow born June 22, 1937 in Wilmington, Del.
Norman Warren Barlow born February 12, 1939 in Wilmington, Del.
Sharon Rose Barlow born May 6, 1941 in Wilmington, Del.

Deaths:

Ida Jane Hanson died 1878, Wilmington, Del.
William C. Hanson died 1887, Wilmington, Del.
Joseph C. Hanson died 1888, Wilmington, Del.
Susan C. Hanson died 1891, Wilmington, Del.

Deaths: (Cont'd).

Joseph C. Hanson died 1896, Wilmington, Del.
Dorothy Shonk Hanson died October 18, 1915, Wilmington, Del.
Harvey Lewis Baldwin died August 19, 1943 while serving in the U.S. Armed Forces.

Genealogical Notes:

```
Dorothy Shonk
  m.
  1) James Lewis        | Sarah Elizabeth Swithenback
  2)                    |
  Jeoffrey Swithenbank  |
                        |                    | Dorothy May Hanson
                                              |
                        William Henry Hanson  |
                                              |
                                              | W. Harry Dawson
```

ANDREW & LYDIA (McCAULEY) HARVEY FAMILY BIBLE

Printed & Sold by M. Carey, Philadelphia, 1817. This Bible was last known to be in the possession of Mrs. Lydia Harvey Greenfield, Elkton, Md.

Marriages:

Andrew Harvey and Lydia McCauley was married February 6, 1817.
Elizabeth Harvey and Daniel McCauley was married February 24, 1820.
Rachel Harvey and John Scarborough was married March 18, 1817.
Andrew Harvey and Lydia Quarll was married October 27, 1842.

Births:

Andrew Harvey was born January 24, 1791.
William Harvey, son of Andrew Harvey Sr. & Susannah was born September 12, 1792.
Elizabeth Harvey, daughter of Do.[sic] [Harvey], was born August 14, 1794.
Lydia Harvey was born September 21, 1796.
Rachel Harvey, daughter of Do.[sic] [Harvey], was born November 17, 1796.

Births:

John Harvey, son of Do. was born February 23, 1799.
Thomas Harvey, son of Do. was born March 25, 1801.
Susannah Harvey, daughter of Do.[sic] was born July 28, 1803.
Mary Harvey, daughter of Do. was born March 8, 1805.
Francis Harvey was born September 5, 1805.
Hannah Harvey was born January 25, 1810.
Lydia Quarll was born February 17, 1810.
Jane Harvey was born March 28, 1812.

[Children of Andrew and Lydia (McCauley) Harvey:]
William Harvey was born November 14, 1817.
Henry Harvey was born December 30, 1819.
Susan Harvey was born December 9, 1822.
Andrew Harvey was born April 12, 1826.
Daniel Harvey was born February 18, 1828.
Francis Harvey was born February 22, 1830.
John Harvey was born July 19, 1832.
Francina Harvey was born February 21, 1835.
Henry Harvey, son of Andrew and Lydia (Quarrl) was born January 10, 1848.

Deaths:

Andrew Harvey, son of William and Rachel, departed this life November 17, 1813, Aged 47 years.
Jane Harvey, daughter of Andrew [Sr.] and Susannah Harvey, departed this life July 20, 1814, Aged 1 year & 4 mos.
Susannah Harvey, daughter of John and Elizabeth Waggoner, departed this life August 5, 1815, Aged 45 years.
William Harvey, son of Andrew [Sr.] and Susannah Harvey, departed this life December 14, 1814, Aged 22 years.
Henry Harvey, son of Andrew & Lydia Harvey, died September 13, 1821, Aged 20 mos & 13 days.
Francina Harvey died February 27, 1835.
John Harvey, son of Andrew & Lydia Harvey, died August 25, 1835.
Lydia Harvey, Consort of Andrew Harvey, died March 13, 1849.
Henry Harvey, son of Andrew & Lydia Harvey, departed this life March 13, 1849. Of such is the Kingdom of Heaven.
Andrew Harvey, son of Andrew [Sr.] and Susannah Harvey, departed this life September 8, 1868, in the 78th year of her age.
Susan Tyson, daughter of Andrew and Lydia [McCauley] Harvey, departed this life February 14, 1897 in the 75th year of her age.
Lydia Harvey, (2nd) wife of Andrew Harvey, departed this life October 17, 1886 in the 77th year of her age.

Deaths: (Cont'd).

Daniel Harvey, son of Andrew & Lydia Harvey, departed this life October 28, 1897 in the 73rd year of his life.
Andrew Harvey, son of Andrew & Lydia Harvey, departed this life March 29, 1904 in the 78th year of his life.

JOHN HAYES FAMILY BIBLE RECORD

Published 1814, Philadelphia. Printed by M. Carey, No. 121 Chestnut Street.

Marriages:

John Hayes and Ann Elizabeth Salisbury was married January 4, 1816 by the Reverend John Sharpley in Kent County, Maryland.
Henry M. Hayes and Eliza Brooks was married April 20, 1821 [probably in Cecil County, Md.]
John T. Gallaher and Hannah Amelia Hayes were married at Chery [sic] Hill in Cecil County, Md. on November 5, 1844 by the Rev. Edward Kennard.
Ethland Brooks Gallaher and James J. McCauley were married at Spring Hill (Childs) by Rev. E. T. Cochel June 20. 1878.
Elsie R. McCauley and Walter Armstrong were married at Antego, [__?] by Rev. A. C. Dixon October 29, 1902.
John Hayes McCauley and Florence E. McCrery were married January 18, 1914, [place not indicated].
Adele Leslie Blackwell and John Clifford Calloway were married in Chesapeake City [Md?] by Rev. Zeigler June 15, 1929.
Walter A. Blackwell, Jr. and Sarah Isabel Bridges were married in Hancock, Md. October 3, 1931.

Births:

John Hayes was born July 14, 1793 in Middletown, Pennsylvania.
Henry Moore Hayes was born February 15, 1798 in Wilmington, Del.
Ann Elizabeth Salisbury was born Marcy 3, 1799 in Kent County, Md.
Eliza Brooks was born August 18, 1801 [place not shown].
John Thomas Gallaher was born at Spring Hill, Cecil County, Md. on September 27, 1813.
[Children of Henry Moore Hayes & Eliza Brooks, all born at White Hall Farm, Cecil County, Maryland:]
Stephen Hayes born April 12, 1822.

Births: (Cont'd).

Hannah Amelia Hayes born January 26, 1824.
Maria Rudulph Hayes born January 6, 1826.

[Children of John T. Gallaher and Hannah A., his wife, all born at Spring Hill, Cecil County, Maryland:]

Henry Evans Gallaher was born August 2, 1845.
Alfred Gallaher was born September 13, 1847.
Maria Amelia Gallaher was born February 18, 1850.
Mary Rebecca Gallaher was born July 24, 1852.
Ann Rudolph Gallaher was born February 18, 1855.
Ethland Brooks Gallaher [daughter] was born March 14, 1857.
Lydia Caroline Gallaher was born April 18, 1860.
John Hayes Gallaher was born October 10, 1862.
Fanny May Gallaher was born May 27, 1865.
Newton Robert Reese Gallaher was born December 24, 1867.
James McCauley was born November 12, 1853.
Walter Armstrong Blackwell was born November 4, 1876, [place not indicated].

Adele Leslie Blackwell was born in North East Md. January 27, 1905.
Walter A. Blackwell, Jr. was born July 17, 1908.
Elsie Roberts McCauley was born at Childs, [Spring Hill, Md.?] March 16, 1879. She has a twin who died shortly after birth.
John Hayes McCauley was born at Antego, [__?] November 1, 1881
Clifford Calloway was born May 17, 1905, [place not indicated].

[Children of John Hayes McCauley & Florence S. McCrery:]

John Hayes McCauley, Jr. was born January 12, 1915.
James Albert McCauley was born June 15, 1917.
Newell (Charles) McCauley was born July 27, 1919.
Barton Brook McCauley was born Marh 11, 1925.

Deaths:

Henry Moore Hayes departed this life July 28, 1828 at White Hall.
Tobias Rudulph died at his residence near Elkton [Md.] on September 11, 1828 about 10 o'clock P.M.
John Hayes died February 19, 1854 at his residence near Cowan Town [__?].
Fanny May Gallaher departed this life on January 3, 1867.

LINEAGE OF MRS ELSIE McCAULEY BLACKWELL
(Mrs. Walter A. Blackwell)
D.A.R. No. 210778

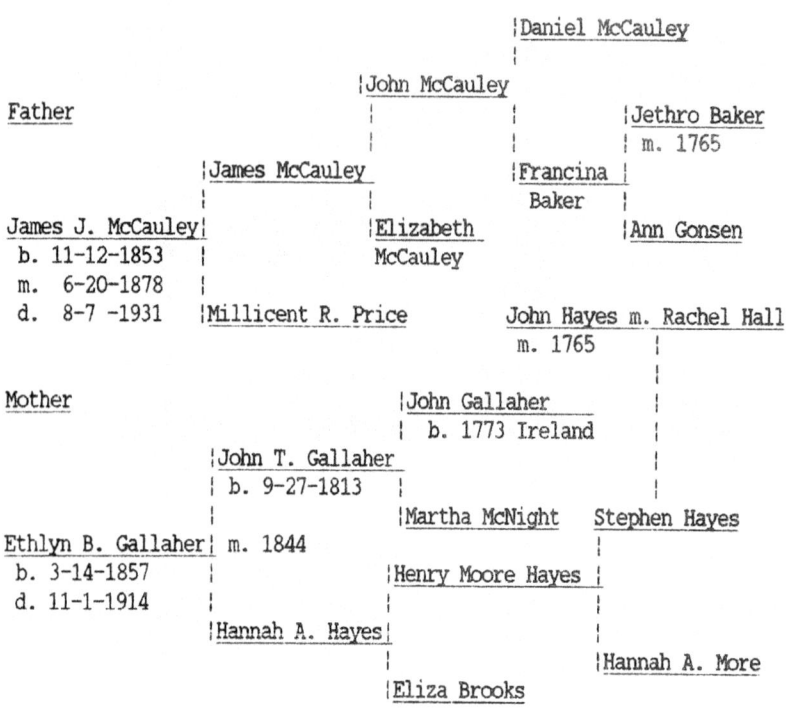

HENKEL FAMILY BIBLE RECORDS

These Bible records are from old Henkel family Bible Records; offical church and cemetary records in New Market, Va., and were originally checked by Miss Cora C. Curry, then Historian of Henkel Family Association then-located at 1420 Gerard St., N. W., Washington.

Marriages:

Rev. Paul Henkel married Elizabeth Nagley in Monterey, Va. November 20, 1776.
Dr. Solomon Henkel (Solomon David) married Rebecca Miller September 10, 1800.
Rev. Ambrose Henkel married 1st Catherine Hoke at Lincoln County, N.C.
                     2nd Mary Kite at Page County, Va.
                     3rd Veronica Heyl.

Marriages: (Cont'd).

Rev. David Henkel married Catherine Heyl at Lincoln County, Va.
Rev. Charles Henkel married Mary Elizabeth.

[Children of Dr. Solomon Henkel:]
Helena married Gideon Rupert June, 1822.
Samuel Godfrey married Susan Coyner November 1, 1832.
Siram Peter married Margaret Coyner.
Solomon David married Sarah Bowman June 11, 1840.
Silon Amos married Elizabeth Shaver August 18, 1842.
Hannah Rebecca married Lewis M. Zirkle October 20, 1846.
Solon Paul Charles married Anna Maria Miller November 16, 1846.
Helea Anna Maria married Rev. David Henkel September 11, 1849.

Births:

Paul Henkel, son of Jacob and Barbara Teeter Henkel, was born December 15, 1754 in Rowan Co., N.C.
Elizabeth Nagley was born September 20, 1757 in Monterey, Va.
Solomon David Henkel was born November 10, 1777 in Pendleton, Va.
Rev. Phillip Henkel was born September 23, 1779 in Pendleton, Va.
Naomi Henkel was born January 5, 1782.
Rev. Ambrose Henkel was born July 11, 1786.
Sabina Henkel was born October 1, 1788.
Rev. Andrew Henkel was born October 21, 1790 in New Market, Va.
Rev. David Henkel was born May 4, 1795 in Staunton, Va.
Rev. Charles Henkel was born May 15, 1798 in New Market, Va.

[Children of Dr. Solomon D. Henkel:]
Helena was born in 1801.
Seorim was born June 2, 1803.
Sylvanus was born February 1, 1805; died the same day.
Samuel Godfrey was born February 16, 1807.
Siram Peter was born March 16, 1809.
Simeon Socrates was born October 9, 1811.
Silon Amos was born August 6, 1813.
Solomon David was born December 9, 1815.
Solon Paul Charles was born February 7, 1818.
Hannah Rebecca was born February 22, 1822.
Helea Anna Maria was born September 18, 1882.

Deaths:

Paul Henkel died November 20, 1776.
Rev. David Henkel died June 5, 1831 in Lincoln Co., N.C.

Deaths: (Cont'd).

Rev. Charles Henkel died February 2, 1841 in Perry Co., Ohio.
Elizabeth Nagley died April 20, 1843.
Dr. Solomon Henkel died August 31, 1847 at New Market, Va.
Rev. Ambrose Henkel died January 6, 1870.
Rev. Andrew Henkel died April 23, 1872 at Germantown, Ohio, buried in Germantown, Ohio.
Rev. Phillip Henkel died October 9, 1883 at Richland, N.C.

[Children of Dr. Solomon Henkel & Rebecca Miller:]
Helena died in January, 1875.
Seorim died February 1, 1804.
Samuel Godfrey died in March, 1863.
Siram Peter died October 17, 1872.
Simeon Socrates died October 2, 1812.
Silon Amos died April 30, 1844.
Solomon David died October 7, 1872.
Solon Paul Charles died May 14, 1882.
Hanna Rebecca died April 13, 1861.
Helea Anna Maria died February 15, 1874.

- All interred in Henkel Lutheran Church Cemetary, New Market, Va. - Cemetary tombstone records verify the above bible records.

[Genealogical Notes:]

The Henkels:- Over two centuries have passed since Rev. Anthony Jacob Henkel, an exiled Lutheran Clergyman, came from Germany to Pa. in 1717. He was one of the founders of the Lutheran Church in America. He died 1728 and for a long time his burial place was not known. His wife Elizabeth was buried at St. Michael's Church, Germantown, Pa. Research instituted 1910 revealed that Rev. Henkel was buried in the same grave as his wife. The Henkel family placed a memorial [t]here in 1917.

Rev. Paul Henkel, a grandson was a prominent Luthera. He was a writer of Hymns, Luteran books and was a pioneer Missionary in Va., N.C., Ky., Tenn., and Ohio.

Rev. Ambrose Henkel with his four brothers established the Henkel Printing House of New Market, Va. in 1806. This is still operating and is the oldes Lutheran Publishing house in America. Engravings were made of wooden blocks.

Rev. Paul Henkel was an intimate friend of Rev. Peter Muhlenberg, who as a Major General of the Rev. gained renown. Every schoolboy knows the story of how Rev. Muhlenburg, after preaching a patriotic sermon, pulled aside his clerical robe, disclosing a Col. uniform. He said the time to fight had come. He gave his robe to Rev. Paul Henkel, his friend and kinsman with the injunction that the robe remain in the family in the ministerial line. Finally, the robe, in order to preserve it, was loaned by the Henkel family to The Lutheran Theological Seminary at Mt. Airy, near Germantown, Pa. For many years the robe was used by the minister at New Market when brides of the Henkel family were married.

Henkel Fort, Pendleton Co. W.Va. was the only Fort in the County utilized by the patriot forces, or, that had any Revolutionary history.

- HENKEL-EASTMAN-STIEGAL-BRIGHT-BUCK-BUSH -
(Mr. and Mrs. Arthur B. Eastman, Newark, Del.)

I. Helen Henkel (Mrs. A. B. Eastman)

```
        1              2              3              4          >5
                                                          |Rev. Paul Henkel|
                                        |Dr. Solomon Henkel|
                       Solomon D.|
                         Henkel  |                  |Elizabeth Nagley
                                 |
Silon Amos Henkel|               |Rebecca Miller
   (father)      |
                 |Sarah Bowman


        5       6       7              8              9        >10
                                                          |Dr. Justus|
                                                          |  Henkel
                                       |George Henkel  |
                       Anthony J.    |
                        |Henkel      |
                |Justus              |Eulales Dantazer
                |Henkel |
                |       |Maria Elizabeth
Jacob Henkel|   (Cont'd. Next Page.)
```

89

90

```
       5       |                                    10
               |                            Johannes Henkel
   Mary Leeter |                           (Chaplain to Queen
                                            Maria of Hungary)


   1            2             3                  4
                                           |Baron Wm. Stiegal
                                           |
                            Jacob Stiegal  |
                            | 1785-1869    |
                            |                |Elizabeth Holtz
                |David Stiegal|
                |             |              |Michael Bright
                |             |              |
  Alice Stiegal|              |Catherine Bright|
     (Mother)  |               1783-1855    |
                |Sarah Siebert               |Louisa [Bright]

       5              6             7              8     >9
  |Michael Bright  Jonathan Bright  Johannes Bright  Balthaser Bright
  | 1732-1814      | 1706-1794      | b. 1662        | 1636-1705
  |Sarah Stoner    Margaret Simons  Anna Katherine   Anna Margaret
                                    Hoffman          Christman
   9
  Christopher Brecht
   1591-1665         |
  Anna [Brecht       |
```

Michael Bright 1732-1814 was a member of the Committee of Observation while Commissionrr of Berks Co. Pa. during the Revolution.

Baron Wm. Stiegal was the famous maker of Stiegal Glass about whom so much has been written.

II. Arthur Bartlett Eastman:

```
       1              2              3              4            5   >6

  Charles Francis  Joseph B.       Moses         Corp. Edward   Ebenezer
     Eastman        Eastman        Eastman         Eastman       Eastman
  | (father)    (Cont'd. Next Page.)
```

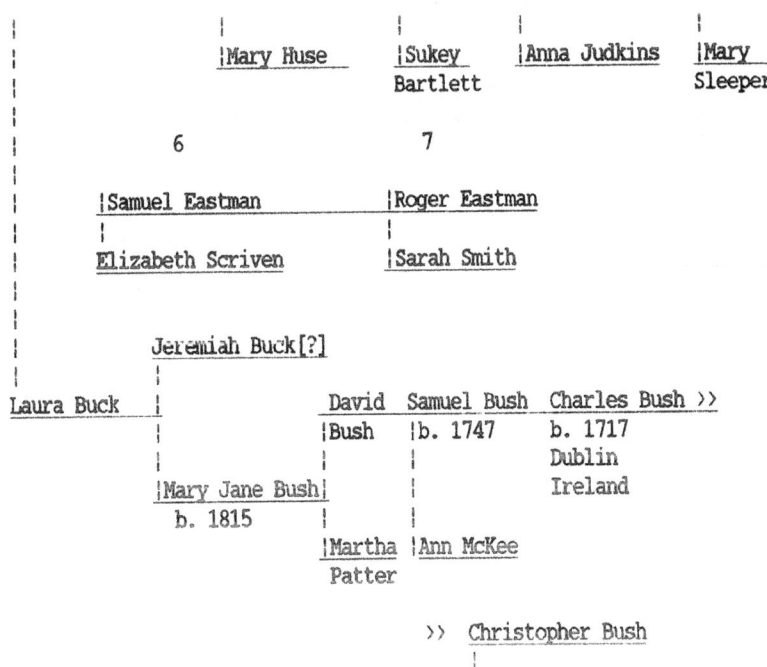

```
                    |Mary Huse      |Sukey          |Anna Judkins    |Mary
                                    Bartlett                        Sleeper

            6                              7

            |Samuel Eastman               |Roger Eastman
            |                             |
            Elizabeth Scriven             |Sarah Smith

            Jeremiah Buck[?]
Laura Buck  |                    David   Samuel Bush  Charles Bush >>
            |                    |Bush   |b. 1747     b. 1717
            |                    |       |            Dublin
            |Mary Jane Bush|     |       |            Ireland
             b. 1815       |     |       |
                                 |Martha |Ann McKee
                                 Patter

                                 >>  Christopher Bush
                                     |
                                     |Elizabeth Erskins
```

The Eastman family is an old New England family, Roger Eastman being the founder. He cam to New England shortly after 1630. Edward Eastman was the Patriot. Edward serve in the capacity of Corporal of a New Hampshire Reg. during the Revolution. Charles Francis Eastman married Laura M. Buck of Delaware. He taught of Prof. Reynold's private school, Wilmington [Del] for sereral years and was Principal for 3 years at Beloit, Wisc. In 1875 he went to Europe to study Greek at Leipsic. While in Europe, he traveled extensively in England, Switzerland, France, Germany and Italy.

The Bushs of Delaware is [sic] a well known old Delaware Family. Charles Bush served as Ensign in the Colonial Militia in 1747. He lived at New Castle. Gov. Douglas Buck and [later] Senator for Delaware and Christopher Ward are cousins.

JOHN HERDMAN FAMILY BIBLE RECORDS

Bible was bought of John Porter in the year of our Lord 1776. It was last known to be in the possession of R. D. Herdman, Dover, Del. John Herdman lived in White Clay Road, New Castle County, Delaware.

Marriage:

John Herdman and Mary Garretson were married February 4, 1800 by the Rev. Mr. Reed of Wilmington.

Births:

I [John Herdman] was born September 29, 1739.
Eleanor Hamilton my wife was born October 15, 1743.
John Herdman was born December 2, 1769.
Mary Garretson, his wife, was born December 23, 1780.
Jefferson Herdman was born December 3, 1800.
John Herdman was born March 10, 1803.
Garretson Herdman was born October 10, 1807.
Beckley and William Herdman, twin brothers, were born January 23, 1810. Beckley a few minutes the ouldest [sic].
James Lawrence Herdman was born on Tuesday, October 29, 1816 about half after five o'clock in the morning.
George Cox was born February 1, 1822.

Deaths:

John Herdman departed this life January 26, 1791, it being the 52 year of his age.
Eleanor Herdman departed this life May 5, 1829, being 85 years, 7 months of age at her Decease.
Garretson Herdman departed this life March 7, 1818.
James Lawrence Herdman departed this life August 14, 1818 in the evening about 11 o'clock.
John Herdman departed this life January 24, 1832, being sixty-two years and seven weeks old on the day of his death.

Notes:

John Herdman - Sergt in Whig Bat. Revolutionary War. Del. Archives 659, 975, 995, 1000, 1084.
Mary Garretson was the daughter of Henry Garretson who was a private in Capt. Robeson's. Co.

EMLEY HOLCOMBE FAMILY BIBLE RECORDS

Bible purchased by Emley Holcombe A.D. 1808. Printed and published by Matthew Carey, No. 122 Market St., Philadelphia, 1803. Last known to be in the possession of Louise Holcombe Boyd, Newark, Del.

Marriages:
(Pg. 677)
Emley Holcombe was married to Mary Skillman at her Father's house by the Reverend Thomas Grant on May 12, P.M. 1803.
Wm. Holcombe, son of Emley and Mary Skillman was married to Martha Wilson on Sunday evening July 30, 1826 at Sullivan, Madison County, New York.
John E. Holcombe, son of Emley and Mary [Skillman] was married to Mary Quick at her Farther's house by the Rev. John F. Clarke on Wednesday, January 26, at 2 Oclock P.M. 1831.
W. H. Holcombe was married 2d time to Mrs. Henrietta Clendenin, widow of Lieut. of the U.S. Army, she being the daughter of Major King, also of the Regular Army.
J. E. Holcombe married 2d time 1849 to Mifs [sic] Sarah Prall daughter of John S. Prall, Esq. Reaville.
(Pg. 678)
Charles O. Holcombe son of John and Mary Skillman was married to Ann Rebecca Barber by the Rev. Wm. Runnels at her father's house, Tiffin, Seneca Co., Ohio on Sunday August 28, 1824.
Charles O. Holcombe was married 2d time to Catherine Taylor Young, widow of Dr. J. Watson Young and daughter of Wm. S. Taylor.
Mary Holcombe, daughter of Emley and Mary S. Holcombe was married to Lewis J. Titus in her Father's house by the Rev. P. O. Studdiford, on Tuesday, September 25, 1838.
Theodore Holcombe, son of Emley and Mary S. Holcombe was married to Sarah Ann Probasco at her father's house by the Rev. Holloway W. Hunt on Wednesday, November 21, 1838.
Alexander H. Holcombe, son of Emley and Mary Skillman Holcombe was married to Mifa Malvina Kay Mentz at her father's house No. 1718 Vine St., Philadelphia by the Rev. Dr. B. Watson assisted by the Rev. Dr. P. A. Studdiford on Thursday, (12 M. noon) April 11, 1867.

Births:
(Pg. 677)
Emley Holcombe, son of Richard and Hannah Holcombe, was born September 21, 1777.
(Pg. 678)
Mary Skillman, daughter of John and Mary Skillman was born December 20, 1779.

Births: (Cont'd).

William Holcombe, son of Emley & Mary Holcombe, was born July 22, on Sunday morning at one o'clock, 1804.
Ellen Ann Holcombe, daughter of Emley & Mary Holcombe, was born April 7, at three o'clock, 1806.
John Emley, son of Emley & Mary Holcombe, was born April 2, on Saturday evening at eleven o'clock, 1808.
Theodore Holcombe, son of Emley and Mary Holcombe was born on Saturday morning July 14, 1810 at 2 o'clock AM.
Charles Ogden Holcombe, son of Emley & Mary Holcombe, was born June 21, on Monday 4 o'clock PM, 1813.
Isaac Skillman Holcome, son of Emley & Mary Holcombe was born on Wednesday Evening, June 5, 1816.
Lewis J. Titus was born February 10, 1817.
Mary Holcombe, daughter of Emley & Mary Holcombe, was born October 24, on Saturday evening at 6 o'clock PM, 1818.
(Pg. 679)
Susannah, Black Girl, was born August 13, 1796.

Children of Alexander Henry Holcombe and Malvina Kay Mentz:
   Freddie born March 10, 1868 at 11:45 PM. — Died March 12, at 10:00 AM.
   Elizabeth Tazewell born March 29, 1869 AT 10 AM.
   William Emley Holcombe born September 17, 1871 at 4:30 PM.
   Alexander Henry [2d] born August _?, 1873 at 8:30 PM.
   Malvina Marguerite born March 31, 1876 at 2:30 AM.
   Emley Mentz Holcombe born May 29, 1879 at 11 PM.

Children of Alexander Henry Holcombe 2d and Margaret Keen Romaine:
   Alexander Henry [III?] born August 17, 1899.
   Margaret Louise born November 23, 1901.
   Malvina Kay born June 24, 1906.
   Adelaide Romaine born September 15, 1907.
(Pg. 680)
   Alexander Henry Holcombe, son of Emley and Mary Holcombe, was born Friday, June 1, 1821.

Deaths: (Pg. 680)

Alexander Henry Holcombe departed this life on Friday, April 9, 1886 at 4:45 PM aged sixty four years ten months and eight days.
Malvina Kay Holcombe passed into rest December 4, 1906.
Ellen Ann Holcombe departed this life Friday, October 2, 1835 aged 29 years five months and 25 days, 12:30 PM at her father's house.
Mary S. Holcombe departed this life Sunday morning, April 17, 1842 at 11:30 AM aged sixty two years three months and twenty seven days, at her own house.

Deaths: (Cont'd).

Emley Holcombe departed this life on Saturday morning, July 11, 1846 at 12:30 AM aged sixty eight years, nine months and twenty days.
John E. Holcombe departed this life on Thursday Feruary 17, 1859 at 4:20 PM aged 50 years, 10 months, and 11 days. (Reaville Cem'y.)
Honorable William Holcombe, Ex-Lt. Gov. of Minnesota, departed this life on Monday September 5, 1870 suddenly at Stillwater, Minnesota aged sixty six year, one month & fourteen days.
Lewis J. Titus died April 10, 1875.
Charles Ogden Holcombe departed this life on December 25, 1890 aged seventy seven years, six months & four days.

Genealogical Notes:

RICHARD HOLCOMBE was a private, New Jersey Troops, Hunterdon Co. N.J. - Revolution.

```
         1              2
                  Mary Skillman
                       |
Richard Holcombe       | Alexander H. Holcombe 1st
  b. 12-3-1752   |     |     1821-1886
  d. 1-26-1835   | Emley Holcombe |
                 |      Malvina Kay Metz
                 | Ann Holcombe
                 |          | 3              4
Hannah Emley     |          |
                            | James Romaine
                                        |
                  Furman Romaine |    | Edward C. Romaine
                                      | b. 6-19-1842
                            Sarah Chapman |          >> 5
                                     Carrie Keen Watkinson |
         5
Margaret Keen Romaine      6
              |
              | Mrs. Louise Holcombe Boyd
Alex H. Holcombe 2nd |      D.A.R.
 b 8-5-1873
```

JAMES HOOPES FAMILY BIBLE RECORDS

Avondale, Pa., Published by Cornish Lamport & Co. New York
This Bible was last known to have been owned by Mrs. Rees Jarmon, Newark, Delaware. It was a gift to her, but none of [those listed] are related to her.

Marriages:

James Hoopes and Mary Anna Bell were married March 18, 1847.

Births:

James Hoopes was born October 10, 1817.
Mary Anna Hoopes was born February 16, 1825.
Elwood Hoopes was born February 15, 1848.
Brinton B. Hoopes was born March 23, 1850.
Tounsend? Hoopes was born September 10, 1852.
Anna Elizabeth Hoopes was born November 11, 1858.
Lewissa L. Hoopes was born January 6, 1856.
James A. Hoopes was born March 23, 1861.
Clifford Chambers Duncan was born July 28, 1892.
Courtland T. Duncan was born January 7, 1897.

Deaths:

James A. Hoopes departed this life April 8, 1861 aged 13 days.
Tousand? Hoopes departed this life August 18, 1885 aged 32 years.
James Hoopes departed this life October 10, 1886 aged 69 years.
Lewissa L. Hoopes departed this life February 23, 1893 aged 37 years.
Mary Anna Hoopes departed this life February 15, 1896 aged 73 years.

Genealogical Chart:

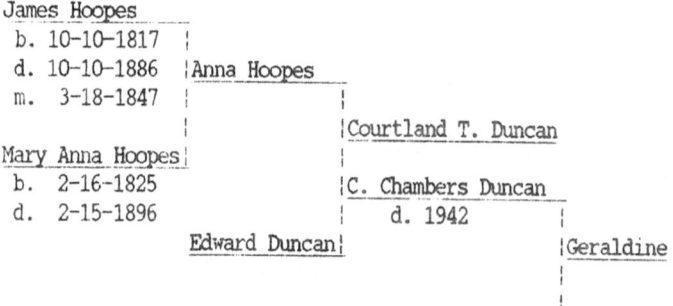

```
James Hoopes
   b. 10-10-1817    |
   d. 10-10-1886    | Anna Hoopes
   m. 3-18-1847     |
                    |           | Courtland T. Duncan
Mary Anna Hoopes    |
   b. 2-16-1825     | C. Chambers Duncan
   d. 2-15-1896     |    d. 1942
               Edward Duncan |              | Geraldine
```

HULL FAMILY BIBLE RECORDS

The Hull Bible issued 1866 by John E. Potter, 617 Sansom St., Philadelphia, Pa. Belonged to Mr. Hull's father from Mar. 13, 1867 until his death and was last known to be in the possession of Mr. John Hull.

Marriages:

Daniel B. Hull and Patience P. Joseph were married July 4, 1854.
John H. Hull and Phebe E. Ferguson were married April 20, 1881 at Chester, Pa.

Births:

Daniel B. Hull was born in Baltimore, Md. on April 14, 1833.
Patience P. Joseph was born in Lewistown, Del. on April 9, 1827.
John Henry Hull was born at Attleboro, Pa. on September 8, 1858.
Samuel Edward Andrews, son of Samuel E. and Patience Andrews, was born at Lumberton, N.J. on January 17, 1843.
Winifred I. Hull, daughter of John H. and Phoebe E. Hull was born at Wilmington, Del. on December 14, 1881.
Elsie M. Hull, daughter of John H. and Phoebe E. Hull was born at Wilmington, Del. on April 13, 1884.
Bertha Hull, daughter of John H. and Phoebe E. Hull was born at Wilmington, Del. on January 14, 1886.
Phebe E. Hull, daughter of John H. and Phoebe E. Hull was born at Wilmington, Del. on March 4, 1888.
James H. Hull, son of John H. and Phoebe E. Hull was born at Rockesson, Del. on November 23, 1892.
John A. Hull, son of John H. and Phoebe E. Hull was born at Wilmington, Del. on September 5, 1894.
Homer W. Hull, son of John H. and Phoebe E. Hull was born at Manington Townswhip, Salem Co., New Jersey on October 23, 1896.

Deaths:

Samuel Edward Andrews died at Pennock Square, Delaware on August 18, 1854.

JAMES JACOBUS FAMILY BIBLE RECORDS

Marriage:

Jacobus Jacobussen married Maritje Kip, who was 4th in descent from Hendrick Hendricksen Kip Jr., magistrate under Dutch rule of New Castle, Delaware on June 3, 1743.

Births:

Our son Brant was born March 26, 1744.
Our daughter Elizabeth was born June 7, 1744.
Our son Jacobus was born December 23, 1751.
Our son Abraham was born November 15, 1752.
— New Style [?] —
Our son Jacobus was born January 11, 1753.
Our son Abraham was born August 3, 1754.
Our daughter Eva was born April 14, 1756.
Our daughter Antje was born January 3, 1760.
Our son Nickase was born August 20, 1762.
Our son David was born December 16, 1764.
Our daughter Maritje was born September 9, 1766.

JONES - PATTEN FAMILY BIBLE RECORDS

Printed and published by M. Carey, No 121 Chestnut St., 1814.
Last known to be owned by the late John B. Miller, Newark, Delware.

Marriages:

Morgan Jones and Mary Patten married May 21, 1818.
Robert Thomas Cochran and Mary F. Patton married September 1, 1853.
James Griffith married Francina Barr [no date given].

Births:

Children of Zachariah and Joanna Jones (nee Joanna Thomas):
Morgan Jones was born July 7, 1758.
Sarah Jones was born August 26 or 27, 1759.
Zachariah Jones was born September 15 or 16, 1768.

Morgan Jones, son of Morgan Jones and Mary, his wife, was born February 6, 1819.
Morgan Jones, second, son of Morgan Jones and Mary, his wife, was born September 4, 1820.

Births (Cont'd).

William James Patten, son of James Patten and Francina, his wife, was born January 22, 1825.
Mary Francina, daughter of James Patton and Francina, his wife, was born June 27, 1827.
George Washington Linsey was born November 22, 1837.
Agnes Elizabeth Linsey was born January 4, 1840.
Francina B. (Barr) Linsey was born July 16, 1800.

Deaths:

Morgan Jones, son of Morgan Jones and Mary, his wife, departed this life March 13, 1820 aged one year, one month and one week.
Morgan Jones Senior departed this life August 25, 1820 aged 62 years, 1 month and 18 days.
Morgan Jones Second, son of M. Jones, Sr., and Mary, his wife, departed this life February 27, 1821.
Mary Jones, wife of Morgan Jones, Senior departed this life September 16, 1821 aged 32 years and 45 days.
James Patten departed this life April 24, 1828.
William James Patton son of James Patton and Francina Patton departed this life August 28, 1852 aged 27 years, 6 months and 28 days.
Mary F. Cochran, wife of R. T. Cochran departed this life Sunday morning, August 1, 1888 aged 62 years, 1 month and 15 days.
James Linsey Sr departed this life September 8, 1858.
Francina B. Linsey departed this life April 12, 1882 aged 82 years, 8 months, 26 days.

Genealogical Notes:

Zachariah and Mary Jones Griffith were 1st cousins.
Morgan Jones B. 1758 and James Griffith, who married Francina Barr were 2nd cousins.

Compiler's Note:

It is not possible to determine from the Bible record, whether Patton and Patten are two different family names, a change in the spelling of the name, or a lack of care in recording the data.

Family Chart:

I.   Morgan ap Rhydderch 1620-30
   d. 1680. m. Jane [Rhydderch] Morgan, who latter married John Griffith and came to America:
         Welch tract near Newark, Delaware

Children [of Morgan & Rhydderich]:

1. Thomas Morgan — Rev. Jenkins Thomas | David Jenkins
                           [Possibly Rev. | Samuel Jenkins
                           Thomas Jenkins] | John Jenkins
                                           | Enoch Jenkins
                                           | Nathaniel Jenkins
                                           | Catherine Jenkins

2. Rev. Abel Morgan | Jane Morgan | Abel Holme
                             | m. John Holme | Martha Holme Edwards
                             | | Enoch Holme
                             | | Hannah Holme Keen
                             | | John Holme
                             | | Pricilla Holme Cox
                             | | Thomas Holme
                             | Rachel Morgan | Jacques Holme
                             | Abel Morgan
                             | Samuel Morgan
                             | Enoch Morgan

3. Rev. Enoch Morgan | Esther Morgan Douglas
                               | Enoch Morgan ... Rev. Samuel Morgan
                                                 Enoch Morgan, Jr.
                               | Rev. Abel Morgan

4. Esther Morgan Jones | Morgan Jones..... | Joshua Jones
       b. Alltgoch, Wales | b. 1697 Wales | Ann Jones Delap
            1678 | d. 6-4-1760 | John Jones
       d. 10-2-1754 | m. Eleanor Evans | Abel Jones
           Welsh Tract | | Zachariah Jones >> ♦
       m. David Jones | | Rev. David Jones
                                 | | Morgan Jones
                                 | | m. Mary Davis
                                 | | Esther Jones Thomas
                               | James Jones
   ♦   [Continued | d. 1786 | Enoch Jones
   ♦♦ Next Page] | m. Susanna | Daniel Jones
                                 | Signed Oath of | James Jones, Jr.
                                 | Allegance | Mary Jones Griffith >> ♦♦
                                 | | Jane Jones Buckingham
                                 | John Jones | Hannah Jones Shields
                                 | Daniel Jones | Esther; Susannah; Marga-
                                 | Jane Jones Passamore   ret.
                                 | Rachel Jones Williams
                                 | Mary Jones Beal

♦ Morgan Jones [son of Zachariah] b. 1758.
♦♦ James Griffith [son of Mary Jones Griffith] m. Francina Barr.
   Francina [Barr] Griffith m. James Patten
                              m. James Linsey

Compiler's Note:

The Heading of the above Chart is as it appears in the Bible Records i. e. "Morgan ap Rhydderch 1620-1630". There is no given name shown for the Morgan who married Jane Rydderch, whose full maiden name first appears in the following chart on John Griffith.

FAMILY CHART

II.   JOHN GRIFFITH 1655-1735
               Wales to Welsh Tract

Married 3 times. Second wife was Jane Rhydderch (Morgan).
                 Third wife was Rachel.

Children of John and Jane (Morgan) Griffith:

1. Daniel
2. Samuel
3. John
4. Rev. Benjamin Griffith m. Sarah Miles daughter of Richard.
5. Sarah who married Col. Thomas Cooch, Cooch's Bridge.

Chart of Rev. Benjamin Griffieth Descendants:-

1. Jane Griffith
   Evans b. 1721 | Sarah
                    | Rachel m. John Powell
                    | John Griffith
2. Rev. Abel Griffith| William Griffith
   1723-1793 | Elizabeth
   m. Sarah Coffin | Martha

   m. Rebecca Miles | Benjamin Miles
                    | m. Eleanor Thomas

3. Sarah Griffith Roberts
   b.1732

(Cont'd. Next Page)

```
                        | John Griffith 1765-1837; m. Rachel Hersey
                        |                         m. Margaret Sharp
                        | Susan Griffith
                        |
4. Joseph Griffith      |
   b. 1733; d. 1773     | James Griffith  | John Griffith
   m. Mary Jones        |   m. Francina   | Joseph Griffith
      daughter of       |      Barr, dau. | Francina Griffith
      * James and       |      of David * |   m. James Patton
        Susanna         |                 |   m. James Linsey  | George
                        |                                      |   Linsey
                        | Catherine Griffith                   | Agnes C.
                        |   m. David Eaton                     |   Linsey
                        |                                      |   m.
                        |                                      |   George
                        | Rebecca Griffith                     |   Miller
                        |
5. Rachel Griffith - Rachel Davis
   m. Abel Davis     m. Joshua Perry
```

Children of Agnes C. Lindsey and George Miller
[Exactly as shown in the Bible Record]

1. John B. Miller   Helen W. Miller
   Newark, Del.   Audrey E. Miller.......D.A.R.
   1866-1843   Francina
   m. Elizabeth Wright   John
2.   William
   James Linsey Miller   Jane
                               Agnes ..................D.A.R.

Revolution:

* James Jones signed oath
* David Barr signed oath

JONES - GILLISPY FAMILY BIBLE RECORDS

These records copied from Bible last known to be in the possession of Mrs. E. Tazwell of Wilmington, Delaware.

Marriages:

Phillip Hicks Jones married Mary Gillispy on October 15, 1815.
[NOTE: This Bible record gives two spellings for Phil(l)ip].

Births:

Phillip Hicks Jones, first son of Wm. and Hannah Jones, was born June 21, 1792.
Mary Gillispy, first daughter of James and Elizabeth Gillispy, was born August 12, 1799.
[Children of Philip and Mary Jones]
Elizabeth Jones, first daughter, was born July 4, 1816.
Wm. Jones, first son, was born December 11, 1818.
Hannah Jones, second daughter, was born February 20, 1821.
Sarah Ann Jones, third daughter, was born April 23, 1823.
George Jones, second son, was born September 27, 1824.
John Wesley Jones, third son, was born February 6, 1826.
Thomas Jones, fourth son, was born May 19, 1827.
Mary Jones, fourth daughter, was born October 14, 1829.
Edith, fifth daughter, was born June 30, 1832.
Joseph Chamberlain, fifth son, was born January 30, 1835.
Philip Reybold Jones, sixth son, was born February 13, 1838.
Henry Harrison Jones, seventh son, was born September 26, 1840.

Deaths:

George Jones died September 25, 1824.
John Wesley Jones died July 9, 1826.
Thomas Jones died December 7, 1828.
Philip Jones died August 19, 1857.
Henry Harrison Jones died June 20, 1864.
Mary Gillspy died November 18, 1868.

CHARLES LEAK FAMILY BIBLE RECORDS

Taken from Bible published by Chas. H. Yost, 805 Market Street., Phila. Penna. (Successors to White & Yost). Lask known to be in the possession of Ida May Leak.

Marriages:

Leak, Charles abd Henrietta Gamble married, Methodist parsonage, Newark, Delaware, August 14, 1867.
Howard Leak married Mary Lutton.

Marriages: (Cont'd).

Charles Wesley Leak married twice [No children; no other information given].
Ida May Leak married John T. Wilson.
George Robert Leak married Mathilda Dean, April 4, 1900.
Wilmer Ernest Leak married Anna Williams in Pasadena, California, 1919.

Births:

Charles Leak, son of Thomas Leak and Mary Walker Leak, was born September 5, 1840 in Philadelphia, Pa.

[Children of Charles and Henrietta Leak]:
  Howard Leak was born February 19, 1869.
  Charles Wesley Leak was born August 30, 1870.
  Walter Leak was born August 30, 1870. -- Bachelor [Twin of Charles, if dates are correct].
  Ida May Leak was born December 8, 1873.
  Wilmer Ernest Leak was born Augut 3, 1875.
  George Robert Leak was born June 13, 1878.
  Henry Clay Leak was born April 15, 1880.   -- Bachelor.
  Edward Elmer Leak was born August 12, 1883.   -- Bachelor.

Alice and Helen Leak, daughters of Howard Leak and Mary Lutton, [dates of birth not given].
Anna and Sarah Leak, daughters of Ida May Leak and John Wilson, [dates of birth not given; Anna deceased - no date].
Delena, Ida May, Roberta, and Violette, daughters of George and Mathilda Leak, [dates of birth not given].

Deaths:

Henry Clay Leak died August 26, 1917.
Walter Leak died December 10, 1932.
Wilmer Ernest Leak died April 3, 1940.
Charles Wesley Leak died July 1, 1941.

[Genealogical Note]:

Thomas Leak came to this country from England and married Mary Walker of Philadelphia. They had nine children Abraham, Charles Wesley, Edward, John, Thomas, Robert, Henry, Emma, and Franklin.

THOMAS AND MARY MACKEY FAMILY BIBLE RECORDS

Printed and published by M. Carey, No. 121 Chestnut Street, Philadelphia, Pa. 1815. This Bible was last known to be in the possession of Miss Audrey Miller, Newark, Delaware. National D.A.R. No. 300292 (her grandfather was John Miller).

Marriages:

John Miller married Mary Mackey [no date given].

Births:

Mary Evans was born September 22, 1764.
Hugh Boyle Mackey was born September 24, 1808.
Mary Mackey was born June 8, 1810.
John Stewart Mackey was born November 4, 1811.
Thomas Lanson Mackey was born September 8, 1813.

Deaths:

Thomas Mackey died December 24, 1816 in the 29th year of his age.
Catharine Evans Mackey died Jan 4, 1817 in the 37th year of her age.
Mary Evans Wilson died April 9, 1830, age 65 years, 7 mos., 18 days.
John Miller died May 27, 1884, age 78 years, 2 mos., 24 days.

THE JAMES LINDSAY FAMILY BIBLE RECORDS

Published by Evert Duyckinck, John Tiebout, G. & R. White and Webster and Skinners of Albany. George Long, Printer 1813. Last recorded as property of Miss Audrey Miller, Delaware Ave., Newark, Del.

Births:

Elizabeth Craig [Lindsay], mother of James Lindsay, was born November 11, 1760. She had 8 children.
James Lindsay was born December 14, 1790.

Deaths:

James Lindsay died September 9, 1858. Believed to be buried in White Clay Creek Cemetary near Newark, Del.

[Lineage Chart of]
John B. Miller
Newark, Delaware

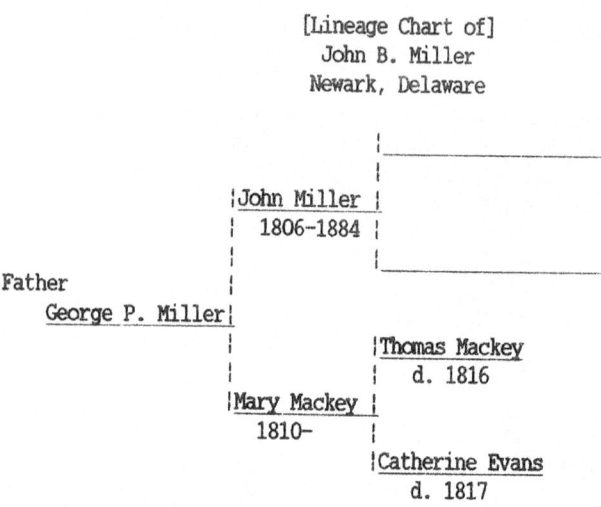

Father
George P. Miller

Mother

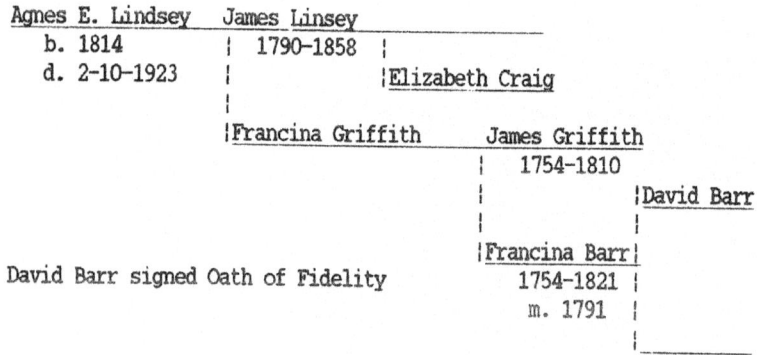

David Barr signed Oath of Fidelity

THE DANIEL McCAULEY FAMILY BIBLE RECORDS

Published July 25, 1803, Matthew Carey, No. 118 Market St., Philadelphia, Pa. Owned, in 1942, by Mrs. Arthur Denny. King James Edition (3rd).

Marriages:

Daniel McCauley and Frances Baker was married March 11, 1781.
Henry and Ann McCauley was married August 12, 1806.
John and Elizabeth McCauley was married January 14, 1808.
James Chesney and Nancy McCauley was married March 10, 1810.

Marriages: (Cont'd).

Andrew Harvey and Lydia McCauley was married February 6, 1817.
Daniel McCauley and Rachel Beard was married December 22, 1825.

Births:

Daniel McCauley was born April 21, 1754.
Frances McCauley was born August 24, 1765.
Henry McCauley, their son, his wife, was born August 12, 1781.
Elizabeth McCauley, their daughter, was born November 8, 1783.
Jethro McCauley, their son, was born January 16, 1786.
Ann McCauley, their daughter, was born January 10, 1789.
James McCauley, their son, was born October 10, 1792.
Lydia McCauley, their daughter, was born September 21, 1796.
Daniel McCauley, their son, was born November 15, 1803.
James McCauley, son of Henry and Ann McCauley, was born October 31, 1807.
Frances McCauley, daughter of John and Elizabeth McCauley, was born October 1, 1808.
James McCauley, their son, was born August 23, 1809.
Absolom McCauley, 2nd son of Henry and Ann McCauley, was born October 10, 1808.
Jethro McCauley, their 3rd son, was born October 10, 1809.
Daniel McCauley, 2nd son of John and Elizabeth McCauley, was born October 14, 1811.
Eliza Ann, daughter of Henry and Ann McCauley, was born was born April 21, 1812.
Francina Ann, daughter of James and Nancy Chesney, was born January 12, 1813.
Harrieta McCauley, daughter of John and Elizabeth McCauley, was born February 21, 1814.
Mary, daughter of James and Nancy Chesney, was born June 12, 1814.
Frances McCauley, 2nd daughter of Henry and Ann McCauley was born July 18, 1814.
Elizabeth McCauley, daughter of John and Elizabeth McCauley, was born July 17. 1816.
John McCauley, son of Henry and Ann McCauley, was born Dec. 29, 1816.
Lydia Ann McCauley, daughter of John and Elizabeth McCauley, was born October 24, 1818.
Daniel McCauley Chesney, son of James and Nancy Chesney, was born February 13, 1819.
Margaret Franc., daughter of Henry and Ann McCauley, was born June 10, 1819.
Mary Jane McCauley, daughter of John and Elizabeth McCauley, was born June 26, 1821.

Births: (Cont'd).

Henry Baker McCauley, son of Henry and Ann McCauley, was born March 10, 1822.
John Henry McCauley, son of John and Elizabeth McCauley, was born July 12, 1823.
Lydia Moriah McCauley, daughter of Henry and Ann McCauley, was born May 25, 1824.

Deaths:

James McCauley, son of Daniel and Frances McCauley, departed this life August 15, 1798, aged 5 years, 10 months, four days.
Jethro, their son, departed this life November 4, 1807, aged 21 years, 9 months, 18 days.
Henry McCauley, their son, departed this life April 5, 1825, aged 43 years, 6 months, 24 days.
John McCauley died May 15, 1836.
Lydia Harvey, daughter of Daniel and Frances McCauley, departed this life March 17, 1837 in her 41st year.
Elizabeth McCauley, their daughter, died May 4, 1867 in her 78th year.
Ann Chesney, their daughter, died December 8, 1874 in her 86th year.
Daniel McCauley, son of Daniel, died September 24, 1877.
Ann Chesney, wife [sic] of James Chesney, died December 8, 1874.

THE JAMES AND SARAH ANN McCAULEY FAMILY BIBLE RECORDS

Published - Hartford 1837 by Judd, Losuies & Co. Loased owned by J. Hayes McCauley -- Leeds, Md.

Marriages:

James McCauley and Sarah Beard were married November 27, 1834.
James McCauley and Milicent R. Price were married August 30, 1849.

Births:

James McCauley was born August 23, 1809.
Sarah Beard was born January 19, 1812.
Milicent Roberts Price McCauley, born December 15, 1816.

[Children of James McCauley and Sarah Beard]:
Elizabeth Baker and Mary Hughes (twins) born August 5, 1835.

Births: (Cont'd).

Male Child born July 24, 1837, died the same day.
John was born October 25, 1838.
Rachel was born December 9, 1840.
Hannah Louise was born June 28, 1843.
[Children of James McCAuley and his wife, Milicent R. Price
Helen Amanda McCauley, born June 4, 1851.
James Jacob McCauley, born November 12, 1853.
Harriet Selena McCauley, born February 24, 1858.

Deaths:

On the 14th day of December 1846, Sarah McCauley, my dearly beloved wife departed this life in the 35th year of her age.
Milicent Roberts Price McCauley died April 18, 1890.
James McCauley died January 25, 1897.
Helen Amanda McCauley died May 4, 1929.
Harriet Selena McCauley died November 22, 1929.
James Jacob McCauley died August 7, 1931.

THE [McCAULEY] - BAKER FAMILY BIBLE RECORDS

Marriages:

Henry Baker married Margaret Hardman, August 4, [or 6] 1667.
Samuel Baker married Rachael Warder, September 4, 1703.
Nathan Baker married Sarah Collett, May 15, 1705.
Mary Ann Baker [daugher of Samuel & Rachael Baker] married Bileo [no date].
Samuell [stet] Baker [son of Samuel & Rachael Baker] married Elizabeth [no date or last name given].
Henry Baker [son of Samuel & Rachael Baker] married Mary [no date or last name given].
John Baker [son of Samuel & Rachael Baker] married Sarah [no date or last name given].
Joseph Baker [son of Samuel & Rachael Baker] married Esther Head [no date given].
Lydia Baker [daughter of Samuel & Rachael Baker] married John Burroughs [no date given].
Margaret Baker [daughter of Samuel & Rachael Baker] married — Somlinson [no date given].
Sarah Baker [daughter of Samuel and Rachael Baker married Abel Janney, April 2, 1733.
Joseph Janney [their son] married Hannah Jones, September 26, 1764.

Marriages: (Cont'd).

Hannah Janney [daughter of Joseph and Hannah Janney] married --- Hopkins.
Henry Baker [son of Nathan and Sarah Baker] married Elizabeth (last name unknown) [no date].
Jethro Baker [son of Henry and Elizabeth Baker] married Ann Gonsen [Bible record also shows Ann Gonsen (Johnson)] in Old Swedes Church, Wilmington, Del., March 20, 1765.
[Children of Nathan and Elizabeth Baker:
Henry married Elizabeth [no maiden name given; NDG].
Jeremiah married Ruth Bonham [NDG].
Nathan married Joyce Yardley [NDG].
Mary married Job Ruston [NDG].
Elizabeth married Robt. Cummins [NDG].
Thomas married Hannah Thackey [NDG].

Births:

Henry Baker was born in England about 1646.
[Children of Henry and Margaret Hardman Baker:]
Samuel Baker was born [in England] August 1, 1676.
Rachael [No Date Given (NDG)].
Rebecca [NDG].
Phoebe [NDG].
Nathan was born January 8, 1864 [in England].
Sarah [NDG].
Henry [NDG].
Margaret [NDG].
[Children of Samuel Baker and Rachael Warder:]
Mary Ann [NDG].
Samuell [NDG].
Henry [NDG].
Nathan [NDG].
Sarah born October 9, 1712.
John [NDG].
Nathan (2nd?) [NDG].
Joseph [NDG].
Benjamin [NDG].
Lydia [NDG].
Margaret [NDG].
Hester [See Genealogical Notes; NDG].
[Children of Nathan and Elizabeth Baker:]
Henry [NDG].
Jeremiah [NDG].
Nathan [NDG].
Mary [NDG].

Births: (Cont'd).

Elizabeth [NDG].
Thomas [NDG].
Jethro Baker, son of Henry and Elizabeth Baker, was born about 1745.
Joseph Janney, son of Sarah Baker and Abel Janney [NDG].
Hannah Janney, daughter of Joseph Janney and Hannah Jones was born May 19, 1774.
Johns Hopkins, son of Hannah Janney and ―― Hopkins, [NDG].

Deaths:

Henry Baker [from England] died before 1703.
Nathan Baker [his son] died before April 5, 1729.
Samuel Baker [son of Henry] died before 1760.
Sarah Collett daughter of Jeremiah (or Jeremy) Collett
Henry Baker, son of Nathan, died in 1768.
Jethro, son of Henry, died in Cecil County, Md., in June, 1777.

Genealogical Notes:

Henry Baker and his wife Margaret Hardman: Members of the Society of Friends. Arrived in Philadelphia with their family July 17, 1684. Settled first in what is now Bucks County, Pa., later bought land in Cecil Co., Md.

ANCESTRY OF ELSIE McCAULEY BLACKWELL

The first record of Henry Baker I appears in the minutes of Lancashire Quarterly Meeting of Friends -

"Henry Baker of Newton, Lancashire, Husbandman, and Margaret Hardman of Aspull, Lancashire, spinster were married 8th mo. 6th, 1667.

The Pennsylvania Historical Society has "A Partial List of Those Families who arrived at Philadelphia, between 1682-1687." Among the entries appears "Mr. Wm. Preeson of the Vine of Liverpoole, arrived 17th day of the 7th mo. 1684 at Philadelphia - among the passengers from Walton in Lancashire, Henry Baker, Margaret his wife, their daughters Rachel, Rebecca, Phebey [sp?], Hester, and their sons, Nathan and Samuel - Mary Beckett and ten [indentured?] servants named John Siddell for 4 yrs., Thos. Fisher, 4 yrs., Hen. Siddell, 4 yrs., Thomas Canby, 4 yrs., Deborah Boothe, 4 yrs., Joshua Lort, 4 yrs., Joseph fferror [sic], 4 years."

Thomas Canby was the son of Benjamin Canby and Mary Baker, a sister of Henry Baker - therefore, his nephew.

Henry Baker was the father of ten children, eight of whom reached maturity and married into prominent families of Pennsylvania and New Jersey.

Through his son Samuel, he was the ancestor of Johns Hopkins, the founder of Johns Hopkins University and Hospital in Baltimore, Md., and through his son Nathan was the ancestor of Charles Robert, R.A. the distinguished artist and author, so highly praised by Ruskin in his "Modern Painters".

Francis, or Francina, Baker McCauley, daughter of Jethro Baker; (See Daniel McCauley Record [above]) was a sister of Lydia Baker Leslie - the mother of Charles Robert Leslie, R.A., of Thomas Leslie who was paymaster of the U.S. Army at West Point for fifty years, of Eliza Leslie, the authoress whose Cook Book passed through fifty-six editions - and who wrote many stories for Godey's Lady Book, and of Patty Leslie who married Henry C. Carey of Philadelphia.

Nathan Baker, son of <u>Henry Baker I</u> married Sarah Collett, May 15, 1705, the daughter of Jeremiah Collett of whom Smith in his History of Delaware Co., Pa., says "He was settled in Chichester before the arrival of William Penn." The records of St. Paul's Church, Chester, Pa., show that he was on of the first Vestrymen of that church being elected April 18, 1704, and served till his death.

Jeremiah Collett married Jane May in 1681 - was trice commissioned as Justice of the Peace [May 13, 1693 and September 25, 1703]. History of Chester Co. Pa., makes frequent mention of him. He was Court Collector, 1844; Sheriff, 1684-83[sic] - also one of the Jury at the first Court of Chester after Penn's arrival.

Henry Baker II, son of Nathan Baker, was the builder of St. Mary Anne's Church, North East, Cecil Co., Md., 1742 and his initials are included with that of rector [sic] and his vestry on the corner-stone. There is proof of an older church in the ancient records of the parish - which state "In consideration of building the aforesaid church, where the old church now stand, and a vestry house, said Henry Baker shall have all the right and title of the old church and vestry house besides 800 pounds." (History of North Elk Parish" by Rev. J. Gibson Gantt B.D.

St. Mary's Cemetary is one of the oldest in Maryland. "In Church Affairs," it says, "There is a stone bearing the date 1590 and another the date 1630" - It was an Indian burying ground - long before the white man came and their bones are often found (they buried their dead standing) when a grave is dug.

Henry Baker II had two sons in the American Revolution, Capt. Jeremiah Baker - for whom a Cecil Co., Md., D.A.R. Chapter is named, (he is buried in St. Mary Anne Cemetery) and Jethro Baker, who was appointed to gather blankets for the army, dury a very cold winter and from them took smallpox and died. Will date June 2, 1777 - was proved June 30, 1777.

Jethro Baker is the Revolutionary Ancestor of Elsie McCauley Blackewll, also of Harvey Bounds, Delaware, S.A.R., through Lydia McCauley Harvey, wife of Andrew Harvey. References - Henry Baker and

Descendants by Miles White, Jr. published in Southern History Association, September and November, 1901.

Jeremiah Collett must have been married three times. According to the Compendium of First Families of America, he married Jane May in 1681, Ann Collett (the mother of Sarah, wife of Nathan Baker) wife of Jeremiah Collett "died ye fifteenth of October 1704 and was buried ye 11th of July 1705" - St. Paul's Church Record, Chester; when Jeremiah Collett died, Nov. 15, 1706, letters of administration were granted to his widow, Weyntie Collett.

```
        Henry Baker I, England
  9     |    &
        | Margaret Hardman

        Nathan Baker
  8     |    &
        | Sarah Collett

        Henry Baker
  7     |    &
        | Elizabeth

        Jethro Baker
  6     |    &
        | Ann Gonsen

        Daniel McCauley
  5     |    &
        | Frances Baker
```

```
           ___John McCauley_____
    4      |    &
           |_Elizabeth McCauley___

           ___James McCauley_____
    3      |    &
           |_Milicent R. Price____

           ___James J. McCauley___
    2      |    &
           |_Ethlyn B. Gallaher___

           ___Walter A. Blackwell_
    1      |    &
           |_Elsie R. McCauley____
```

ALEXANDER McDONALD FAMILY BIBLE RECORDS

Marriages:

Alexander McDonald [II], son of John McDonald, who was the son of Alexander McDonald [I], married Mary McClister [NDG].

Births:

Alexander McDonald [II] was born September 13, 1790.
Mary McClister McDonald was born November 25, 1788.
[Their Children:]
Louesa McDonald was born April 21, 1815.
John McDonald was born August 11, 1816.
Sally McDonald was born November 11, 1817.
James Watkins McDonald was born January 26, 1819.
Margaret McDonald was born May 4, 1820.
Ambrose McDonald was born June 18, 1822.
Elizabeth McDonald was born January 27, 1825.
Charles McDonald (of North Platte, Neb.) was born October 25, 1826.

Deaths:

Alexander McDonald [II] deceased November 28, 1873.
Mary McDonald deceased August 26, 1846.
[Their Children:]
    Louesa McDonald deceased March 11, 1818.
    Sally McDonald deceased April 24, 1819.
    James W. McDonald deceased September 22, 1827.

Deaths: (Cont'd).

Elizabeth McDonald deceased October 30, 1840.
Ambrose McDonald deceased April 25, 1852.
John McDonald deceased September 18, 1864.
Margaret McDonald deceased October 13, 1870.
Charles McDonald deceased April 22, 1919. (North Platte, Neb.—
above record from his family Bible.

ROBERT MONTGOMERY FAMILY BIBLE RECORDS

Printed by Samuel Pagester, Paternoster Row, Philadelphia. Published by J. J. Lippincott & Co. 1848. Purchased by Robert Montgomery, Mill Creek, H[undre]d. New Castle, Delaware, October 20, 1849. Last known owner: Mrs. Harry I. Garrett, Strickersville, Pa.

Marriages:

Robert Montgomery and Sarah Ann Smith were married May 19, 1847.
George Q. Montgomery and Louisa D. Stern were married May 18, 1875.
Saresa J. Montgomery and James M. Ewing were married December 23, 1869.
Anna Margaret Montgomery and Joseph B. Ewing were married December 25, 1872.
John Henry Montgomery and Annie Lizzie Gregg were married November 26, 1876.
Mary Smith Montgomery and John C. Vansant were married February 3, 1881.
Elizabeth K. Montgomery and Harry I. Garrett were married December 29, 1886.

Births:

Robert Montgomery was born November 25, 1822.
Sarah Ann Smith was born August 28, 1823.
George Quincy Montgomery was born February 6, 1848.
Saresa J. Montgomery was born April 6, 1850.
Anna Margaret Montgomery was born October 7, 1852.
John Henry Montgomery was born May 2, 1854.
Mary Smith Montgomery was born November 8, 1856.
Emily Montgomery was born December 28, 1859.
William Smith Montgomery was born November 25, 1861.
Elizabeth K. Montgomery was born August 20, 1865.

Deaths:

Emily Montgomery died June 4, 1860, aged 5 months, 7 days.
Saresa J. Montgomery, wife of James M. Ewing died November 28, 1876.
Robert Montgomery died December 15, 1900.
Sarah A. Smith, wife of Robert Montgomery, died January 29, 1903.
George Q. Montgomery died October 16, 1903.
Louisa D. Stern, wife of George Q. Montgomery, died January 10, 1896.
William Smith Mongtomery died December 8, 1912.
Joseph P. Ewing, husband of Anna Margaret Montgomery, died January 22, 1924.
James W. Ewing, husband of Saresa J. Montgomery, died September 20, 1926.
Mary Smith Montgomery, wife of John C. Vansant, died November 8, 1929 on her 72nd birthday.
John C. Vansant, husband of Mary Smith Montgomery, died September 2, 1935.
Anna M. Montgomery, wife of Joseph B. Ewing, died November 27, 1837, aged 85 years.

DANIEL McKINLEY & MARY S. ERWIN FAMILY BIBLE RECORDS

Bible last known to be owned by Mrs. Angie Perkins, Newark, Delaware. Published 1829 by T. Kinnersley, New York.

Marriages:

Daniel McKinley and Mary S. Erwin were married February 17, 1825.

Births:

Daniel McKinley was born March 1, 1798.
Mary S. [Erwin] was born May 7, 1802.
[Their Children:]
John McKinley was born December 25, 1825.
Samuel Erwin McKinley was born July 22, 1828.
Caroline Amanda McKinley was born June 3, 1829.
Mary Jane McKinley was born September 16, 1831.
Daniel Spencer McKinley was born January 16, 1834.
Harriet Ann Erwin McKinley was born July 21, 1836.

Deaths:

Samuel Erwin McKinley departed this life August 9, 1828.

Genealogical Note:

This bible came to Mrs. Angied Perkins from the Joseph W. Brooks family. (All descendants of J.W. Brooks are dead). Mrs. Perkins [did] not know the connection of this family with the Brooks family.

JOHN McINTIRE FAMILY BIBLE RECORDS

Marriages:

Robert McIntire (Antier) married Ann [date & maiden name not given].
John McIntire married Mary [date & maiden name not given].
William McIntire married Jane Brookins 1793.
Anna McIntire married William McKean 1796. [See James McKean Bible].
Thomas McIntire married Maggy Phillips 1811.
Thomas McKean [son of Anna and William McKean] married Julia Miller March 26, 1835.
William Thomas McKean [son of Thomas and Julia Miller McKean] married Edith Emogene Patridge June 9, 1875.

Births:

John McIntire was born to Robert and Ann McIntire [No Date Given].

[Children of John and Mary McIntire;]

William
Thomas
John [II]
Lewis
Anna was born in 1778.
Sarah
Mary [II]

William McKean [husband of Anna] was born in March 1772.
Thomas McKean [son of William and Anna] was born May 16, 1802.
William Thomas McKean [probably son of Thomas and Julia Miller McKean] was born August 24, 1844.

Deaths:

Robert McIntire died between August 16, 1775 and June 28, 1789.
John McIntire died in Cecil Co. Md., February 16, 1816.
Anna McIntire died March 16, 1844, age 66.

Deaths: (Cont'd).

William McKean died January 13, 1857, age 84 years, 10 months.
Thomas McKean died August 19, 1879.
Julia Miller McKean died April 16, 1862; buried in Jacksonville, Center Co., Pa.
William Thomas McKean died January 23, 1924.
Edith Emogene Patridge [his wife] died December 27, 1924.

Genealogical Notes:

John McIntire: Revolutionary Patriot; Signed Oath of Fidelity in Cecil Co., Md.
Florence McKean Knight, great-great-grandaughter of John McIntire, National No. D.A.R. 110399.

References:

McKean Genealogies by Cornelius McKean p 52-53 Thomas McKean Bible.
Md. 1790 Census p. 43. North Milford hundred, Cecil Co.
Hist of Del (Scarf) vol 2, p 9345; Assessments 1804.
History of Center Co. Pa. p 345.
Bradford Co. [Pa?] Historical Society.

JAMES McKEAN FAMILY BIBLE RECORDS

Marriages:

James Scott married Sarah in 1747.
James McKean married Jane Scott (Head of Christina Presbyterian Meeting House, Newark, Del.) 1769.

[Their Children]:

William married Anna McIntire [1796 per McIntire Bible Record].
James married Esther Black [No Date Given].
Rebecca married John Doffins [NDG].
Andrew married Catherine Bedell [NDG].
John married Mary Mauier [NDG].
Robert married Martha [NDG; No maiden name given].
Benjamin married Lucy [NDG].
Samuel married Julia McDowell [NDG].
Jane married John [NDG].

Births:

James McKean was born in Cecil Co., Md. in 1745.
Jane Scott, daughter of James and Sarah Scott, was born in 1751.
[Their Children]:
Allen was born in 1770.
William was born in 1772.
James was born in 1774.
Rebecca was born in 1776.
Andrew was born in 1777.
John [NDG].
Robert [NDG].
Benjamin was born in 1784.
Samuel was born in 1787.
Jane [NDG].

Deaths:

James Scott died January 20, 1781 in battle. Estate Adm. November 2, 1782.
James McKean died in Burlington, Pa., January 4, 1797.
Jane Scott died in 1813.

Revolutionary War Service:

James McKean was a Private in Capt. Hugh McClellan's Co., Eighth Battalion, Cumberland Co. Militia 1780-1782, Alexander Brown, Colonel.

James Scott was a Private in Capt. Peter Jacquette's Co., Col. David Hall's Delaware Regiment. He enlised March 10, 1780 for the war; was transferred, exact date unknown, to the 1st Co. of the 2nd Battalion in Colonel Williams Regt., serving in the Southern Army and his name appears on a muster roll of that organization for the months July, August, and September, 1780, dated Hillsborough, N.C. Sept. 1780 and the records show he died Jan 20, 1781 in battle. Del. Archives Vol 1, p. 118.

THE PRICE-BLACKWELL FAMILY BIBLE RECORDS

Family Biles last known to be in the possession of the McCauley and Blackwell families. Ref. St. Stephen's Parish Register, Earleville, Cecil Co., Md. Wills Cecil Co. Md. Courthouse.

Genealogical Note:

William Price I came from Wales with two sons early in the 17th century.

Marriages:

William Price II married Margaret [Date and Maiden Name Not Given].
William Price III, eldest son of William Price II, married Mary Hyland, sister of John and Nicholas Hyland and daughter of Col. John Hyland and Mary Darrington, [in] 1665.
[Their Children:]
    Andrew married Elizabeth Perry [in] June 1725.
    Richard married Sarah Clark July 27, 1726.
    John married Mary [Date & Maiden Name Not Given].
John, son of John and Mary Price, married Teresha Terry, June 31, 1776.

Blackwell Lineage
Jacob Price, son of John and Teresha Price, married Millicent Hendrickson, June 20, 1801.
Milicent Roberts Price, daughter of Jacob and Teresha Terry Price, married James McCauley, August 1849. [See McCauley Family above].
James Jacob McCauley married Ethlyn Brooks Gallaher, June 20, 1878. [See McCauley Family above].
Elsie Roberts McCauley, daughter of James J. and Ethlyn Gallaher McCauely, married Walter Armstrong Blackwell October 29, 1902.
    [See Hayes Family above].

[Their Children:]
Adele Leslie Blackwell married John Clifford Calloway [NDG].
Walter A. Blackwell, Jr. married Sara Isabel Bridges.

Births:

William Price II was born about 1626.
[Children of William Price III and Mary Hyland:
William was born September 18, 1699.
Richard was born January 10, 1702.
Andrew was born November 17, 1704.
Hyland was born January 13, 1709.
John was born about 1712 ?

John and Mary Price Children:
John was born February 19, 1740.
Joseph was born December 1, 1741.
Henry was born April 4, 1745.

Blackwell Lineage
Jacob Price, son of John and Teresha Price, was born March 30, 1784.
Millicent Price, daugher of John and Teresha Price, was born December 15, 1816.

Births: (Cont'd).

James Jacob McCauley, son of James and Milicent Price McCauley, was born November 12, 1853.
No dates given for the births of Adele Leslie Blackwell and Walter A. Blackwell, Jr., children of Elsie Roberts McCauley and Walter Armstrong Blackwell.

Deaths:

William Price III died in 1721. Ref will Cecil Co., Md.
John Price, husband of Teresha Terry Price died September 29, 1853.
Millicent Roberts Price died April 18, 1890.
James Jacob McCauley died August 7, 1931.

THE JOHN PRICE FAMILY BIBLE RECORDS

Printed by T. Wright and W. Gill, Printers to the University (Oxford) and sold by R. Baldwin and S. Crowder, in Paternoster Row, London and by W. Jackson, in Oxford 1770.

Marriages:

John Price married Forisho Foarry (Theresa Terry) Welsh Ancestry June 31, 1776. [See Price-Blackwell Family above].

Births:

...Children born unto said John
Hugh T. Price was born April 21, 1777.
Vachal T. Price was born June 17, 1778.
John T. Price was born November 23, 1779.
Jacob Price was born March 30, 1781.
[Daughter, no name given, born to John T. Price about September 1806.]

Deaths:

My son John T. Price departed this life about 12th November 1807, leaving one little girl aged about fourteen months.
My son Hugh T. departed this life about the 4th day of October, 1811.
Toroshea Price, wife of the above said John Price departed this life November 27, 1815.
    Note [in original]: This Bible is incomplete. Refer to will.

THE JACOB PRICE FAMILY BIBLE RECORDS

Published by M. Carey, Philadelphia 1815.
Last known to be owned by J. Hayes McCauley, Leeds, Md.

Marriages:

Jacob Price and Millicent Hendrickson married June 25, 1801. [See Price-Blackwell Family above].
John H. Price and Deborah Carlyn married April 1, 1827. [Later loose-leaf insert gives name as Conlyn and date as April 1, 1828].
Jacob Price and Martha Wilson married June 16, 1831.
William V. Wilson and Eliza Ann Price married March 8, 1832.

Births:

Children of Jacob and Millicent Hendrickson Price:
  Tereshe T. Price was born May 20, 1802.
  John H. Price was born March 12, 1804.
  Lilbune Price was born March 5, 1806. [Spelled "Lilbun" in death entry}.
  Elizer A. Price was born March 20, 1808.
  Hugh T. Price was born August 9, 1810.
  Vachel T. Price was born July 20, 1814.
  George W. Price was born November 21, 1818 (not clear).
  Mary Matilda Price was born Mary, 13, 1820.

George Washington Chandlee was born June 14, 1823.
Additional Births on Loose Leaf:
William Price Price was born March 2, 1828.
Eliza Jane Price was born June 7, 1830.
John Hyland Price was born July 25, 1831.
Edward T. Price was born September 28, 1833.
Josephine Price was born July 9, 1835.
Ella Price was born January 10, 1838.
Children of Jacob and Martha Wilson Price [entered in bible]:
  Helen Maria Price was born October 21, 1833.
  Joseph Wilson Price was born December 24, 1835.
  Sarah Amelia Price was born August 12, 1838.

Deaths:

Millicent R. Price died August 23, 1828.
Hugh F. Price died September 8, 1829.
Lilbun Price died April 23, 1840. [Spelled "Lilbune" in Birth entry].
Jacob Price died September 20, 1853.

THE RAWLINGS FAMILY BIBLE RECORDS

Printed New York, by D. Fanshaw, for the Amer. Bible Society, 1831.

Note: This Bible came to me from my mother, Mary Caroline Rawlings
... who died Feb. 27th, 1937. Her mother, Caroline (Wood) Atkinson,
mar. Frederick Rawlings 13th Jan. 1841.
August 23, 1943.   Eleanor B. Wilkins Cooch.

Marriages:

Samuel and Caroline Atkinson were married Thursday, May 28, 1835.
Caroline (Wood) Atkinson married Frederick Rawlings, January 13, 1841.

Births:

Frederick Rawlings was born August 28, 1802.
[Samuel Atkinson was born in 1804].
Caroline Wood was born April 26, 1814.
John Henry Atkinson was born April 16, 1836.
Samuel Oliver Atkinson was born December 4, 1838.
Elizabeth A. Rawlings was born October 19, 1841.
Richard Cromwell Rawlings was born June 23, 1844.
Robt. B. Rawlings was born November 13, 1846.
Mary Caroline Rawlings was born December 3, 1849.

Deaths:

Samuel Rawlings died 13th January, 1839 in the 34th year of his age.
Frederick Rawlings died November 25, 1851.
Caroline Rawlings died April 14, 1854.
Robert B. Rawlings died 23 minutes past 10, August 3rd, 1871 after ten
    days sickness with typhoid fever (at Easton, Maryland), with bright
    hope of immortality. Among his last words were "We must do our
    part and the Lord will do the rest."
Mary Caroline Rawlings [Wilkins] died February 27, 1937.

REED-SIPPLE FAMILY BIBLE RECORDS

Records from the Reed family Bible Published and sold by Kimber and Sharpless [also from Reed Family Record].

Marriages:

John Newell married Mary Edmonds.
George Wilson married Patience [Maiden name not given].

Marriages: (Cont'd).

Henry Newell married Margaret Wilson May 15, 1762.
Waitman Sipple married Marian Townsend.
Elias Sipple [son of Waitmen] married Ann Newell [daughter of Henry] November 23, 1786.
James Reed married Elizabeth Davis November 29, 1797.
Jehu Reed [their son] married Margaret Sipple [daughter of Elias] "on Tuesday the 9th day of January, 1827 at 3 o'clock in the evening".
Lydia Sipple [daughter of Elias] married a [Mr.] Norris [NDG].
Ann Sipple [daughter of Elias] married John Saxton [NDG].
Tabitha Sipple [daughter of Elias] married Captain James Grier [NDG].
James H. Reed [son of Jehu] married Emma Rebecca Chrisman in Pottsville, Pa., September 30, 1857.
Jehu Reed married [second] Mary Moor on Saturday, about 11 o'clock on June 10, 1837.

Births:

Henry Newell was born December 7, 1741.
Elias Sipple was born September 13, 1759.
Ann Newell was born March 17, 1768.
James Reed was born November 3, 1770.
Elizabeth Davis was born January 2, 1778.

[Children of Elias and Ann Newell Sipple:]
    Henry Newell Sipple was born December 21, 1787.
        Departed this life aged eight years, 1 month, 11 days.
    Lydia Sipple was born June 1, 1790.
    Elijah (?) Sipple was born May 25, 1794.
    Ann Sipple was born May 27, 1798.
    Margaret Sipple was born July 4, 1801.
    Tabitha Sipple was born October 4, 1804.
[Children of James Reed and Elizabeth Davis:]
    John Reed was born December 4, 1798.
    Joel Reed was born January 8, 1801.
    Thomas Reed was born October 20, 1802.
    Jehu Reed was born May 5, 1805.
    Mary Reed was born October 16, 1807.
    Henrietta Reed was born June 18, 1810.
    Elizabeth and Margaret Reed were born April 6, 1813.
    James Reed [II] was born October 1, 1815.
    Isaack Reed was born January 12, 1819.
[Children of Bengaman and Mary Moor:]
    Bengaman Moor [II] was born February 17, 1823.
    Susan Moor was born December 2, 1827.

Births: (Cont'd).

John M. Moor was born August 29, 1829.
Hester Ann Moor was born December 25, 1831.
[Children of Jehu Reed and Margaret Sipple:]
   Elizabeth Ann Reed was born March 21, 1828 on Friday about 12 o'clock.
   James Henry Reed was born December 6, 1829 on Sunday about 11 o'clock in morning daytime.
   Elias Sipple Reed was born July 9, 1832 about 9 o'clock on Monday morning.
   Jehu Reed was born October 10, 1834 on Friday about five o'clock in the afternoon.
   Emma Rebecca Chrisman was born at Pottsville, Pa., Wednesday, January 6, 1836.
   [Children of Jehu Reed and Mary Moor:]
   Marietta Reed was born January 3, 1839.
   Clayton M. Reed was born April 22, 1840, Wednesday between Day Brake [sic] and sunrise.
   Thomas Reed was born on Wednesday, April 13, 1843.
   [Children of James H. Reed and Emma Rebecca Chrisman:]
   C.W. Reed, our first born, came the 4th day of February-Friday-1859.
   Henry Newell Reed, our second son, was born on Saturday, December 28, 1861.
[Others:]
Chares Evans Reed was born September 24, 1888, at 4 o'clock P.M. at 630 Berkly St., Camden, N.J.
Emma Gillespie Reed was born December 9, 1889, 6 P.M. Monday at Linden Hall, Newark, Del.
George Gillespie Evans Reed was born August 24, 1897 — Tuesday, 5 P.M. at 515 Second St., N.E. Washington, D.C.
Albert Chrisman Reed was born October 31, 1899—Tuesday at 6:10 P.M. at 515 Second St., N.E. Washington, D.C.
Henry Newell Reed, Jr. was born November 13, 1896 at Newark, Delaware.

Deaths:

Henry Newell Reed died February 1, 1796, aged eight years, 1 month, and 11 days.
Ann Sipple [wife of Elias] deceased October 6, 1804 between five and six o'clock in the morning.
Elias Sipple deceased January 27, 1805 at 7 o'clock in the evening.
John Reed [son of James and Ann Reed] deceased October 30, 1805, aged 8 years 11 months.
Joel Reed [also their son] deceased November 8, 1801, aged 10 months.
Margaret Reed [their daughter] deceased April 19, 1813 aged 11 days.

Deaths: (Cont'd).

Isaack Reed [also their son] deceased October 22, 1823 aged 4 years, 9 months.

Elizabeth Ann Reed [daughter of Jehu Reed and Margarett Sipple] deceased being 7 mo. and 3 days old [October 24] 1828.

Elizabeth Reed [sister of Margaret] departed this life March 16, 1831 on Wednesday night aabout 12 o'clock.

Elijah B. Sipple [son of Elias] departed this life September 9, 1833 at 10 o'clock at night in the 39th year of his age.

Henrietta Downs departed this life June 11, 1834.

"Unlucky to the most worthy and affectionate Mother—Margarett Reed [wife of Jehu] deceased October 18th 1834 in the evening of the 9th days of her illness aged 33 years, 3 months, 14 days."

James Reed (the elder) departed this life October 7, 1844. Age 73 years, 11 months and 4 days.

Mary Reed, wife of Jehu Reed, departed this life October 1, 1864.

James Reed departed this life September 19, 1867. Aged 51 years, 11 mo. and 28 days.

Thomas Reed [son of James and Ann Reed] deceased April 26, 1869 - 66 years, 6 months & 6 days. Was kind to the poor & ripe in wisdom as in years.

Jehu Reed departed this life November 30, 1880 — aged 75 years, 6 months, and 25 days.

Emma Rebecca Chrisman departed this life in [Pottsville, Pa.] Monday evening, last day of February, 1904. Aged 68 years, 1 month and 23 days.

James Henry Reed [son of Jehu Reed and Margaret Sipple] died December 29 [30?], 1911.

Henry Newell Reed, Sr. died November 13, 1823.

Henry Newell Reed, Jr. died August 29, 1933.

Charles E. Reed died October 18, 1937.

Reed Family Record

Henry Newell, son of John Newell of Kent County, Del. and Mary, his wife, whose maiden name was Edmonds of Murderkill Neck was born December 7th, 1741 and married Margarett, daughter of George and Patience Wilson, May 15th, 1762, and settled on the place where his father lied and died, now A.D. 1900 the property of Caleb B. Williams.

Their daughter Ann was born there March 17th, 1768. Elias Sipple, son of Waitman and Mariam, his wife, whose maiden name was Townsend, was born 13th of September 1759 and married Ann Newell November 23rd, 1786. Their only son surviving youth married Mary, daughter of General Potter at Denton, Md., whose son and daughter both deceased without issue. Lydia [Sipple] married a Norris, the father of Richard and John K. Norris. Ann Sipple married John Saxton. The fifth child of said Elias Sipple and Ann Newell was Margarett Sipple, born July 4, 1801. Their 6th was Tabitha, who married Capt. James Grier. Margarett Sipple Married Jehu Reed Jan. 9th 1827. Jehu Reed wasborn near Snowhill, Md. May 5th 1805. His father, James Reed, who owned and operated a farm and sawmill in that locality came to Kent Co., Del. in 1810 and died on the now Hubbard Place, October 7th, 1844. Born Nov. 3rd, 1770. Aged 73 years 11 mo. days.

James H. Reed was born on the (Hueston?) Farmy (Saxton Place) Dec. 6th 1829, Sunday 11 A.M. Elias S. Reed was born at Reed Place July 9th, 1832. Jehu P.[?] Reed October 10th, 1834.

Emma Rebecca Chrisman, daughter of Samuel and Catherine Searles Chrisman was born at Pottsville, Pa. Jan. 6th, 1836. She married James H. Reed at that place Sept. 30th 1857. On a farm where they went to reside, called Oakland, a mile south of Milford, Del. their two sons were born as follows:

Charles W. Reed was born Feb. 4th, 1859.
Henry Newell Reed was born Dec. 28, 1861.

JAMES REYNOLDS FAMILY RECORDS

The following are taken from an old Medical Book belonging to James Reynolds last known to be in the possession of John R. Ernest, Newark, Delaware.

Births:

James Reynolds was born April 29, 1793.
Sarah Reynolds, his wife, was born April 11, 1796.
[Their Children:]
Elizabeth Reynolds was born December 11, 1814.
James Reynolds [II] was born November 31, 1817.
Ann Reynolds was born November 17, 1819.
Permelia Reynolds was born September 8, 1821.
Sarah Reynolds [II] was born October 31, 1823.
William Reynolds was born December 24, 1825.
Martha Reynolds was born May 26, 1828.
Letisha Reynolds was born December 17, 1830.
Andrew C. Reynolds was born October 12, 1832.
William R. [possibly P.] Reynolds was born September 2, 1835.

Deaths:

Sarah Cathrin [sic] Reynolds was born December 8, 1839.
William Reynolds departed this life June 3, 1833.
Elizabeth Hobson, wife of John Hobson [Reynolds - Cole Records give as Hodson], and daugher of James Reynolds, Sr. and Sarah, his wife, departed this life May 17, 1844.
James Reynolds, Sr., son of John Reynolds and Ann, his wife, departed this life February 23, 1847 in the 54th year of his age.
John Reynolds, son of James Reynolds and Sarah, hiw wife, departed this life September 8, 1850.
Sarah Reynolds, wife of James Reynolds, Sr., and daughter of Perrigrin Cole and Elizabeth, his wife, departed this life Febrruary 15, 1855, in the 59th year of his [sic] age.
William Perrigrine Reynolds died at Townsend, Delaware August 29, 1928.

REYNOLDS - COLE FAMILY BIBLE RECORDS

The following names copied from the Reynolds family Bible last known to be in the possession of Mrs. Richard Hodgson, Townsend, Delaware.

Marriages:

James Reynolds, Sr. and Sarah Cole were married March 31, 1814.
Elizabeth Reynolds and John Hodson [James Reynolds Records give as Hobson] were married December 18, 1834.
John Reynolds and Elizabeth Heverin were married November 21, 1838.
Ann M. Reynolds and Isaac Price were married January 2, 1842.
Permelia Reynolds and Lambert Seemans were married April 28, 1842.
James Reynolds, Jr. and Mary A. Reynolds were married January 1rd [sic] 1844.
Martha Reynolds and James Harris were married September 3, 1846.
William P. Reynolds and Addie Roberts were married May 14, 1857.
Sarah C. Reynolds and Henry Pratt were married February 14, 1860.
Andrew C. Reynolds and Sallie Cheffins were married November 21, 1861.

Births:

James Reynolds, Sr., son of John and Ann, his wife, was born April 29, 1793.
Sarah Reynolds, wife of James Reynolds, Sr. and daughter of Perrigrine Cole and Elizabeth, his wife, was born April 11, 1796.

[Their Children:]

Elizabeth Reynolds was born December 17, 1814.
John Reynolds was born April 22, 1816.
James Reynolds was born November 21, 1817.
Ann M. Reynolds was born November 17, 1819.
Permelia Reynolds was born September 8, 1821.
Sarah P. Reynolds was born October 31, 1823.
William P. Reynolds was born December 24, 1825.
Martha Reynolds was born May 26, 1828.
Letisha Reynolds was born December 17, 1830
Andrew C. Reynolds was born October 12, 1832.
William P. Reynolds was born September 2, 1835.
Sarah C. Reynolds was born December 8, 1839.

Deaths:

Sarah P. Reynolds departed this life August 29, 1831.
Letisha Reynolds departed this life September 28, 1831.
William Reynolds died June 3, 1833.
Elizabeth Hobson (Hodson?) died March 27, 1844.
John Reynolds departed this life September 8, 1850, aged 34 years, 4 months, and 17 days.
Andrew C. Reynolds died March 13, 1870.
James Reynolds departed this life February 23, 1847 in the 54th year of his age.
Sarah Reynolds, wife of James Reynolds, departed this life February 15, 1855.
Permelia Reynolds died July 21, 1874.
Elizabeth Reynolds, wife of John Reynolds and daughter of David Heverin and Jane, his wife, departed this life August 17, 1853.

ANDREW COLE REYNOLDS FAMILY BIBLE RECORDS

The following is taken from the family Bible belonging to Andrew C. Reynolds, Warwick, Md. and related family Bibles.

Marriages:

James Reynolds married Sarah Cole, March 31, 1814. [Parents of Andrew Cole Reynolds].
James G. Cheffins married Elizabeth [Cheffins - Parents of Sarah Elizabeth Cheffins].
Isaac Price married Ann M. Reynolds January 2, 1842.*

Marriages: (Cont'd).

Andrew Cole Reynolds married Sarah Elizabeth Cheffins November 21, 1860 at Smyra, Kent County, Delaware at 9 o'clock (night) by Piner Mansfield.

James Ulysses Grant Reynolds, their son, was married to Frances Louise Price on August 14, 1889 at St. Anne's Church, Middletown, Delaware by the Rev. Joseph Beers.

[Children of James Ulysses Grant Reynolds and Frances Louise Price:]
James Price Reynolds was married to Helene Hester Rogers on June 13th [year not given] at #171, 3rd, Anita Dive, Brentwood Heights, California by the Rev. Phipip [sic] A. Easley, rector of St. Stephen's Episcopal Church of Hollywood, California.
Mary Frances Reynolds was married to Morgan Joseph Kavanagh, Jr. on November 24, 1920 at Cheyenne, Wyoming.

Annie Elmer Ellsworth Reynolds married John Fagen Ernest December 4, 1879.

John Reynolds Ernest married Mildred Brown May 14, 1915.

Births:

John Reynolds was born before 1764 in Appoqunimink Hundred. He took the Oath of Allegiance, New Castle Co., Del. August 17, 1778.
James Reynolds, his son, was born April 29, 1793 near Smyrna, Del.
Sarah Cole, daughter of Peregrin Cole, was born January 11, 1796 in Appoqunimink Hundred.
Isaac Price was born December 15, 1813.*
Ann M. Reynolds, wife of Isaac Price, was born November 17, 1819.*
John Fagen Ernest was born November 21, 1850 in Elkton, Md.

[Children of Andrew Cole Reynolds and Sarah Elizabeth Cheffing:]
Annie Elmer Ellsworth Reynolds was born Wednesday, April 23, 1862 at 9:25 PM.
James Ulysses Grant Reynolds was born Friday, October 23, 1863 at 8:50 PM near Townsend, Newcastle County, Delaware.
Lillie May Price Reynolds was born Wednesday night, May 16, 1866 at 54 minutes past 12 o'clock.
Andrew Cole Reynolds [Jr.] was born Tuesday night, January 25, 1870 at 8:45 PM.

Mildred Brown was born in Indianapolis, Ind. on December 12, 1891.
James Price Reynolds was born at 1806 South 15th St., Philadelphia, Pa. on February 16, 1892 at 3:40 PM.
Mary Frances Reynolds was born at 1239 South Broad St., Philadelphia, Pa. on August 30, 1893 at 5:50 PM.
Jacqualine Ernest, daughter of John Reynolds Ernest and Mildred Brown was born August 15, 1920.

Deaths:

John Reynolds died at Smyrna, Del. in 1820. [His will of October 5, 1820 was probated October 10, 1820. Original will is on file in the Delaware Archives, Dover, Delaware, p. 820.]
James Reynolds died at Smyrna, Del. February 23, 1847. [Letters of Administration for his estate were issued on March 2, 1847 - See Will Record U. Volume 1, Page 435, New Castle County, Delaware.]
Sarah Cole died February 15, 1855.
Isaac Price died November 29, 1866. Age, 52 years 11 months 24 days.
Andrew Cole Reynolds departed this life March 13, 1870 at 9:30 AM, near Townsend, Del. [Letters of Administration on his estate were issued on March, 25, 1870. Recorded in Wilmington, DE, in Will Record Book B Volume 2, Page 13, New Castle County, Delaware.]
John Fagen Ernest died in Elkton, Md. on March 8, 1916.
Sarah Elizabeth Cheffins died at Warwick, Md. May 5, 1920.
James Ulysses Grant Reynolds died at Trona, California September 4, 1936; buried at Inglewood Cemetery, Inglewood, California, September 8, 1936.

THOMAS SAWYER & MARGARET LEWDEN FAMILY BIBLE RECORDS

[Last known to be] in the possession of Mrs. Kirk E. Baxter, 1085 S. Boulevard, Springfield, Mo. Printed by and for George Grierson, Printer to the King's most Excellent Majesty, at the King's Arms and two Bibles in Essex Street MDCCLII (1752). Stickers pasted on inside of Bible read: J. Wilson, bookbinder and Bookseller and Stationer, Wilmington, Delaware.

Marriages:

Thomas Sawyer and Margaret Lewden married April 16, 1761.
Rebecca Sawyer married Laurence Hanson.
Joseph Sawyer married [1st] Mary Murray November 11, 1788; [2nd] Susan Osborne February 16, 1804.
Robert Sawyer married Mary Turner.
Lewden Sawyer married [1st] Mary Steele, [2nd] Hannah Allen, [3rd] Ebby Burdick.
Margaret Hanson married George B. Sawyer.
Thomas Lewden Sawyer, son of Lewden and Ebby Sawyer, married [1st] Henrietta Carpenter, September 7, 1839.
Thomas Lewden Sawyer, married [2nd] Martha Parsons [no date given].
George Meggeson Sawyer, son of Thomas Lewden Sawyer and Henrietta Carpenter, and Virginia Stephens were married November 30, 1871 by Rev. James Waterman in Christ Church, Springfield, Mo.

Marriages: (Cont'd).

Carrie Eva Sawyer, daughter of G. M. and Virginia Sawyer, and Kirk E. Baxter were married May 19, 1891 by the Rev. Kirk Baxter at Springfiled, Mo. on National Boulevard.
Lewden M. Sawyer, son of G. M. and Virginia Sawyer, and Eliza M. Stone were married May 31, 1922 by Rev. A.G. Van Elden in St. Mary's Church, Galena, Kansas.

[Children of Caroline E. Sawyer and Kirk E. Baxter:]
Mary Virginia Baxter married George Weir McDonald November 12, 1914.
Kirk Sawyer Baxter married Eugene Firld December 18, 1915.

Births:

George M. Sawyer, son of Thomas L. and Henrietta Sawyer, was born June 10, 1848 in Gallatin, Tennessee.
[Children of Thomas Sawyer and Margaret Lewden:]
Rebecca Sawyer was born Monday, January 25, 1762 at 4:00 AM.
Joseph Sawyer was born Thursday, December 8, 1763.
Hannah Sawyer was born Thursday, May 8, 1765 at 3:00 PM.
Margaret Sawyer was born Sunday, January 25, 1767 between 2 and 3 AM.
Lewden Sawyer was born May 20, 1769. - Died September 6, 1770.
Robert Sawyer was born March 21, 1772.
Lewden Sawyer was born August 27, 1773.
[Children of Joseph Sawyer and Mary Murray:]
Margaret Sawyer was born December 1789.
William M. Sawyer was born August 3, 1792.
Ann Sawyer was born April 1, 1795.
[Children of Lewden Sawyer, son of Thomas Sawyer & Margaret Lewden:]
Joseph
Margaret
Jane
Rebecca
George
Lewden
Thomas Lewden Sawyer [was born to Lewden and Ebby Sawyer - no date].
[Children of Thomas Lewden Sawyer and Henrietta Carpenter:
Clarentine
Catherine
Harriett
Elizabeth
George M. Sawyer was born June 10, 1848 in Gallatin, Tennessee.
Edward R.
Henrietta

Births: (Cont'd).

Eva
Annie
[Children of Thomas Lewden Sawyer and Martha Parsons:]
Charlie
Etta
Anna
[Children of George M. Sawyer and Virginia C. Stephens:]
Carrie Eva was born in Springfield, Mo. October 21, 1872.
Lewden McCullah [Sawyer] was born in Springfield, Mo. September 22, 1874.
Robert Meggison [Sawyer] was born in Springfield, Mo. December 20, 1877.
Fannie Isabella was born in Springfield, Mo. June 5, 1880.
Helen was born in Springfield, Mo. August 19, 1882.
Rebecca Hanson Meggison [Sawyer] was born in Springfield, Mo. June 23, 1888.
[Children of Carrie E[va] Sawyer and Kirk E. Baxter:]
Kirk Sawyer [Baxter] was born April 6, 1892 [in Springfield, Mo.]
Mary Virginia was born April 10, 1895 [in Springfield, Mo.]
[Child of Kirk Sawyer Baxter and Eugene Firld:]
Barbara Dale Baxter
[Children of Mary Virginia Baxter and George Weir Malcolm:]
Kirk
Weir
John Baxter [Malcolm]
George Sawyer [Malcolm].

Deaths:

Margaret Sawyer, daughter of Thomas Sawyer and Margaret Lewden, died in the Spring of 1777.
Margaret Sawyer, daughter of Joseph Sawyer and Mary Murray, died September 1790 aged nine months.
Mary Sawyer, wife of Joseph Sayver, died May 6, 1802 at 7:00 AM.
William Sawyer, their son, died February 22, 1829 in the 37th year of his age.
Joseph A. Sawyer, son of William and Ann Sawyer, died in April 1846.
Joseph Sawyer died at New Castle, Del. on August 4, 1847 in the 84th year of his age.
William Sawyer, son of William and Ann Sawyer, died in April 1849.
Ann M. Denks?, wife of Michl H. Denks and daughter of Joseph and Mary Sawyer died August 4, 1854 aged 59 years, 4 mos. and 4 days and was entered her Father's vault in the old Quaker burial ground, New Castle, Delaware.

Deaths: (Cont'd).

John A. Stephens, father of Virginia Stephens & Springfield, Mo. Postmaster was killed during a raid on Springfield in the [18]50s.
Henrietta Sawyer died in 1857.
Henrietta Sawyer, wife of Thomas Lewden Sawyer, died August 23, 1859.
Robert Meggison Sawyer, son of G. M. and Virginia Sawyer, died December 30, 1898 age 21 years.
George M. Sawyer died of Bright's disease at his home on National Boulevard, Springfield, Mo. April 28, 1895 at 12:30 AM age 47.
Virginia Stephens, wife of George M. Sawyer, died of paralysis April 23, 1918, at 12:30 AM age 65 years. Both are buried in Maple Park Cemetary, Springfield, Mo. Survived by the following children: L. M. Sawyer, Mrs. R.W. Fugitt, Mrs. Perry Enslen, and Mrs. Guy Mace, all of Springfield, by Mrs. Kirk Baxter of Belle Fourche, S.D.; two brothers: John Stephens of Muscatine, Iowa, and Will Stephens of Beatrice, Nebraska, and one sister, Mrs. John R. White of Springfield, Mo.

[Adapted from a Family Tree Diagram in this Bible Record:]

Joseph Sawyer married Margaret Lewden, April 16, 1761.
    Joseph Sawyer [his son] married Mary Murphy and Susan Osborne.
        1. William Sawyer married Ann Johnson.
        2. Ann Sawyer married Judge Finks.
    Robert Sawyer married Mary Turner.
        1. Joseph Sawyer married Eliz. Stevens and Eliz. Scribner.
            Children: Emma, Louis, Joseph, Ogden, Lizzie & Anna.
        2. Robert Sawyer married Martha Ellison.
    Lewden Sawyer married Mary Steele, Hannah Allen & Ebby Burdic.
        1. Joseph A. Sawyer married Mary Hathaway.
            Children: Ella, Robert, Lewden, Joseph, Allen, Mary.
        2. Margaret Sawyer.
        3. Jane married William Allen.
            Children: William, Margaret married Norton; Mary married Arthur Stevenson.
        4. Rebecca married Thom Ellison.
        5. George married Rebecca [maiden name not given].
        6. [Thomas] Lewden Sawyer married Henrietta Carpenter and Martha Parsons.
            Children: 1. Charlie [Sawyer].
                      2. Etta.
                      3. Anna.
                      4. Eva married Will Stevens.
                      5. George M. married Virginia Stevens.
                          Children: Carrie, Lewden McCullah, Robert, Fannie, Helen, Rebecca.

THOMAS ALEXANDER SMITH FAMILY BIBLE RECORDS

Family Bible [last known to be] in the possession of Mrs. Elsie (Smith) Dutton -- 183 West Main Street, Newark, Delaware.

Marriages:

Abraham Van Arsdale married Elsie June 19, 1771. "... by word of mouth to Elsie Smith Dutton from Alice Van Arsdale, Christmas Holidays, 1917."
Sylvester Smith married - first - Sarah Elizabeth Cullett June 12, 1845.
James Harrison Frazer was married to Alice Van Arsdale Clayton at Plymouth, Michigan by Rev. Joshua Anderson Clayton (Presbyterian) on January 25, 1853.
Abraham Van Arsdale married Elsie Baird, June 19, 1771.
Joshua Anderson Clayton married Margaret Skillman.
James Harrison Frazer married Alice Van Arsdale Clayton.
Thomas Alexander Smith was married to Adah Clayton Frazer at Ridgely, M. E. Church, Caroline Co., Md. by the Rev. F.C. McSorley on September 10, 1878.
Alice Anita Smith was married to Dr. Walter Mills Carmine, Ridgely, Md. M.E. Church by the Rev. John Jones.
Elsie Sylvester Smith was married to George Elliott Dutton, Ridgely, Md. M.E. Church by the Rev. Howard T. Quigg.
Thomas Alexander Smith, Jr. married Jennie Austin of Birmingham, Alabama, June 4, 1921. At home.

Births:

Elsie Baird was born August 9, 1752.
Joseph Skillman was born March 12, 1768.
Abraham Van Arsdale was born December 2, 1771, Harlinger, N.J.
Elsy Van Arsdale was born February 3, 1780.
Margaret Skillman was born March 22, 1803, Middlebush, N.J.
Joshua Anderson Clayton was born February 10, 1805, Florida, New York.
Sylvester Smith was born February 8, 1822, Mispillion Hundred, Kent Co., Delaware.
James Harrison Frazer was born September 28, 1824 [possibly 1823] Rupert, Vermont.
Sarah Elizabeth Gullett was born April 18, 1825, Mispillion Hundred Kent Co., Delaware.
Alice Van Arsdale Clayton, daughter of Abraham Van Arsdale and Elsie Baird was born May 12, 1830, Murean, Saratoga County, N.Y.

Births: (Cont'd).

Thomas Alexander Smith, son of Sylvester Smith and Sarah Elizabeth Gullett, was born September 3, 1850, Mispillion Hundred, Kent County, Delaware.

Adah Clayton Frazer, daughter of James Harrison Frazer and Alice Van Arsdale Clayton, was born December 3, 1853 in Detroit, Michigan.

[Children of Thomas Alexander Smith & Adah Clayton Frazer:]

Ethel Smith was stillborn, March 18, 1880.
Alice Anita Smith was born Feb 11, 1881, Ridgely, Caroline County, Md.
Elsie Sylvester Smith was born July 11, 1883, Ridgely, Caroline County, Md.
Thomas Alexander Smith, Jr. was born June 19, 1889, Ridgely, Caroline County, Md.
Alice Carmine, daughter of Alice Anita [Smith] & Dr. Walter Mills Carmine, was born February 18, 1913 at Sparrows Point, MD.
George Elliott Dutton, son of Elsie Sylvester Smith and George Elliott Dutton, was born June 18, 1913 at Newark, Delaware.
Eugenia Carmine, daughter of Dr. W.M. and Alice Anita Carmine, was born September 18, 1919 at St. Helena, Maryland.

Deaths:

Elsie Baird died October 6, 1801.
Abraham Van Arsdale died April 4, 1821.
Sarah Elizabeth Gullett died at age 27, October 18, 1852
Joshua Anderson Clayton died December 26, 1870, Plymouth, Michigan.
Margaret Skillman died June 2, 1894, Detroit, Michigan.
Sylvester Smith died March 28, 1898, Ridgely, Maryland.
James H. Frazer died May 27, 1903, Ridgely, Maryland, age 79.
Emma Catherine Shaner, wife of Chas. Van Arsdale Frazer, died at Pottsville, Pennsylvania, November 7, 1912 of pneumonia, age 47 years.
Alice Van Arsdale Clayton died May 5, 1919, Ridgely, Maryland, age 88.
Dora Skillman, wife of Joshua Anderson Frazer, died at Elizabeth, N.J. summer of 1919.
Mary Leura [sic] Roberts Frazer, wife of Emory D. Frazer [no date given].
Thomas Alexander Smith died at Newark, Delaware April 30, 1932.
Adah Clayton Frazer Smith died at Newark, Delaware December 21, 1933.

WILLIAM SMITH FAMILY BIBLE RECORDS

"This record is take from my Grandfather, William Smith's family bible, purchased in 1834. The fly leaf of the bible has been lost. There is no record of when it was printed or who by. This book is now mine".   Mrs. Harry I. Garrett, Strickersville, Pa.
Cooch's Bridge Chapter, D.A.R.

Marriages:

William Smith married Mary DeHaven on the tenth day of May, 1821.

AGES
He was twenty-three years, three months and ten days old.
She was eighteen years old.

His age	years	mo	Days
	23	3	6
Her age	18	0	0
Difference	5	3	6

Sarah Ann Smith married Robert Montgomery [No date given].
Mary Jane Smith married William Armstrong [NDG].
John D. Smith married Annie Garrett [NDG].

Births:

John Smith, father of William Smith, was born in Ireland in 1769.
Isabella Smith, mother of William Smith, was born in Ireland in 1769.
William Smith was born February 4, 1797.
Adam Smith was born July 13, 1798.
John Smith was born June 29, 1800.
Mary Smith was born June 29, 1802.
Isabella Smith was born May 17, 1804.
George Smith was born September 10, 1806.
Eliza Jane Smith was born June 28, 1810.
Children of William and Mary Dehaven Smith
John Smith was born November 11, 1821.
Sarah Ann Smith was born August 28, 1823.
George I. Smith was born July 31, 1826.
Mary Jane Smith was born February 14, 1829.
William H. Smith was born October 31, 1831.
James (? poss. Jacob) Reed Smith was born March 7, 1834.
James P. Smith was born January 11, 1837.
Samuel D. Smith was born October 23, 1839.
Elizabeth Smith was born September 26, 1842.
Winfield Scott Smith was born April 28, 1847.

Deaths:

William Smith departed this life at 1 PM Thursday, September 24, 1863 aged 66 years and 7 months.
John D. Smith departed this life at 5:00 AM, Janaury 5, 1881 aged 59 years - 9 mos. - 29 days.
Mary Smith, wife of William Smith, departed this life February 18, 1882 at 4:00 AM. Aged 78 years - 9 mos. - 8 days.
Samuel DeHaven Smith, MD departed this life February 6, 1898 AT 9 PM, aged 58 years - 11 mos - 13 days.
Jacob Reed Smith departed this life July 16, 1900, aged 66 years - 4 mos - 9 days.
Robert Montgomery, husband of Sarah Ann Smith, departed this life December 15, 1900 age 78 years.
Sarah Ann Smith Montgomery departed this life January 29, 1903, aged 79 years - 5 mos - 1 day.
William Armstrong, husband of Mary Jane Smith, departed this life July 15, 1903 age 80 years.
George I. Smith departed this life January 25, 1905, aged 78 yrs - 5 mos - 28 days.
Annie Garrett Smith, wife of John D. Smith departed this life February 25, 1905.
James P. Smith died November 28, 1911 aged 74 years.

LINEAGES

Of Mrs. Ernest Frazier, Mrs. Harlan C. Herdman, Miss Anna Frazer & Mrs. Anna Frazer Jones

MacDonough-Hyland-Foard-Smith [-DeHaven]
[Adapted from Bible Record Charts]

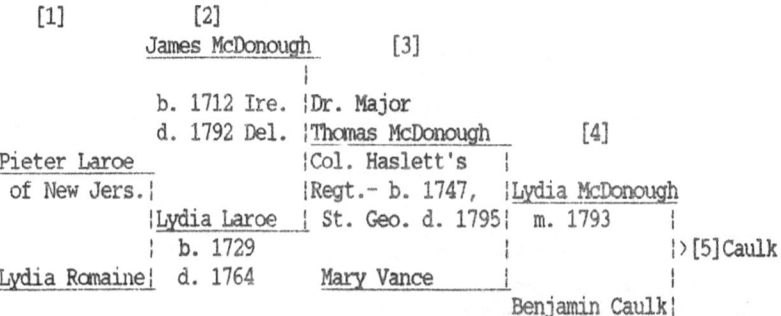

(Cont'd. on Next Page)

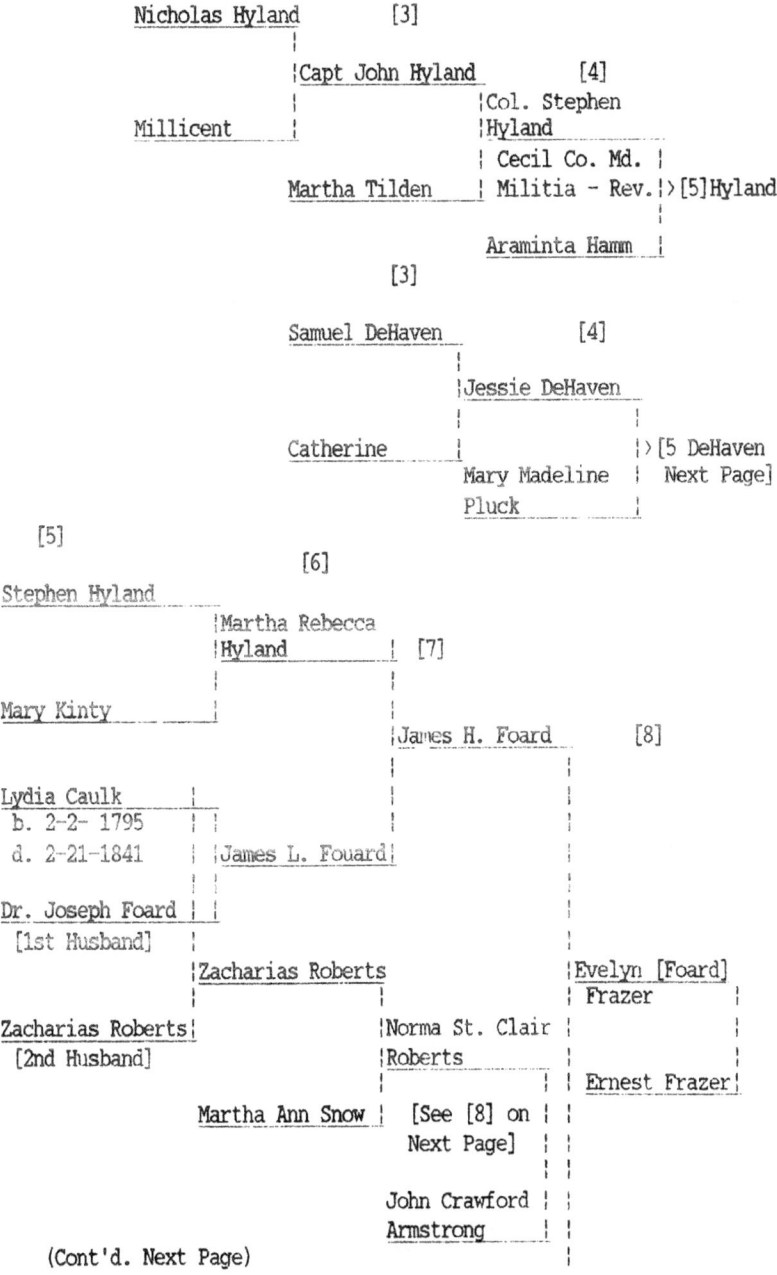

[5]

Mary DeHaven

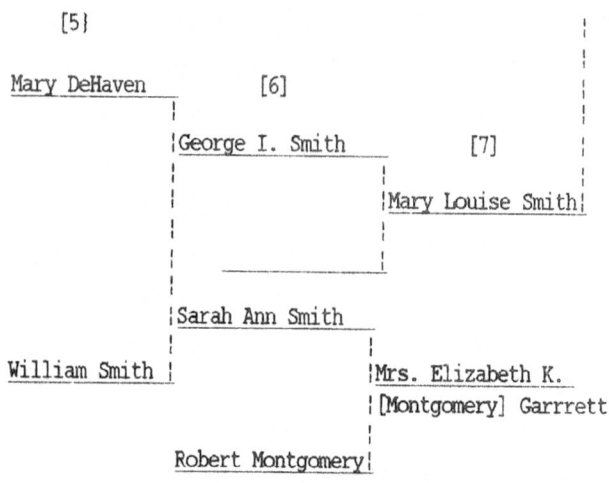

William Smith

Robert Montgomery

[6] George I. Smith

[7] Mary Louise Smith

Sarah Ann Smith

Mrs. Elizabeth K. [Montgomery] Garrrett

[8]

Frances Crawford Armstrong
1861-1920

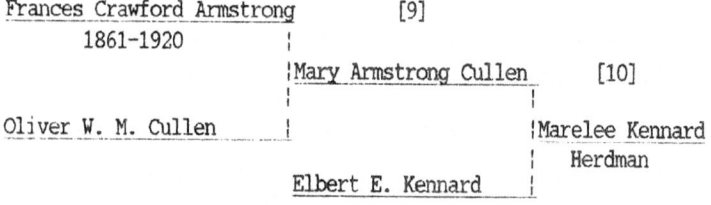

Oliver W. M. Cullen

[9] Mary Armstrong Cullen

Elbert E. Kennard

[10] Marelee Kennard Herdman

Genealogical Notes:

Col. Stephen Hyland assisted in establishing American Independence while acting in the capacity of Col. Cecil Co. [Md.] militia.

Maj. Thomas MacDonough assisted in establishing American Independence while acting in the capacity of Major, Del. He was the father of Commodore McDonough, [sic] Lake Champlain.

First Samuel DeHaven loaned money to Continental Congress to support the Revolution. He fought as a private. Second Samuel DeHaven was a grandson of Peter DeHaven.

References: See Wm. Smith Bible Records, Robert Montgomery Family and DeHaven Family Bible Records Above.

THOMAS STEEL FAMILY BIBLE RECORDS

Dated 1832 - MCarty and Davis, 171 Market St. Philadelphia, Pa.
I. Ashmead & Co. printers.

Marriages:

James Steel married Elizabeth Mahaffey July 26, 1777.
Allen Steel, their son, was married to Ruth Sharp May 21, 1792 by Rev. Conden.
Thomas Steel married Mary Huggins September 12, 1826.
Robert Huggins Steel married Louisa Hossinger.
John Thomas Steel married Elizabeth Ellen Garrett.
Hudson Steel married Louisa Warren.
George W. Steel married [1st] Mary Elden Mote.
George W. Steel married [2nd] Ruth Ann Tuft.
Ada Laura Steel married William Joseph Davis of Elkton, Maryland June 28, 1895.
Harriet Louisa Steel married George T. Johnson.
Clara Elizabeth Davis married John Henry Minster November 2, 1921.
John Miller Davis married Sara Erma Roney August 26, 1926.
Ada Carolyn Johnston married Roger Pennington Watkins October 18, 1941.

Births:

Thomas Steel, son of Allen and Ruth Steel, was born August 11, 1802.
Mary Huggins Steel, wife of Thomas Steel, was born February 10, 1803.

<u>Children of Thomas and Mary Huggins Steel</u>
Robert Huggins Steel was born July 20, 1829.
John Thomas Steel was born Mary 6, 1831.
Caroline Steel was born June 23, 1834.
Adeline Steel was born June 23, 1834.
Lucinda Steel was born September 8, 1836.
Hudson Steel was born November 19, 1838.
George W. Steel was born August 9, 1843.

<u>Children of John Thomas and Elizabeth Garrett Steel</u>
Anna Lucinda Steel was born July 27, 1861.
Robert E. Steel was born April 9, 1863.
William T. Steel was born August 16, 1864.
John Edwin Steel was born September 24, 1866.
Mary Elizabeth Steel was born August 2, 1869.
Ada Laura Steel was born February 1, 1871.
Harriett Louisa Steel was born July 26, 1876.

Births: (Cont'd).

Children of Ada Laura Steel and William Joseph Davis
Clara Elizabeth Davis was born September 7, 1896.
John Miller Davis was born October 4, 1904.
Children of Harriett Louisa Steel and George T. Johnson
Mary Alive [sic] Elizabeth Johnston [NDG].
Ada Carolyn Johnston [NDG].
Children of Clara Elizabeth Davis and John Henry Minster
John Davis Minster was born April 16, 1923.
William Davis Minster was born September 19, 1928.
Child of John Miller Davis and Sara Erma Roney
Robert Miller Davis was born March 30, 1930.

Deaths:

Caroline Steel August 16, 1837.
Lucinda Steel February 14, 1860.
Anna Lucinda Steel June 8, 1862.
Robert E. Steel July 29, 1863.
Mary Huggins Steel May 20, 1869.
William T. Steel November 29, 1870.
Thomas Steel February 18, 1880.
Robert H. Steel November 21, 1899.
Elizabeth Garrett Steel, wife of John Thomas Steel, February 2, 1908.
Hudson Steel July 12, 1909.
John Thomas Steel December 13, 1913.
George W. Steel February 27, 1921.
Harriett Louisa Steel June 11, 1932.
John Edwin Steel February 28, 1933.
Mary Elizabeth Steel June 19, 1937.

Historical Note:

Head of Christiana Church [Delaware] and Cemetery stands on ground leased to the Trustees of Head of Christiana Church by Allen Steel, son of one James Steel and father of Thomas Steel for nine hundred and ninty nine years or until there ceased to be services held there in the service of the Lord in which instance the property [would] revert to the farm adjoining, from which it was taken. The deed [was] in the possession of George T. Johnston's family that of Harriett Louisa Steel Johnston.

John Thomas Steel was Sunday School Superintendent and Eldre of the church from the age of 21 years. Andrew Kerr [see lineage chart next page] signed the Oath of Fidelity before James Black.

James Steel signed the Oath of Fidelity before Justice Richard Bond.

James Steel, Jr. signed the Oath of Fidelity before Justice Richard Bond March 1778.

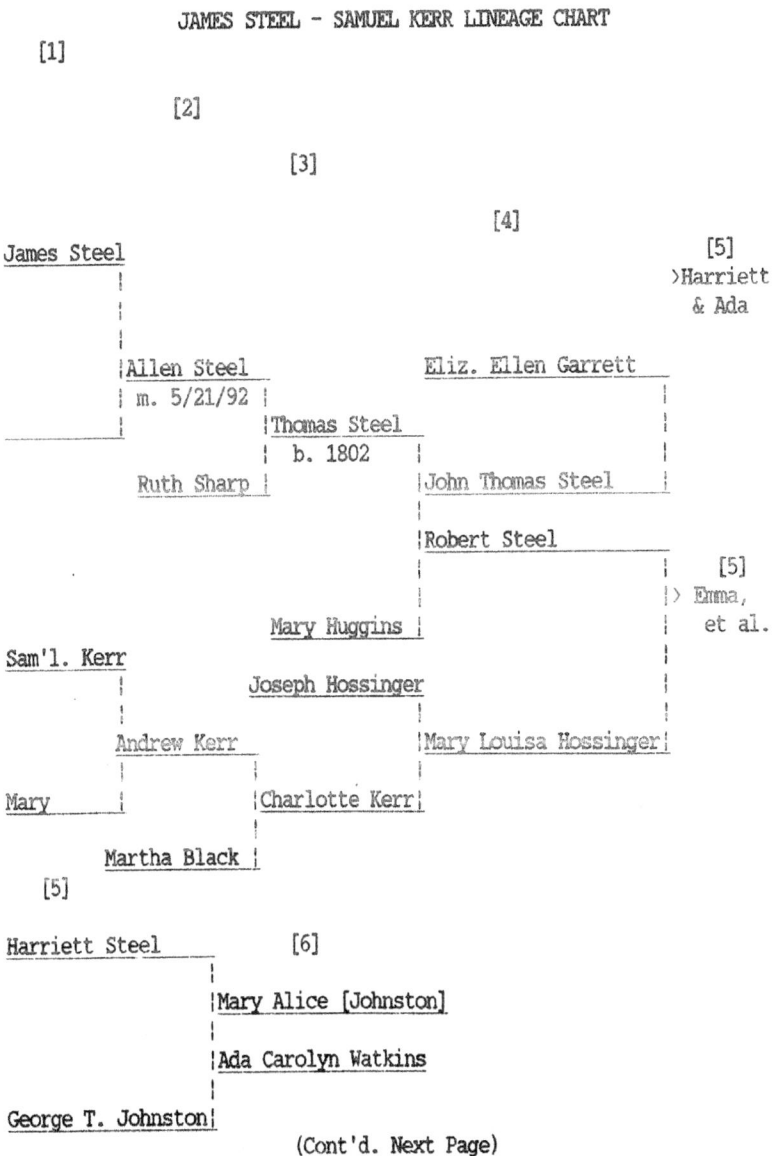

(Cont'd. Next Page)

Ada Laura Steel
                Clara Elizabeth Davis   m. John Henry Minster.
                John M. Davis   m. Sara Roney.
William Joseph Davis

[5]

Jones
           [6]
        Robert T. Jones

Emma Steel

James H. Steel
        Catherine Steek

Louisa Garrett

Dr. Walter H. Steel
        Paul, Walter, Rosalie, Justin, Phoebe, Dean,
        & Louise [Steel]

Katherine Pie

SAMUEL VAIL FAMILY BIBLE RECORDS

Published in New York by A. J. Johnson 1870.

Marriages:

Samuel C. Vail and Martha B. Cantwell were married April 18, 1872 by Rev. H.S. Thompson.
Clara Cantwell Vail and Caleb Newbold Price were married July 8, 1896 at home by Rev. Davidson.
Agnes Pennington Vail and Joseph Naglee Reeves were married December 1, 1910 at Saulisbury, Md by Rev. David Howard.
Julia Blake Higgins and John Fletcher Price, son of Clara Vail and Caleb Newbold Price were married in New York City June 12, 1928.

Births:

Clara Cantwell Vail was born February 13, 1873.
Alice Smith Vail was born December 24, 1874.
Agnes Pennington Vail was born October 13, 1878.
John Fletcher, Son of Clara Vail and Caleb Newbold Price was born Tuesday, November 30, 1897.
Clayton Vail Price was born Thursday, February 15, 1900.
Julian Cantwell Newbold Price was born Sunday, October 2, 1904.
Mary Louise, daughter of Julia Higgins and John Fletcher Price was born June 11, 1936.

Deaths:

Caleb Newbold Price died June 23, 1921 at Carney's Point, N.J.
Martha Cantwell Vail died December 9, 1922.
Samuel Cleaver Vail died June 12, 1923.
Joseph Naglee Reeves died August 23, 1927.
Alice Smith Vail, daughter of Martha C. and Samuel Vail died Monday, April 18, 1938.

ALEXANDER WILSON FAMILY BIBLE RECORDS

Published by Kimber and Sharpless, 1852. [Last known] Owner:-
Mrs. Sara Wilson Slack, Newark, Deleware.

Marriages:

Alexander Wilson and Sarah Jane Clendenin were married December 30, 1852.
John T. Wilson and Ida May Leak were married December 24, 1895.
Norman Slack and Sarah Etta Wilson were married November 11, 1926.

Births:

Alexander Wilson was born October 28, 1829.
John H. Wilson was born March 7, 1831.
John T. Wilson was born November 6, 1853.
Elija J. Wilson was born February 20, 1855.
William R. Wilson was born March 7, 1858.
Annie Elizabeth Wilson was born January 14, 1898.
Sarah Etta Wilson was born October 3, 1900.
Jon Wilson Slack, son of Norman Slack and Sarah E. Wilson Slack, was born June 1, 1937.

Deaths:

John H. Wilson died September 21, 1853 aged 22 years and 6 months.
Alexander Wilson died January 16, 1896.
Elija J. Barton [?] died January 29, 1909.
Sarah J. Wilson died July 2, 1913.
Annie E. Wilson died December 22, 1917.
William R. Wilson died October 4, 1917.
John T. Wilson died May 22, 1930.

STEPHEN WILSON FAMILY BIBLE RECORDS

[Last known to be] in the possession of Henry Wilson, Hockessin, Delaware.

Marriages:

Stephen Wilson married Lydia _____ _____.
Alice Wilson married [1st _____ Jackson; 2nd _____ Chandler.
Ebenezer Edmunds married Mary Gale.
S. Edmund married Rachel Sabin.
David Wilson married Sarah Hadley.
Emily Edmunds married Nathaniel Brainard.
Stephen Wilson [son of David Wilson] married Sarah Mitchell.
Jay Brainard married Mary Melissa Wells.
Edward Wilson married Sara Moore.
Cora Brainard married Leon W. Gilmore.
Henry P. Wilson married Marian Gilmore.

Births:

Alice Wilson was born May 26, 1775.
Stephen Wilson was born September 30, 1762.
Lydia Wilson was born November 6, 1772.
[Children of Stephen and Lydia Wilson:]
    David Wilson was born October 20, 1795.
Sarah [Hadley] Wilson [wife of David] was born November 11, 1795.
    Jonathan Wilson was born May 13, 1798.
    Pusey Wilson was born September 13, 1800.
    Sarah Wilson was born September 5, 1803.
    James Wilson was born April 28, 1806.
    Josiah Wilson was born August 9, 1817.
[Children of David and Sarah [Hadley] Wilson:]
    Stephen Wilson was born August 18, 1822.
    Phoebe H. Wilson was born March 16, 1824.

Births: (Cont'd).

Eliza Wilson was born February 28, 1826.
Lydia P. Wilson was born August 15, 1828.
Hadley Wilson was born April 7, 1831.
Sarah Mitchell Wilson [wife of Stephen] was born March 19, 1832.
[Children of Stephen and Sarah Mitchell Wilson:]
Emilie P. Wilson was born November 6, 1856.
Joseph M. Wilson was born October 5, 1858.
Eliza R. Wilson was born April 15, 1863.
David H. Wilson was born March 14, 1865.
Edward S. Wilson was born February 24, 1873.
Sara C. Moore [wife of Edward S. Wilson] was born February 19, 1877.
[Children of Edward and Sara C. Wilson:]
Ethel C. Wilson was born March 25, 1908.
Henry P. Wilson was born April 7, 1909.
Edwards S. Wilson, Jr. was born October 30, 1911.
Marian Gilmore [wife of Henry P. Wilson] was born April 3, 1914.
James Herbert Wilson was born December 13, 1914.
[Children of Henry Palmer and Marian Gilmore Wilson:]
Henry Palmer Wilson, Jr. was born March 25, 1942.

Deaths:

Lydia Wilson died November 1, 1810.
Pusey Wilson died October 25, 1818.
Stephen Wilson died August 23, 1820.
Hadley Wilson died June 24, 1832 aged 1 year, 2 mos., 17 days.
Sarah Hadley Wilson died February 2, 1844, aged 48 years, 2 mos., 27 days.
Alice Wilson died December 13, 1856 aged 81 years, 6 mos., 17 days.
David Wilson died June 25, 1869 aged 74 years, 6 mos., 5 days.
Phoebe H. Wilson died August 18, 1870 aged 46 years, 5 mos., 2 days.
Stephen Wilson [son of David Wilson] died April 28, 1899 aged 77 years, 8 mos., 9 days.
Sarah Mitchell Wilson died December 27, 1906 aged 74 years, 9 mos., 8 days.
David H. Wilson died August 4, 1906 aged 41 years.
Joseph M. Wilson died April 28, 1924 aged 66 years.
Emilie Wilson Palmer died August 2m 1932 aged 76 years.
Edward S. Wilson died January 18, 1941.
Sara C. Wilson died March 7, 1942 aged 65 years, 1 mo., 16 days.

Historical Note:

Ebenezer Edmunds of Dudley, Mass. served at Lexington Alarm in Capt. Nathaniel Healey's Co.

LINEAGE OF HENRY P. WILSON
Hockessin, Delaware

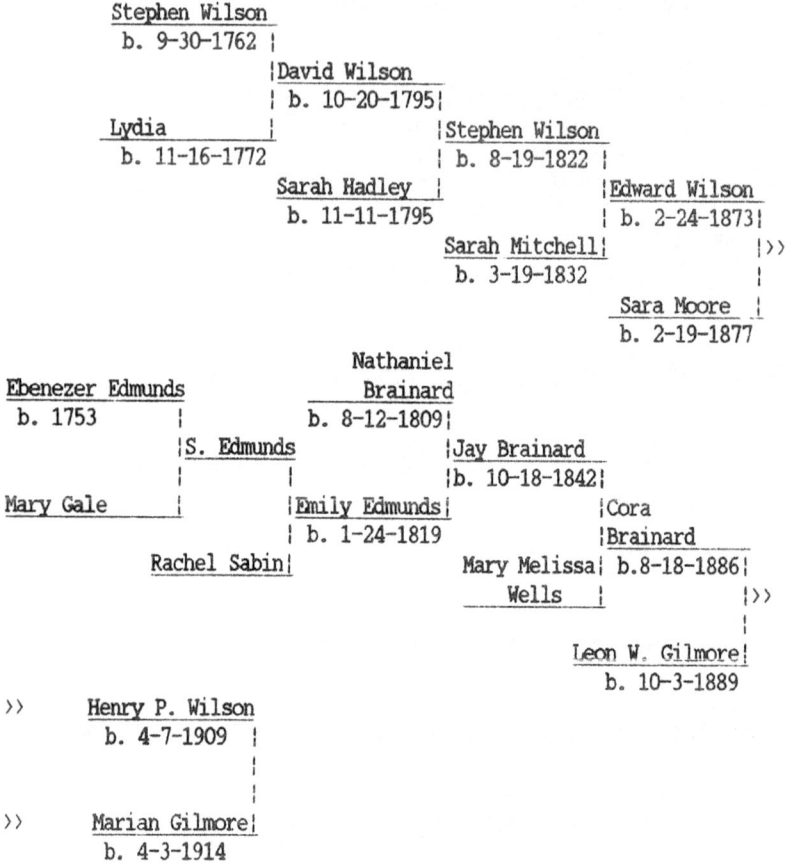

JOHN WITT FAMILY BIBLE RECORDS

Record from Old Bible Printed in Edinburgh by Adrian Watkins his Magesty's [sic] Printer. Published - MCDDLVI (1756). Bible was found in home of Miss Emily C. Thomas, daughter of Richard L. Thomas of North East, Maryland.

Marriages:

Mr. John Witt was married to Miss Isabella Arnold July 15, 1781. Isabella Witt was married to Joseph Ingraham January 31, 1793.

Births:

John Witt was born December 8, 1784.
William Ingraham was born August 1793.
Stephen Colver, son of Stephen and Isabella Colver was born in
Baltimore, January 31, 1803 — Died October 21, 1804.

Deaths:

William Ingraham died December 23, 1795.
Stephen Colver died at Wasshington [DC] February 9, 1809.
Sarah Sergeant, wife of Alling Sergeant departed this life September
29, 1854, aged 54 years.

THOMAS WOLLASTON FAMILY BIBLE RECORDS

5th .. Mo 27th .. 1793. Printed and sold by Isaac Collins
Trenton M.D.CC.XCI (1791).

Marriages:

Thomas Wollaston married Hannah _____.
Joseph Chambers married Amy Thompson.
Jeremiah Wollaston, their son, married Mary Chambers, daughter of
Joseph and Amy Chambers on January 14, 1807.
Thomas Wollaston of Stanton, Delaware married Minerva Pennock of
Londongrove.
Sarah Wollaston [daughter of Jeremiah Wollaston] married a Pennock.

Births:

Joseph Chambers was born January 23, 1745 (old style).
Amy Thompson was born February 6, 1745 (old style).
Jeremiah Wollaston was born June 29, 1765.
[Children of Joseph & Amy Chambers:]
Sarah Chambers was born July 24, 1769.
Elizabeth Chambers was born November 13, 1770.
William Chambers was born October 26, 1772.
James Chambers was born March 16, 1775.
Mary Chambers was born August 13, 1777.
William Chambers was born December 8, 1780.
Joseph Chambers was born December 21, 1782.
Amy Chambers was born May 4, 1787.
[Children of Jeremiah & Mary Wollaston:]
Eliza Wollaston was born December 28, 1807.

Births: (Cont'd).

Amy Wollaston was born April 29, 1809.
Isaac Wollaston was born November 18, 1810.
Thomas Wollaston was born November 26, 1812.
Joshua Wollaston was born August 5, 1815.
Sarah Wollaston was born July 15, 1818.

Deaths:

William Chambers departed this life April 16, 1775.
James Chambers departed this life November 1, 1777.
Joseph Chambers departed this life October 8, 1801 aged 59 years, 8 mos. and 15 days.
Amy Thompson Chambers departed this life March 1, 1806 aged 61 years and three weeks.
Jeremiah Wollaston departed this life March 30, 1825 between ten and eleven o'clock at night.
Mary Wollaston, his wife, departed this life December 31, 1856 between nine and ten at night.
Eliza Wollaston departed this life July 4, 1864 about two o'clock in the afternoon.
Joshua Wollaston departed this life June 8, 1870 aged 54 years, 10 mos. and 3 days.
Sarah Wollaston Pennock departed this life February 12, 1879 at 8:30 AM aged 60 years, 6 mos. and 27 days.
Isaac Wollaston departed this life April 12, 1893 at 12 o'clock noon, Aged 82 years, 4 mos. and 25 days.
Thomas Wollaston departed this life March 8, 1896 at 3:15 AM aged 83 years, 3 mos. and 11 days.
Ann[?] Wollaston departed this life September 16, 1899 at 10:15 PM aged 90 years, 4 mos. and 18 days.
Minerva Wollaston, wife of Thomas Wollaston departed this life April 7, 1902 at 3:40 PM. Age 81 years 11 mos. and 27 days.

Note from News Clipping:

Thomas Wollaston, one of the oldes citizens of New Garden Township, died at his home a mile or two south of New Garden meeting house on Sunday morning, of pneumonia, after an illness of little over a day. Mr. Wollaston was born near Stanton, Delaware 84 years ago, and soon after reaching his majority he married Minerva Pennock, of Londongrove, who survives him at the age of 78 years. 48 years ago he took posession of the property on which he died and where he ramined until his death. There are surviving nine children of the marriage: Mrs. Mary Paxon of New Garden; Mrs. Annie Atkinson, of Bucks County; Pusey, Ellwood, Frank, and Emma Wollaston of Lewisville;

Mrs. Ida Craig of New Garden and William P. [Wollaston] who live on the home property.... He was a member of New Garden Friends meeting.

[LINEAGE OF THOMAS WOLLASTON]

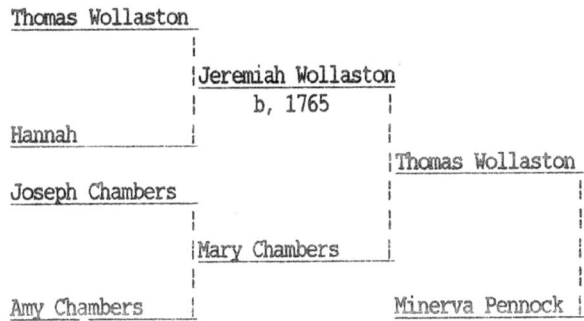

Thomas Wollaston

Hannah

Joseph Chambers

Amy Chambers

Jeremiah Wollaston
b, 1765

Thomas Wollaston

Mary Chambers

Minerva Pennock

WOOD - JENNINGS FAMILY BIBLE RECORDS

Published by Edmund Cushing 1834 Lunenburg, Mass.
Bible [was last known to be] in possession of Mr. Willard J? Wood, Newark, Del.

Marriages:

John K. Wood and Sarah Jennings were married February 22, 1832.
Enos E. Wood married [1st] Ann Pilling December 1862.
Enos E. Wood married [2nd] Alice A. Flinn June 1874.
Willard Franklin Wood married Bertha E. Price August, 1907.
Herbert Franklin Wood married Elizabeth M. Lee June 1933.

Births:

John K. Wood was born December 29, 1806.
Sarah Jennings, his wife, was born February 2, 1815.
[Children of John K. Wood and Sarah Jennings:]
    Mary Ann Wood was born May 11, 1835.
    Enos Evert Wood was born December 24, 1836.
    John Wesley Wood was born May 3, 1840.
    Sarah Elizabeth Wood was born February 3, 1843.
    Francina Wood was born February 22, 1845.
    Martha Jane Wood was born March 12, 1847.

Births: (Cont'd).

John Nelson Wood was born January, 1850.
Sylvester Alexander Wood was born April 17, 1852.
Mary Pilling Wood, daughter of Enos Wood & Ann Pilling, was born June 25, 1864.
Mary Flinn Wood, daughter of Enos Wood & Alice A. Flinn, was born May 25, 1875.
Willard Franklin Wood, son of Enos Wood & Alice A. Flinn, was born September 21, 1877.
Herbert Franklin Wood, son of Willard Franklin Wood and Bertha E. Price, was born April 14, 1911.

[Children of Herbert Franklin Wood & Elizabeth M. Lee:]
Willard Harvey Wood was born March 5, 1934.
Edna Elizabeth Wood was born July 3, 1936.

Deaths:

John Wesley Wood departed this life June 7, 1842.
Mary Ann Wood departed this life Mary 9, 1858 aged 22 years, 11 mos. and 29 days.
John K. Wood departed this life April 27, 1856.
Mary Pilling Wood died February 17, 1872.

[LINEAGE OF W. H. WOOD]

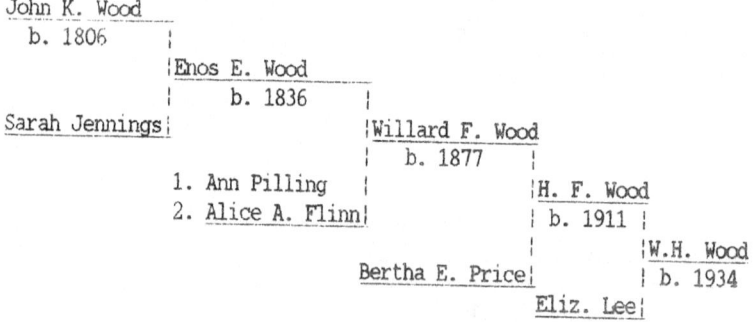

```
John K. Wood
   b. 1806        |
                  | Enos E. Wood
                  |    b. 1836      |
Sarah Jennings |                    | Willard F. Wood
                                    |    b. 1877      |
                  1. Ann Pilling    |                 | H. F. Wood
                  2. Alice A. Flinn |                 |   b. 1911  |
                                                      |            | W.H. Wood
                                    Bertha E. Price|  |            |  b. 1934
                                                      Eliz. Lee|
```

WOODWARD-LYNAM-JARMON FAMILY BIBLE RECORDS

The Comprehensive Bible, Old and New Testaments, Published in 1860 in Philadelphia by J. B. Lippincott & Co. [Last known] owner: Mrs. Reese S. Jarmon, Newark, Delaware.

Note: See LYNAM Family Records Immediately Below.

Marriages:

Ellen B. Lynam and John H. Woodward were married March 1, 1860.
Lizzie A. Woodward and J. Howard Mitchell were married February 12, 1883.
Emilie M. Woodward and John F. Richards were married December 29, 1892.
Anna M. Woodward and Alfred C. Sterling were married December 24, 1894.
Clara A. Sterling and Rees S. Jarmon were married August 30, 1916.
Norma Jane Jarmon and William H. Dawson were married July 3, 1941.
Mildred M. Jarmon and Edward Coates Pierson, Jr. were married October 3, 1942.

Births:

John H. Woodward was born November 8, 1835.
Ellen B. Lynam [daughter of John R. and Elizabeth McFarland Lynam] was born February 9, 1839.
Children of John and Ellen B. Woodward:
Lissie [?] A. Woodward was born February 12, 1862.
Anna M. Woodward was born December 24, 1864.
Emilie M. Woodward was born November 17, 1867.
Clara A. Stirling, daughter of Alfred C. and Anna M. Sterling, was born January 14, 1896.
Children of Clara and Rees S. Jarmon:
Mildred M. Jarmon was born February 22, 1918.
Norma Jane Jarmon was born April 8, 1919.

Deaths:

John R. Lynam departed this life November 12, 1883.
Eliza Lynam departed this life February 3, 1892.
John W. Woodward departed this life August 9, 1894 aged 59 years.
Ellen B. Woodward departed this life March 25, 1917 aged 78 years.
Grace Richards Clark departed this life September 13, 1917.
Lizzie A. Mitchell died September 16, 1933.
Howard Mitchell died October 20, 1933.
Emilie M. Richards died July 20, 1936.

Revolutionary War Record

Joseph Woodward served in 1st Co., 3rd Bat West Bradford twp., Chester Co. Pennsylvania as a private.
5th Series, Pa Archives p. 565, 569, 574, 580.
3rd Series, Pa Archives p. 77, 196, 320, 557, 676.

Genealogical Notes:

1

James Woodward   2
|Joseph Woodward   3
| b. 11-4-1737 |
Ann Pyle | d. 5-31-1812 |Abner Woodward   4
          m. 11 - 1760 | b. 3-17-1765
                         | d. 4-19-1846
         Rebecca Martin| m. abt 1798 |Joseph Woodward
          b. 3-23-1739 | b. 11-12-1799|
          d. 12-30-1831 | d. 2- 5- 1875|
                         Mrs. Eliz. Clark| m. 1- 5- 1826|
                         Harlan
                         b. 9-13-1776
                         d. 9-18-1844   Mary Klair
                                              b. 3-30-1808
                                              d. 7-21-1898

5

John Woodward   6
b. 11-8-1834
d. 8-7-1893 |Anna Mary Woodward   7
m. 3-1-1860 | b. 12-24-1854
                 | d. |Clara Stirling
Ellen Bird Lynam| m. 12-24-1894 | b. 1-14-1896
                                      | m. 8-30-1916
                    Alfred C. Stirling| DAR No. 312086
                    b. 4-24-1860
                                         Rees Staton Jarmon|

[WOODWARD] - LYNAM FAMILY RECORDS

The Lynam Family were Swedes originally from Sweden. Most of the older ones are buried in Old Swedes Church yard at Wilmington, Delaware.

Marriages:

John Loinan married Catharina Didrickson [probably around 1744-1747].
John Lynam married Ann Springer on December 26, 1769.
Joseph Lynam married Joanna Stancast.
Jacob Lynam married Mary Rothwell.
Catherine Lynam married David Stidham.
Ann Lynam married John Armor.
Thomas Lynam married Eleanor Robinson.
Hannah Lynam married Vincent Robinson.
John R. Lynam married Eliza McFarlin November 5, 1829.
William Robinson Lynam married Mary Peterson.
Albert Jefferson Lynam married Mary Jane Stidham.
Thomas James Lynam married 1st Margaret Medill; 2nd Mary Jane Medill.
Eleanro R. Lynam married James Bracken.
James K. Lynam married Elizabeth Derickson.
Sarah McK. Lynam married Willizam Z. Derickson.
Thomas P. Lynam married Mary Stidham.
Robert F. Lynam married Elizabeth Flinn.
Sarah E. Lynam married Howard Flinn.
Ellen Bird Lynam married John H. Woodard.*
Osburn W. Lynam married Addie Davis.
Annie Maria Lynam married Edward Cranston.
John R. Lynam married Lavina Lyman.
Mary R. Lynam married Edward McCallister.
Louetta Lynam married Charles Brown.
Adelaide S. Lynam married [1st] Thomas Jones; Married [2nd] Pusey Pennock in 1905.
Lizzie A. Woodward married J. Howard Mitchell.*
Anna Mary Woodward married Alfred C. Sterling.*
Emilie Woodward married John F. Richards.*
Grace Richards married Rees Clark February 9, 1912.
John W. Richards married Anna McCarns in January, 1914.
Henry C. Mitchell married Lydia Webster October 24, 1914.
Ellen H. Mitchell married Howard Wollaston June 26, 1915.
Anna Mary Richards married Frank Stafford January 20, 1916.
Clara Adelaide Sterling married Rees S. Jarmon August 13, 1916.*
Irene Richards married Henry Mote April 12, 1919.
Francis H. Richards married Betsy Fleming October 20, 1933.

*See Woodward-Lynam-Jarmon Records above.

Marriages: (Cont'd).

Emilie L. Mitchell married Gates Gillmore June 20, 1935.
Joseph Mitchell married Betsy Moore June 6, 1936.
Mildred B. Richards married Wayne Nesbit June 8, 1936.
Paul Mitchell married Ruth Hoopes September 10, 1936.
Norma Jane Jarmon married William H. Dawson July 3, 1941.
Robert Stafford married Mable Murray in February 1942.
Mildred M. Jarmon married Edward Pierson October 3, 1942.
Martha W. Mitchell married Ernst S. Lomax July 13, 1944.

Births:

John Loinan was born in 1722.
Catharina Didrickson was born in 1716.
Their Children:
John Lynam was born in 1747.
Ann Lynam was born in 1751.
Catharina Lynam was born March 22, 1753.
[Children of John Lynam and Ann Springer:]
   Joseph Lynam was born October 11, 1770.
   David Lynam, M.D. was born April 3, 1773.
   Jacob Lynam was born was born August 3, 1775.
   Catherina Lynam was born December 23, 1777.
   Andrew Lynam was born October 9, 1779.
   Ann C. Lynam was born April 26, 1782.
   Hannah Lynam was born June 1, 1783.
Joanna Stancast, wife of Joseph Lynam, was born August 16, 1783.
   Thomas Lynam was born November 14, 1784.
Eleanor Robinson, wife of Thomas Lynam, was born August 14, 1787.
Children of Thomas and Eleanor Robinson:
   John R. Lynam was born February 22, 1808.
   William Robinson Lynam was born June 3, 1809.
   Robert Vincent Lynam was born September 9, 1810.
   Christina Ann Lynam was born May 17, 1812.
   Lewis Harry Lynam was born October 1, 1813.
   Albert Jefferson Lynam was born July 10, 1815.
   Thomas James Lynam was born February 27, 1817.
   Penrose Bull Lynam was born February 11, 1819.
   Eleanor R. Lynam was born September 14, 1820.
   James K. Lynam was born January 2, 1824.
   Sarah McK. Lynam was born October 9, 1925.
Children of John R. & Eliza Lynam:
   Thomas P. Lynam was born in 1833.
   Robert F. Lynam was born in 1835.
   Lewis Lynam was born in 1836.
   Sarah E. Lynam was born February 12, 1837.

Births: (Cont'd).

Ellen Bird Lynam was born February 9, 1839.
Osburn W. Lynam was born in 1841.
Annie Maria Lynam was born November 8, 1842.
John R. Lynam was born in 1844.
Mary R. Lynam was born in 1846.
Louetta Lynam was born November 7, 1853.
Adelaide S. Lynam was born September 22, 1856.
Children of John H. and Ellen Bird Lynam Woodward:*
   Lizzie A. Woodward was born February 12, 1862.
   Anna Mary Woodward was born December 24, 1864.
   Emilie M. Woodward was born November 17, 1867.
* See Woodward-Lynam-Jarmon Records
Children of Lizzie A. & J. Howard Mitchell:
   Henry C. Mitchell was born September 8, 1884.
   Ellen H. Mitchell was born September 4, 1837.
   Joseph Mitchell was born April 8, 1890.
   Irwin J. Mitchell was born March, 1892.
   Emilie L. Mitchell was born June 10, 1894.
   Paul W. Mitchell was born November 22, 1898.
Child of Anna Mary and Alfred Sterling:
   Adelaide Sterling was born January 14, 1896.
Children of Emilie M. and John F. Richards:
   Grace Richards was born in February, 1894.
   Anna Mary Richards was born January 9, 1896.
   Irene Richards was born May 29, 1898.
   Mildred B. Richards was born March 1, 1905.
   Francis H. Richards was born June 22, 1907.
Children of Henry C. & Lydia Mitchell:
   Martha W. Mitchell was born January 12, 1917.
   Hannah R. Mitchell was born May 30, 1919.
   Joseph Mitchell was born August 23, 1929.
Children of Ellen H. & Howard Wollaston:
   Eleanor M. Wallaston was born January 8, 1917.
   J. Paul Wollaston was born December 11, 1919.
   Charles T. Wollaston was born November 5, 1923.
Children of Clara S. & Rees S. Jarmon:
   Mildred M. Jarmon was born February 22, 1918.
   Norma Jane Jarmon was born April 8, 1919.
Children of Grace & Rees Clark:
   Emilie Clark was born December 19, 1912.
Children of Anna Mary & Frank Stafford:
   Edythe & Kathryn Stafford (Twins) born May 21, 1918.
   Robert Stafford was born August 2, 1921.
Child of Anna & John W. Richards:
   Alexander F. Richards was born July 7, 1916.

Births: (Cont'd).

Children of Francis & Betty Richards:
John T. Richards was born September 19, 1935.
Laura Ann Richards was October 7, 1936.

Deaths:

John Loinan died in 1768.
Ann Lynam died in 1786.
Catharina Didrickson [wife of John Loinan] died in 1791.
Andrew Lynam died in 1805.
John Lynam died December 16, 1830.
Lewis Lynam died in 1836 [the year of his birth].
Sarah McK. Lynam died October 30, 1852.
Eleanor Robinson [wife of Thomas Lynam] died in February, 1855.
Thomas Lynam died February 22, 1870.
Joseph Lynam died January 4, 1872.
John R. Lynam died November 12, 1883.
Irwin J. Mitchell died July 13, 1893 [in the 2nd year of his life].
John H. Woodward [husband of Ellen Byrd Lynam] died August 9, 1894.
Thomas Jones [husband of Adelaide S. Lynam] died in 1895.
Mary Stidham [wife of Thomas P. Lynam] died in November, 1897.
Osburn W. Lynam died January 5, 1898.
Howard Flinn [husband of Sarah E. Lynam] died January 30, 1898.
Annie Maria Lynam died Mary 29, 1905.
Robert F. Lynam died October 27, 1909.
Thomas P. Lynam died June 10, 1913.
Edward McAllister [husband of Mary R. Lynam] died November 19, 1915.
Lavina Lynam [wife of John R. Lynam] died in 1916.
Grace Richards died in September, 1917.
Elizabeth Flinn [wife of Robert F. Lynam] died September 30, 1920.
Edward Cranston [husband of Annie Maria Lyman] died February 12, 1922.
Sarah E. Lynam died March 25, 1825.
John R. Lynam died September 27, 1926.
Mary R. Lynam died October 20, 1929.
Lizzie A. Woodward died September 16, 1933.
J. Howard Mitchell [husband of Lizzie A. Woodward] died October 23, 1933.
Louetta Lynam died in March, 1934.
Emilie M. Woodward died in July, 1936.
Adelaide S. Lynam died January 9, 1945.

LYNAM-WOODWARD-STERLING-JARMON [LINEAGE]

[1]
John Lyman   [2]
  b. 1722 |John Lynam   * [3]
                          | m. 1769
Catharina Didrickson| |Thomas Lynam   [4]
  b. 1716 |
                 Ann Springer| |John R. Lynam
                                         |
                          Eleanor Robinson|
                                                         |> [5]
                 John Hays
                   b. 1764
                   d. 1831 |Sarah Hays
                              |
                 Elizabeth | |Eliza McFarlin|
                                          |
                          Robert McFarlin|

[5]
Ellen Lynam   [6]
                       |Anna Mary Lynam   [7]
                       |
John B. Woodward| |Mrs. Rees Jarmon
                       | D.A.R.
                 Alfred C. Sterling| Newark, Del.

  * John Lynam served in Capt. Pierce's Co. Revolutionary War.

SAMUEL YOUNG DESCENDANTS' RECORDS

Prepared [originally] by Wilbur Wilson, Newark, Delaware.

Historical Note:

Samuel Young was born in Belfast, Ireland; came to America and bought a tract of 300 acres 6.7 miles N.E. 12 miles E. Mern'd [sic], known as Little Baltimore. He died October 14, 1777 and is buried in Red Clay Creek Cemetary.

Marriages:

Samuel Young married Jane Kincaid.
Rebecca Young married Willam Wilson.
Samuel Wilson married Margaret Walker.
Jane Wilson marrried William Thomson.
Rebecca Wilson married George Walker.
George Wilson married [1st] _____ Barton.
George Wilson married [2nd] Lavina Casho.
Mary Wilson married David Scott.
Samuel Young Wilson married Elizabeth Schultz.
Elizabeth Wilson married _____ Moody.
William Wilson married Martha Elizabeth Mitchell.
Lewis Wilson married Sallie Degott.
Jane Thomson married Samuel Geaskins.
Rebecca Jane Walker married William Brown.
Sarah Jane Geaskins married William J. Wilmer.
Adelaide Brown married Willie Westlake.
Samuel G. Wilmer married Evelyn Westlake.
Adelaide Wilmer married Webster Price.
Isabelle Wilmer married Paul Darrington.
Frank Scott married Rachel Wilson of Elkton

Births:

[Children of Samuel Young and Jane Kincaid:]
 Jane Young was born February 6, 1741.
 Elizabeth Young was born April 14, 1743.
 Rebecca Young was born March 6, 1745
 Sarah Young was born February 23, 1747
 Margaret Young was born March 10, 1731.
[Children of William Wilson and Rebecca Young:]
 Elizabeth Wilson was born in October, 1773.
 Mary Ann Wilson was born in January, 1776.
 Jane Wilson was born February 14, 1778.

[Children of William Wilson and Rebecca Young:] (Cont'd).
Rebecca Wilson was born January 29, 1782.
Martha Wilson was born July 22, 1788.-|
Samuel Wilson was born July 22, 1788.- |
[Children of William Thomson and Jane Wilson:]
1. John Thomson was born March 14, 1799. Mary Berryman 10-20-1889 [sic].
2. Rebecca Thomson was born 1802. Henry C. Blumnar [Husband?].
3. Isabella Thomson [No Date Given].
4. Jane Thomson [NDG].
5. William Wilson Thomson was born January 10, 1809.
6. George Thomson was born in 1811.
7. Samuel Young Thomson [NDG].
8. Stephen Thomson 9- 2.26-1818 [sic].

[Children of Rebecca Wilson Walker:]
Samuel Cochran Wlker was born in 1802.
Margaret Walker was born in 1804.
William Wilson Walker was born in 1806.
David Washington Walker was born in 1809.
Rebecca Jane Walker was born in 1812.
Jerome Walker was born in 1815.
Josiah Walker was born in 1818.
Elizabeth Ann Walker was born in 1820.
Mary Ann Walker was born in 1824.

[Children of Samuel Wilson and Margaret Walker:]
Rebecca Wilson [No Date Given].
David Wilson [NDG].
George [NDG].
Mary Wilson [NDG].
Margaret Ann Wilson [NDG].
Samuel Young Wilson [NDG].
Elizabeth Wilson [NDG].
William Wilson was born in 1816.

[Children of Jane Thomson and Samuel Geaskins:]
Sarah Jane Geaskins [NDG].

[Children of Rececca Jane Walker and William Brown:]
Thomas Brown [NDG].
Adelaide Brown [NDG].
Willis Westlake Brown [NDG].

Samuel G. Wilmer, son of Sarah Jane Geaskins and William G. Wilmer [NDG].
Evelyn Westlake, daughter of Adelaide and Willis Westlake [NDG].
Children of George and _____ Barton:
Lewis Wilson [NDG].
Margaret Wilson [NDG].

Births: (Cont'd).

Children of Mary Wilson and David Scott:
  Ella Scottt [NDG].
  Frank Scott [NDG].
Children of William and Martha Elizabeth Mitchell:
  Wilbur Thomas Wilson was born May 2, 1853.
  Annie Luisa Wilson was born July 14, 1855.
Children of Lewis Wilson and Sallie Degott:
  Willard Springer Wilson [NDG].
  Barton Wilson [NDG].
[Children of Frank Scott and Rachel Wilson:]
  Edith Scott [NDG].
  David Scott [NDG].
  Elizabeth Scott [NDG].
  [Plus two others: Names not given].
[Children of Samuel G. Wilmer and Evelyn Westlake:]
  Adelaide Wilmer was born July 7, 1891.
  Isabelle Wilmer [NDG].
Wilmer Price, son of Adelaid Wilmer and Webster Price [NDG].

Deaths:

Samuel Young died October 14, 1777 and is buried in Red Creek Cemetery.
Margaret Walker died in 1832.
William Wilson Thomson died December 31, 1862.
Jane Wilson died October 25, 1869.
Rebecca Wilson died March 14, 1872.

LINEAGE OF MR. WILBUR[?] WILSON, Newark, Del.

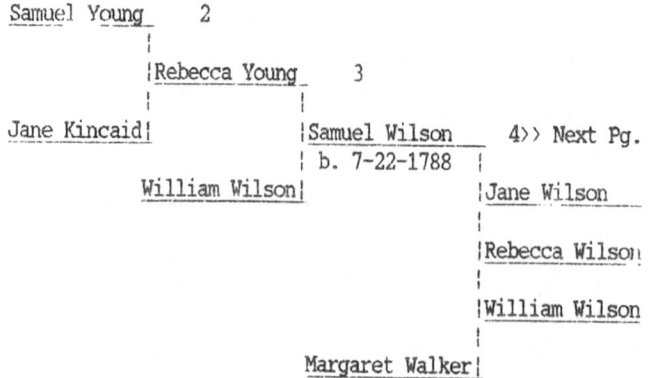

163

LINEAGE OF MR. [WILMER PRICE]

```
    4
Jane Wilson        5
                  Sarah Jane Geaskins    6
William Thomson                         Samuel G. Wilmer   7 >> 8
                          William J. Wilmer                  below
                                                          Adelaide Wilmer


                                                          Webster Price


                                                          Isabelle Wilmer


                                                          Paul Darrington

                                      Evelyn Westlake


                     8
               >>>   Wilmer Price
```

INDEX

ADAM
  Capt. Nath. 36
ADAMS
  Amyane 63; Ann Jane 47
ADAMSON
  Patrick 67; Violet 20, 67, 68
ALDRIDGE
  Ann Elizabeth 77; Elizabeth Booth 76, 77; Francis 76, 78; Fredus 78; John 76-78; John Gottier 76-78; John Stockton 77; John Stogden 77; Rev. Fredus 76, 77; Sophia Cosden 76; William Spry 77, 78; Wm. Spry; 76
ALEXANDER
  Amos 47, 50, 63; Henry 74; Mary 47, 48, 50, 63; Rev. James 71
ALLEN
  Ann Kirkwood 74; David 71, 74, 75; Hannah 131, 134; Margaret 134; Mary 61, 62, 134; Sutia Ann Kerr 74, 75; William 134
ALRICH
  Samuel 10
ANDERSON
  Edna 65, 66; Margaretha Ruth 80
ANDRESON
  Hester Jane 39
ANDREWS
  Patience 97; Samuel E. 97 Samuel Edward 97
ARCHER
  Pamelia 18
ARIS
  Parson Nile 33
ARMITAGE
  Martha Gillespie 69, 70; Mary 70; Rebecca 70; Samuel; 69, 70

ARMOR
  John 155
ARMSTRONG
  Annie C. 6; Annie S. 6, 7; Ernest 6, 7; Fannie 6; Florie B. 7; Frances Crawford 140; Frank L. 6, 7; James C. 6, 7; John Crawford 139; John R. 38; Mabel 6, 7; Mary 38; Mrs. Elsie 12; Rachel 51; Robert 12; Susan Jean 2; William 38
ARNOLD
  Isabella 148
ATKINSON
  Annie 150; Caroline 123; Caroline Wood 123; John Henry 123; Samuel 123; Samuel Oliver 123
AUSTIN
  Jennie 135
BAIRD
  Elsie 135, 136
BAKER
  Benjamin 110; Capt. Jeremiah 113; Elizabeth 109-111; Frances 106, 113; Francina 86; Henry 109-112; Henry I, 111-113; Henry II, 112, Hester 110, 111; Jeremiah 110; Jethro 86, 110-113; John 109, 110; Joseph 109, 110; Lydia 109, 110; Margaret 109, 110; Margaret Hardman 110; Mary 109, 110, 112; Mary Ann 109, 111; Nathan 109-113; Phoebe 110, 111; Rachael 109, 110; Rachael Warder 110; Rachel 111; Rebecca 110, 111; Samuel 109, 111, 112; Samuell 109, 110; Sarah 109, 110; Sarah

BAKER (Cont'd.)
　Collett 113; Thomas 110, 111
BALDWIN
　Harvey Lewis 80, 82
BARBER
　Ann Rebecca 93
BARLOW
　Henry E., III 81; Henry E., Jr. 80, 81; John L. 81; Norman Warren 81; Phyllis L. 81; Sarah Elizabeth 81; Sharon Rose 81
BARNES
　Rev. Albert 18
BARON
　Martha 20, 67
BARR
　David 102, 106; Francina 98, 99, 101, 102, 106; Robert 10
BARTLETT
　Sukey 91
BARTON
　Elija J. 146; Miss 60, 161
BAXTER
　Barbara Dale 133; Kirk E. 132, 133; Kirk Sawyer 132, 133; Mary Virginia 132, 133; Mrs. Kirk 134; Rev. Kirk 132
BEACH
　Martha E. 25
BEAL
　Mary Jones 100
BEARD
　Eliza 1, 2; Elizabeth 2; Hugh 1-4; Jane Ann 1, 2; John 1-3; Margaret 1, 2; Marie 1, 2, 5; Marion 1, 2; Rachel 1, 2, 107; Sarah 108
BECKETT
　Mary 111
BEDELL
　Catherine 118
BEDWELL
　Marguerite Dorothy 80

BEERS
　Rev. Joseph 130
BEESON
　Captain Thomas 43; Mary 40
BELL
　Mary Anna 96
BENNETT
　Anna M. 4
BERNITZ
　Frances 57
BERRYMAN
　Mary 161
BIDDLE
　Ann 9; Louisa 9; Louise 11 Spencer 9, 11
BILEO
　Mr. 109
BLACK
　Esther 118; James 47, 142; Jos. 69; Martha 143; Martha E. 25; Mary 71, 74, 75
BLACKWELL
　Adele Leslie 84, 85, 120, 121; Elsie McCauley 86, 111, 113; Emily 6; Ephraim W. 6, 8; Fannie 6; Florence 6; Harry Martindale 8; Jacob 6, 8; Lizzie 6, 7; Mary Ann 6; Mary Frances 7; Mrs. Walter; A. 86; Phileman 6, 8; Sarah Ann 6; Stella Worrall 8; Theodore 6; Theodore J. 6, 8; Theodore Jefferson 7; Walter A. 8, 114; Walter A., Jr. 8, 84, 85, 120, 121 Walter A., Jr. 84; Walter Armstrong 8, 84, 85, 120, 121
BLAIR
　Mr. 70
BLUMNAR
　Henry C. 161
BOCKUS
　Mary 51
BOND
　Justice Richard 143

BONHAM
Ruth 110
BOOTH
Ebenezer 76, 78; Elizabeth 78
John Wilkes 76
BOOTHE
Deborah 111
BOULDEN
Amelia J. 10
Annie F. 9; David 9, 10;
Edward 9; Elisha 10;
Elizabeth 10; Fanny 10;
Francina 9, 10; George 9,
10; George, Jr. 10; Hannah
9; Hannah Griffith 9; James,
Sr. 10; Jesse 9, 10; Louisa
9, 10; Martha 10; Mary M.
10; Mary Matilda 9; Olivia
10
BOUNDS
Harvey 113
BOWMAN
Jamima 33; Maj. Edward 44;
Sarah 87, 89
BOYD
Mrs. Louise Holcombe 95
BRACKEN
James 155
BRAINARD
Cora 146, 148; Cora A. 11
Cora Aurelia 11; Jay 11,
146, 148; Nathaniel 11,
146, 148; Perces E. 11;
Perces Emily 11; Willis O.11
BRATTON
N. V. 32
BRECHT
Anna 90; Christopher 90
BRECKENRIDGE
Alexander 32; Doak 30; Doke
30, 31; George 32; Jane 32;
John Doak 32; Mary Doke 32;
Robert 32
BREWER
F. 74
BRICE
Annie J. 44; Ella W. 44

BRIDGES
Sarah Isabel 84, 120
BRIGG
Mary E. 30; Mary Elizabeth 81
BRIGHT
Balthaser 90; Catherine 90;
Jonathan 90; Louisa 90;
Michael 90
BROOKE
H. 74
BROOKINS
Jane 117
BROOKS
Alfred G. 14
Eliza 13, 84, 86; Elizabeth
13; Francis C. 14; Henry L.
12; J. Armstrong 13; Jacob
13; James 13; James C. 13,
14; James Thomas 12, 14;
John Heralon 13; Joseph
Armstrong 13; Joseph M. 13;
Joseph W. 12, 13, 117;
Josiah 13; Mary 12; Mary G.
I. 14; Mary Julia 13; Mary
Paulson Armstrong 13; Mary
S 12; Rachel Hays 13, 14;
Rachel Jane 12; Robert
Lewis 13; Sarah Ann 12;
Smith R. 14; Theodore C.
12; Thomas 13; Wensruer 13;
William 12; William Kean
13; William W. 12, 14;
William Webb 13
BROWN
Adelaide 160, 161; Charles
155; Col. Alexander 119;
Martha E. 16; Mildred 130;
Mildred K. 44; Thomas 161;
William 160, 161; Willis
Westlake 161
BRYAN
Anna E. 15; Anna M. 15;
Anna M. Bennett 15; Anna
M., Sr. 15; Annie E. 15;
Carrie Watkins 15; Charles
15; Charles A. 14, 15;
Charles A., Jr. 15; Charles

BRYAN (Cont'd).
A., Sr. 15; Elizabeth 70;
Estella G. 15; Estella Grace
15; Florence B. 15; Florence
Bennett 15; George 70; Jesse
Bennet 15; Jessie B. 15;
Mary Gibson 15; Nora M.(or
W.) 15; Rebecca 70; Stella
56; William G. 15; William
Guy 15
BUCK
Gov. Douglas 91; Jeremiah
91; Laura 91
BUCKINGHAM
Jane Jones 100
BURDICK
Ebby 131, 134
BURGOYNE
Cyrus F. 54; Esther F. 53
BURNS
Mary Emma 38; Robert 38
BURROUGHS
John 109;
BUSH
Christopher 91; Mary Jane 91
BUTERBAUGH
Helen G. 79-81
CALKINS
John 118; Lucy 118
CALLOWAY
Clifford 85; John Clifford 84; Leslie Blackwell 8
CAMBRONA
Rev. W. I. 15
CAMPBELL
Artie 56; Benjamin 15, 56; Catharine Ann 54, 55; Catherine 56; Charles 56; Corrie 56; David 56; Elizabeth 56; Ellie May 15; Elsie 56; Emma 56; Estella 15; Estella Bryan 15; Ethel 56; Florence 56; Frank 56; Freddie B. 15; George 56; Gilbert 56; Harry 56; Jack 56; Jane Jackson 56; John 56; Johnson 56; Julia 56; Laura 56; Lillie 56; Margaret 56; Marian 56; Mary 56; Olive 56; Samuel 56; Sarah 56; William 56
CANBY
Benjamin 112; Thomas 111
CANN
Clara 23, 24; Mrs. Ola 37; Ola 38; Olivia Boulden 10; T. A. 10
CANTWELL
Martha B. 144
CAREY
Henry C. 112
CARLYN
Deborah 122
CARMINE
Alice 136; Alice Anita 136; Dr. W.M. 136; Dr. Walter Mills 135, 136; Eugenia 136
CARPENTER
Henrietta 131, 132, 134
CARROLL
Joseph 1; Mary Hughes 1-3, 5
CARSON
Walter 70
CARTER
Rachel 58
CASHO
Lavina 160
CATON
Capt. John 57
CAULK
Benjamin 138; Lydia 139
CAZIER
Abraham 16, 17; Araminta 16 17; Charles Evans 16; Cornelia 17; Cornelia Foard 16; John C. 16, 17; M. L. 16; Maria Louisa 17; Martha J. 16; Martha Jane 16, 17; Millicent 16, 17; Rebecca 16, 17; Thomas 16, 17; Thomas C. 16, 17; Thomas Coke 16, 17

CHAMBERLAIN
Anna 18; Annie 18, 19;
Charles T. 18; Clara 19, 72
Dr. Joseph 18; Dr. Palmer
18-20; Elizabeth 19; George
18; Hannah 19; James 19;
John 18; John Pyle 18;
Joeph 18, 19; Josephine 19;
Kate 18; Margaret 18, 19;
Martha 18, 19; Mary 18, 19;
Mary Emma 19; Rev. Pierce
18, 19; Robert 17, 19, 21;
Samuel 18
CHAMBERS
Amy 149; Amy Thompson 150;
Anna 38; Elizabeth 149;
Isaac 38; James 149, 150;
Joseph 149, 151; Mary
149, 151; Sarah 149;
William 149, 150
CHANDLEE
Ann Elizabeth 21; Annie
50, 63; Annie E. 47; Annie
Elizabeth 62; Annie G. 63;
Benjamin 22; Edward E. 22;
Elizabeth 63; Elizabeth G.
21; Ellis 21, 22, 63;
George W. 21; George
Washington 122; Henry
Peters 21; Isaac 22; Jacob
Edwin 21; Millicent Rebecca
21; S. W. 21; Sidney W. 21,
63; Sydnianne 21; Teresa
Maria 21; Teresa Price 21;
Teresa T. 21; Teressa F.
62; Veazey John 21; William
Ellis 21
CHANDLER
Mr. 146
CHEFFINS
Elizabeth 130; James G.
129; Sallie 128; Sarah
Elizabeth 129-131
CHESNEY
Ann 108; Daniel McCauley
107; Francina Ann 107;
James 106-108; Mary 107;
Nancy 107
CHICK
Elder F. A. 15
CHRISMAN
Catherine Searles 127; Emma
Rebecca 124-127; Samuel 127
CHRISTMAN
Anna Margaret 90
CHURCHILL
Mr. 56
CLARK
Emilie 157; Grace 157;
Grace Richards 153; Henry
54; Rees 155, 157; Sarah
120
CLARKE
Rev. John F. 93
CLAYTON
Adelaide 24; Adelaide Young
23; Alice Van Arsdale 135,
136 Edgar 24; Edgar
Lockwood 23, 24; Eugene 23,
24; Fannie L. 23; Frances
24; Henry 23, 24; Jeanette
23; Joshua 22-24; Joshua
Anderson 135, 136; Lydia A.
23, 24; Macomb 23, 24;
Martha 24; Martha E.
Lockwood 24; Mary Wilson
23, 24; Rev. Joshua
Anderson 135; Richard 23,
24; Thomas 23, 24; Thomas,
Esquire 23
CLENDENIN
Mrs. Henrietta 93; Lieut;
Sarah Jane 145
CLINGEN
Esq. William 25; Frances
25; Jane 25; Martha B. 25;
Martha Black 25; William,
Jr. 25
COCHEL
Rev. E. T. 84
COCHRAN
Mary F. 99; R. T. 99;
Robert Thomas 98

COFFIN
   Sarah 101
COHES
   Benjamin L. 58
COLE
   Elizabeth 128; Perrigrin 128; 130; Sarah 128, 129, 131
COLES
   Benjamin 58
COLGAN
   Deborah 59; Isabella 58; James T. F. 58; Joseph 58; Mary 58; William 58
COLLETT
   Ann 113; Jeremiah 111-113; Sarah 109, 111-113; Weyntie 113
COLLINS
   Annie Snow 26-28; Charles Parker 26-28; Charles Robert 27; Charlotte 27; James 26, 27; John 26, 28; Joseph 27; Parker 26, 28; Roseanna Jane 27; William 27
COLVER
   Isabella 149; Stephen 149
COMPTON
   Anna Mary 29; James Clifford 29; Rev. 65; William P. 28, 29
CONDEN
   Rev. 141
CONLYN
   Deborah 122
COOCH
   Col. Thomas 101; Eleanor B. Wilkins 123
COOK
   Ann 58
COOPER
   Catherine 58; Sary A. 58
CORNOG
   Abner 29; Abraham 29; Abram Ethelbert 28; Anna Maria 28, 29; Catharine L. 28, 29; Franklin H. 29;

Harriet C. 29; Harry 28, 29; Isabella C. L. 28, 29; Isabelle Love 29; Sarah T. 29; Stephen Love 28, 29; Ulysis 28
COSDEN
   Catherine 76, 77; Jeremiah 77; Rev. Jeremiah 76
COVERDILL
   Mary S. 12, 14
COWHERD
   Marjory 2, 3
COX
   George 92; Pricilla Holme 100
COYNER
   Margaret 87; Susan 87
CRADDOCK
   B. Howard 44;
CRAIG
   Elizabeth 106; Ida 151; Rev. George 52
CRAMBER
   Hannah 36, 37
CRANSTON
   Edward 155, 158
CROOKS
   Alfred 31; Amos A. 30; Amos Alexander 30, 32; Anna Elizabeth 30-33; Benjamin Harrison 30, 31; David Groves 30, 31, 33; E. B. 30; Eliza 31; Ezra 30 Ezra Breckenridge 30-33; Fannie 31; Harrison 31; James D. 30; James David 30-32; James Lasher 30-32; Jas. David 31; John William 30-31; Margaret 30, 31; Mary 30; Mary Clementine 30-31; Mary E. 30; Mary Elizabeth 33; Mary Elizabeth Groves 33; Mary Lasher 33; Miss 30; Rev. E. B. 32; Robert Franklin 30-32; Robert Turpin 30-31; Scott Breckenridge 33;

Usal 32; Usual 30, 32;
William 31
CROPPER
Elizabeth Bradley 42, 43;
Ens. Levin 43
CROSSAN
James 53
CRUMPTON
Clarey 34; Curtis 33, 35;
Elizabeth 34; Jamima 35;
John 33-35; Leasbeth 34;
Margaret Ann 34; Mary 34;
Mesia 34; Sallie 34, 35;
Sally 34; Susanna 34;
Thomas 34
CUBBAGE
Alice J. 55; Alice Jane
Frazier 55; Benjamin 57;
Benjamin C. 55; Benjamin,
Jr. 57; Calvin 54, 55, 57;
Helen 57; Helen Catharine
55; Milton 57; Milton
Frazier 55
CULLEN
Mary Armstrong 140; Oliver
W. M. 140;
CULLETT
Sarah Elizabeth 135
CUMMINS
Robt. 110
DALTON
Frances 56; Frances
Elizabeth 54;
DANTAZER
Eulales 89
DANTZ
Ruth Elizabeth 47; Theo R.
47, 49
DARRINGTON
Mary 120; Paul 160
DAVIDSON
Rev. 144
DAVIS
Abel 102; Addie 155; Alfred
56; Beulah Campbell 56;
Clara Elizabeth 141, 142,
144; Elizabeth 124; John M.
144; John Miller 141, 142;
Mary 100; Rachel 102;
Robert Miller 142; William
Joseph 141
DAWSON
Dorothy May 79-81; George
Hamlin 80; John Edgar 80,
81; Martha 81; W. Harry 80,
82; Willa Virginia 81;
William H. 156; William H.
Jr. 153; William Harry 81;
William Harry, Jr., 80, 81;
DEAN
Martha 54, 57; Mathilda
104; Sarah 56
DEGOTT
Sallie 160, 162
DeHAVEN
Catherine 36-38; Edward 37;
Jacob 37; Jesse 36, 37;
Mary 36, 38, 137, 140; Mary
Madeline Pluck 37; Peter
37, 140; Samuel 36, 37,
139, 140; William; 36, 37
DELAINE
Ernest M. 45; Joseph 44
DELAP
Ann Jones 100
DENKS
Ann M. 133; Michl H. 133
DERICKSON
Elizabeth 155; Willizam Z.
155
DICKEY
A. Elizabeth 39; Amor C.
39; Benjamin 39; Benjamin
Lewis 39; C. Parmer 39;
Charles A. 39; Charles H.
39; Charles Hayes 40;
Charles Hays 39; Eliza D.
39, 40; Elizabeth 39, 40;
Elizabeth B. 39; Hettie 39;
Joseph 39; Lydia J. 39, 40;
Margret 39; Thomas 39, 40
DIDRICKSON
Catharina 155, 156, 158, 159

DIXON
  Ann 40; Hannah 40; Isaac 40; James 41; Jehu 40; John 40; Martha 40; Mary 40; Phebe 40; Rev. A. C. 84; Samuel P. 40; Sarah 41
DOAK
  Ann 32; Mary 32; Samuel 32;
DOFFINS
  John 118
DORSEY
  Charles Anna 42; Charles Henry 42, 43; Col. John 41-43; Crucinda 42; Edward 41, 42; Elizabeth 42; Elizabeth Bradley Cropper 42; Elizabeth Cropper 43, 44; Elizabeth Ellen 42, 43; Elizabeth Straughan 42; Henrietta Straughan 42; Joshua 41-43; Margaret Watkins 42, 43; Nicholas 41, 42; Sarah 43; William N. W. 42; William Nicholas 42; William Nicholas W. 42; Wm. Nicholas W. 43
DOUGLAS
  Esther Morgan 100
DOWNS
  Clara Breckenridge 33; Henrietta 126; Mary Roberta 33; Robert Bingham 32, 33
DRAPER
  Mr. 7
DULANEY
  Mary Ellen 45; Nellie B. 45 Willie B. 45
DUNCAN
  C. Chambers 96; C. R. 32; Clifford Chambers 96; Courtland T. 96; Edward 96; Geraldine 96; Kitty 26, 28
DUTTON
  Elsie Smith 135; George Elliott 135, 136; George Elliott, Jr. 136

EARLE
  George 18
EASTMAN
  Arthur Bartlett 90; Corp. Edward 90; Ebenezer 90; Joseph B. 90; Moses 90; Mrs. A. B. 89; Roger 91; Samuel 91
EATON
  David 102
EDMONDS
  Mary 123, 126
EDMUNDS
  Ebenezer 146-148; Emily 11, 146, 148; S. 146, 148
EDWARDS
  Martha Holme 100
ELIASON
  Fannie Boulden 10; Frank 10
ELLIOTT
  Francis 70
ELLISON
  Charles S. 23; Louisa Boulden 10; Martha 134; Thom 134; William S. 10
EMERY
  Rebecca 54
EMLEY
  Hannah 95
EMORY
  Deborah 58
ENSLEN
  Mrs. Perry 134
ERNEST
  Charles L. 45; Charles R. 44, 45; Charles Randolph 45; Douglas Ellsworth 44, 45; Douglass Ellsworth, Jr. 45; Elijah C. 45; Fagan 44, 45; George W. 44, 45; Gladys 45; Jacqualine 130; Jacqueline 45; James 44, 45; James Mitchell 44; James Mitchell, Jr. 45; John F. 44, 45; John Fagen 130, 131; John R. 44; John

Reynolds 45, 130; Lillian
45; Martha Ann 45; Martha V.
44, 45; Mary E. 44, 45; Mary
Natalie 45; May 44, 45;
Nellie Grant 45; Rosalynd
Jane 45;
ERSKINS
   Elizabeth 91
ERWIN
   Mary S. 116
EVANS
   Agnes Armitage 74, 75
Agnes G. 74; Agnes
Gillespie 71-75; Amos A.
48; Anna B. 74; Anne M.
74, 75; Catherine 106;
Charles B. 74, 75; David
51, 52; Dr. John 46;
Eleanor 47, 48, 100; Eli
51, 52; Elizabeth 51, 52;
Emma M. 74; Eugenia 74, 75;
Fanny 74; Frank S. 46;
Frank Sappington 46; George
48; George G. 71, 72, 74,
75; Hannah 47, 72, 73;
Hannah C. 74; Harriet N.
75; Helen 46; Isabel Creigh
46; Isabella 46-48; James
48, 49; Jane Griffith 101;
Jean 47; Jennie 46; Jennie
B. 46; Jesse 51, 52; John
46-51, 63, 70-73; John
Alexander 46; John L. 74;
John W. 71-74; Josephine
Rebecca 46; Lena 75; Levi
H. 48; Louis P. 74, 75;
Margaret 47-49; Margaret
Ann 71, 72; Margaret Ann
Evans 73, 74; Margaret G.
74, 75; Mark 48, 49; Mary
20, 47, 49, 51, 70-72, 105
Mary C. 72, 73; Mary Exton
75; Mary S. 74, 75; Mary
W. 74, 75; Rebecca N. 46;
Rees 51; Robert 46-50;
Robert, Jr. 47, 50;

Roberta 46; Ruth 51; Sarah
47, 48, 50, 51, 63, 64;
Susan W. 74; Thomas 51, 52;
Thomas, Jr. 51; W. Rowland
46; William 48; William D.
71-75; William Rowland 46
EVERETT
   Nell Elizabeth 26
EVES
   Eliza 70, 73; Mary 70, 73;
William D. 70
EWING
   James M. 115;Joseph B. 115
FEMLEY
   Rev. F. A. 14
FERGUSON
   Phebe E. 97; Rebecca J. 25
FFERROR
   Joseph 111
FINKS
   Judge 134
FINLEY
   Mr. 56; Rev. James 47; Rev.
Wm. 46
FIRLD
   Eugene 132, 133
FISCHER
   Andrew 2
FISHER
   Thos. 111
FITZSIMMONS
   Flora 41, 42
FLEMING
   Betsy 155
FLINN
   Alice A. 151, 152;
Elizabeth 155, 158; Howard
155, 158
FOARD
   Ann 11; Cornelia 16; Dr.
Joseph 139; James 38; James
H. 139; John 16, 17
FOARRY
   Forisho 121
FOUARD
   James L. 139

FOULK
William 54; Aquila 52, 53; Candace 52, 53; Elizabeth 53 Esther 53; Hannah 52, 53; Jacob 53; John 52-54; John, Jr. 53; Maria 53; Naomi 52, 53; Sarah 52, 53; Stephen 53; Susan 53; Susanna 52; William 52-54; William Sharpley 52

FRANCE
Rev. 65

FRASHIER
Alexander 58; Catherine Meria 59; Deborah 58, 59; Deborah Ann 59; Elizabeth 58; Isabella 58; James 57-59; Job Meredith 58; Margaret Jane 59; Mary Ann 59; Rebecca 59; Rebecca Ann 59; Sarah 59; Thomas E. 57-59; Thomas E., Jr. 59; Thomas Emory 58; Whiteley H. 59; William 57-59; William M. 60

FRAZER
Adah Clayton 135; Anna 37, 38; Annie F. Boulden 10; Chas. Van Arsdale 136; Emory D. 136; Ernest 139; Evelyn (Foard) 139; James H. 136; James Harrison 135; Joshua Anderson 136; Martha Boulden 10; Mary Leura Roberts 136; Mrs. Ernest 37, 38; William H. 10

FRAZIER
Ada 55; Agnes 60; Albert 57; Alice 57; Alice J. 54, 55; Alice Jane 55; Amanda 55; Bedford R. 60; Benjamin 55, 57; Benjamin C. 54; Benjamin Campbell 55; Blaine 57; Calvin Job 55; Catharine 57; Catharine A. 55; Catharine Campbell 56; Clarence J. 55; Edward 57; Ephraim 57; Ephraim R. 54, 55; Ephraim Rittenhouse 55; Ernest 57; Eva 57; Fanny C. 55; Frances Elizabeth 55; George 57; George Emerson 55; Harry 57; Irvin 57; John B 55 Job M. 55, 56; John 56; John E. 54; John Emery 55; Lt. James 54, 57; Lucinda 60; Margaret 57; Mary Campbell 55; Minnie R. 55; Rebecca Ruth Meredith 55; Ruth 57; Samuel 55; Samuel D. 55, 57; Samuel M. 54, 56; Samuel W. 55; Thomas Emery 54, 55; William 57; William Edward 54, 55; William M. 60

FRAZOR
James 57, 60

FRY
Rev. Christian 65

FRYMIRE
Ruth Anna 34; Ruthanna Harrington 34; Thomas L. 34

FUGITT
Mrs. R.W. 134

FURGUSON
Margaret 76, 78

GALE
Mary 146, 148

GALLAHER
Alfred 85; Ann Rudolph 85; Anna 61; Anna Maria 61; Annie E. 62; Annie Maggie 62; Edwin Henry 62; Elizabeth 61; Elmer Hanna 61; Emma Bell 62; Ethel Viola 61; Ethland Brooks 84, 85; Ethlyn B. 86, 114; Ethlyn Brooks 120; Fanny 61; Fanny May 85; Frederick Stanley 61; Henry Evans 85; Isabella 48, 49, 61, 64;

Jane 61; John 61, 62, 86;
John E. 63; John Evans 47,
48, 50, 62, 63; John Evans
64; John Hayes 85; John T.
61, 84-86; John Thomas 61,
84; Leon Henry 61; Lydia
Caroline 85; Margaret 61;
Margaret Jane 47; Margaret
Jean 48; Maria Amelia 85;
Martha 50, 61; Martha Ann
47, 48, 64; Martha Jane 64;
Martha McNight 62; Martha
Rebecca 62; Mary 47, 48,
62, 64; Mary Amelia 61;
Mary Ellis 62; Mary Rebecca
85; Moses 61; Newton Robert
Reese 85; R. S. 50; Robert
47-50, 62-64; Robert
Hamilton 47, 48, 63; Robert
Henry 61; Robert Sidney 62;
Robinson 61; Sara Terressa
62; Sarah 49, 62, 63; Sarah
Amelia 47, 48, 64; Stewart
61; William 61; William J.
62; William Jackson 61;

GAMBLE
Allan 64; Bertha 64; Harlow
64; Harry 64; Henrietta
103; Samuel 64; Susanne
Pritchard 64; William 64;
William M. 64

GANTT
Rev. J. Gibson 112

GARRETSON
Henry 92; Mary 92

GARRETT
Anna Rebecca 66; Annie 66,
137; Annie R. 66; Clinton
H. 65; Clinton Humphrey 66;
Eliz. 38; Eliz. Ellen 143;
Elizabeth 66; Elizabeth
Ellen 141; Ella J. 66; Ella
R. 66; Evan 65, 66; Evan H.
65, 66; Harry 66; Harry I.
65, 115; Leon C. 65, 66;
Leon Clinton 66; Lizzie 66;
Louisa 144; Lucie Isobel
65, 66; Mary Rebecca 66;
Mrs. Elizabeth 37; Mrs.
Elizabeth K. (Montgomery)
140; Mrs. Mary Rebecca 37
Robert Anson 65, 66; Sarah
65; Sergeant Major Clinton
H. 66

GASSAWAY
Col. Nicholas 43

GATCHELL
Elizabeth 1, 5

GEASKINS
Samuel 160, 161; Sarah Jane
160, 161, 163

GEBHART
Karen Ruth 81; Thomas Pyle
80, 81; George Bertha 28

GIBBS
Joseph C. 60; Mildred
Redgrave 57, 60; Gibson
Mary D. 15

GILLISPIE
Agnes 69-71; Archibald 68;
Capt. John 67; Elizabeth
68, 69, 101; Emma 73;
Francina 102, 106; Francina
[Barr] 101; Franklin 70,
71, 73; George 20, 71, 73;
George, Jr. 70 71; Hannah
69-71; Henry 73; Jennie 73;
John 73; John F. 73;
Margaret 70, 71; Martha 69;
Mary 69-73; Mary A. 73;
Rebecca 20, 69; Rev. George
20, 68, 69; Rev. John 20,
67, 68; Rev. Patrick 68;
Robert 68; Samuel 69, 71;
Susan 73; Thomas 70, 71;
Thomas J. 71, 73; William
73

GILLISPY
Elizabeth 103; James 103;
Mary 103

GILLMORE
Gates 156

GILMORE
Leon W. 146, 148;

GILMORE (Cont'd).
    Marian 146-148; Marion
    Clarabel 11; Wanda
    Maria 11
GILPIN
    Justice Joseph 78
GOLDEN
    Harry S. 2
GONSEN
    Ann 86, 110, 113
GOTTIER
    Ann Elizabeth 76; Ann
    Elizabeth Booth 78;
    Elizabeth 76, 77; Elizabeth
    Booth 76; Francis 76, 78;
    Francis Booth 76-78;
    Francis, Sr. 76, 77; John
    76, 78; Margaret 76, 77;
    Margaret Ferguson 76;
    Rebecca 77
GRAHAM
    Rev. Robert 65
GRANT
    Fanny Gallaher 62; Rev.
    Thomas 93
GRAY
    Amanda R. 54; Carried 47
GREENFIELD
    Mrs. Lydia Harvey 82
GREER
    Ann 48; Bernard L. 47, 48;
    Bernard Lewis, Jr. 48
GREGG
    Annie Lizzie 115
GRIER
    Capt. James 124, 127
GRIFFITH
    Benjamin 101; Catherine
    102; Daniel 101; Elizabeth
    101; Francina 102, 106;
    Francina [Barr] 101;
    Griffith 10; Hannah 10;
    James 98, 99, 101, 102,
    106; John 99, 101, 102;
    Joseph 102; Martha 101;
    Mary Jones 99-101; Rachel
    101, 102; Rebecca 102;
    Rev. Abel 101; Rev.
    Benjamin 101; Samuel 101;
    Sarah 101; Susan 102;
    William 101
GROVES
    Hiram D. 32; Mary E. 30,
    32; Mary Elizabeth 31, 33
GUEST
    Elizabeth 40; Elizabeth A.
    39; Nathan 39, 40
GULLETT
    Sarah Elizabeth 135, 136
GUM
    Lavina Curtis 34, 35;
    Manaen 34, 35
HADLEY
    Sarah 146, 148
HALL
    Ada 57; Ada V. 54; Cecily
    18; Col. David 119; Rachel
    86
HAMILTON
    Eleanor 92; Esther 1, 4;
    George F. 65; Hans 1, 4;
    James 1, 4; Mary 1, 4;
HAMM
    Araminta 139
HAMMOND
    Mary 26-28; Sophia Cosden
    Aldridge 77, 78
HANSON
    Arnold 81; Dorothy May
    79-82; Dorothy Shonk 81,
    82; Ella N. 79, 80; Ella
    Pyle 80, 81; Emma Spencer
    80, 81; George F. 79, 80;
    George Foote 81; Helen C.
    80; Ida Jane 80, 81; James
    F. 81; James L. 79, 80;
    Joseph C. 80-82; Laurence
    131; Margaret 131; Martha
    M. 80; Martha Miller 79;
    Robert Lewis 81; Ruth Anna
    81; Susan C. 80, 81;
    William H. 80; William
    Henry 79, 80, 82

177

HARDMAN
Margaret 109, 111, 113
HARLAN
Eliz. Clark 154; George Fisler 47; Sarah Amelia 63
HARRINGTON
Henry Ridgely 34; Henry Ridgely [Jr.?] 34; Marion Lee 2-3; Mrs. H. Ridegley 35; Ruthanna Wilson 34; Tillie; W. 36; Virginia Walter 34
HARRIS
James 128
HARVEY
Andrew 82-84, 107, 113; Andrew, Sr. 82; Daniel 83, 84; Do. 82; Elizabeth 82; Francina 83; Francis 83; Hannah 83; Henry 83; Jane 83; John 83; Lydia 82, 83, 108; Lydia McCauley 113; Mary 83; Rachel 82, 83; Susan 83; Susannah 82, 83 William 82, 83
HASLETT
Col. 36, 138
HATHAWAY
Mary 134
HAYES
Anna B. 16; Hannah A. 85, 86; Hannah Amelia 84, 85; Henry M. 84; Henry Moore 84-86; John 84-86; Maria Rudulph 85; Stephen 84, 86
HAYS
Elizabeth 159; John 159; Rachel 14; Sarah 159
HEAD
Esther 109
HEALEY
Capt. Nathaniel 147
HENDRICKSON
Milicent 63; Millicent 120, 122
HENKEL
Anthony J. 89; Barbara Teeter 87; Dr. Solomon 86, 88, 89; Hannah Rebecca 87; Helea Anna Maria 87; Helen 89; Helena 87, 88; Jacob 87, 89; Johannes 90; Justus 89; Maria Elizabeth 89; Mary Elizabeth 87; Naomi 87; Paul 87; Rev. Ambrose 86, 88; Rev. Andrew 87, 88; Rev. Anthony Jacob 88; Rev. Charles 87, 88; Rev. David 87; Rev. Paul 86, 88, 89 Sabina 87; Samuel Godfrey 87; Seorim 87, 88; Silon Amos 87; Simeon Socrates 87; Siram Peter 87; Solomon D. 89; Solomon David 86, 87; Solon Paul Charles 87; Sylvanus 87
HERDMAN
Beckley 92; Eleanor 92; Garretson 92; James Lawrence 92; Jefferson 92 John 92; Marelee Kennard 140; William 92
HERSEY
Rachel 102
HEVERIN
David 129; Elizabeth 128; Jane 129
HEYL
Catherine 87; Veronica 86
HIGGINS
Julia 145; Julia Blake 144
HITCHENS
Charles 56; Herbert 56; Robert 56
HOBSON
Elizabeth 128, 129; John 128
HODGSON
Elizabeth Gillespie 72; James 72; Jas. 70; Robert H. 72
HODSON
John 128

HOFFMAN
 Anna Katherine 90
HOKE
 Catherine 86
HOLCOMBE
 Adelaide Romaine 94;
 Alexander H. 93; Alexander
 H., 1st 95; Alexander Henry
 94; Alexander Henry, 2d 94
 Alexander Henry, III 94;
 Ann 95; Charles O. 93;
 Charles Ogden 94, 95;
 Elizabeth Tazewell 94;
 Ellen Ann 94; Emley 93, 95;
 Emley Mentz 94; Freddie 94
 Hannah 93; Honorable
 William 95; Isaac Skillman
 94; J. E. 93; John E. 93,
 95; John Emley 94; Malvina
 Kay 94; Malvina Marguerite
 94; Margaret Louise 94;
 Mary 94; Mary S. 94; Mary
 S. 93; Mary Skillman 93;
 Richard 93, 95; Sussanah
 (Black Girl) 94; Theodore
 93, 94; W. H. 93; William
 94; William Emley 94; Wm.
 93
HOLLINGSWORTH
 Col. Henry 47; Zebulon 47
HOLLOWAY
 Jane 27; John Laws 26-28;
 John Laws, III 27; John
 Laws, Jr. 26; William D. 27
HOLME
 Abel 100; Enoch 100;
 Jacques 100; John 100;
 Thomas 100
HOLMES
 George 42
HOLTON
 Dorothy C. 57; Wm. 57
HOLTZ
 Elizabeth 90
HOOPES
 Anna Elizabeth 96; Brinton
 B. 96; Elwood 96; James 96;
 James A. 96; Lewissa L. 96;
 Mary Anna 96; Ruth 156;
 Tounsend 96; Tousand 96
HOPKINS
 Johns 111, 112; Mr. 110,
 111
HOSSINGER
 Joseph 143; Louisa 141;
 Mary Louisa 143
HOWARD
 Rev. David 144
HOWELL
 Millicent 77; Stanley Vail
 80
HUGGINS
 Mary 141, 143
HUGHES
 Elisha 1, 3, 5; Mary 1, 5
 Thomas 1, 3, 5
HULL
 Bertha 97; Daniel B. 97;
 Elsie M. 97; Homer W. 97;
 James H. 97; John A. 97;
 John H. 97; John Henry 97;
 Phoebe E. 97; Winifred I.
 97
HUNT
 Rev. Holloway W. 93
HUSE
 Mary 91
HYLAND
 Capt. John 139; Col. John
 120; Col. Stephen 139, 140;
 John 120; Martha Rebecca
 139; Mary 120; Millicent
 16, 17, 139; Nicholas 120,
 139; Stephen 139
INGRAHAM
 Joseph 148; William   149
ISRAEL
 Jane P.   25
JACKSON
 Mr. 146; Sarah Jones 7
JACOBUSSEN
 Abraham 98; Antje 98; Brant
 98; David 98; Elizabeth 98;
 Eva 98; Jacobus 98;

Maritje 98; Nickase 98
JACQUETTE
 Capt. Peter 119
JANNEY
 Abel 109, 111; Hannah 110,
 111; Joseph 109, 111
JARMON
 Clara 153; Clara S. 157;
 Mildred M. 153, 156, 157;
 Mrs. Rees 159; Norma Jane
 80, 153, 156, 157; Rees S.
 153, 155, 157; Rees Staton
 154
JARVIS
 Francis 5; Mary Eliza 5
JEMES
 Lt. John 9; Sarah Whatley 9
JENKINS
 Catherine 100; David 100
 Enoch 100; John 100;
 Nathaniel 100; Rev. Thomas
 100; Samuel 100
JENNINGS
 Sarah 151, 152
JERVIS
 Francis 1-3; Marie Beard 1,
 3; Mary Eliza 1, 2, 4
JOHNSON
 Alexander 42, 43; Ann 134;
 Ann Gonsen 110; Churchman
 19; Edward 19; Elizabeth
 2, 3, 42; George T. 141;
 Hannah 20, 69, 70; James
 18, 19; Joseph 19; Margaret
 Chamberlain 18; Margaretta
 19; William 56
JOHNSTON
 Ada Carolyn 141, 142;
 George T. 142; Harriett
 Louisa Steel 142; Mary
 Alice 143; Mary Alive
 Elizabeth 142
JONES
 Abel 100; Daniel 100; David
 100; Edith 103; Elizabeth
 103; Enoch 100; Esther 100;
 Esther Morgan 100; George
 103; Hannah 103, 109, 111;
 Henry Harrison 103; James
 100, 102; James, Jr. 100;
 Joanna 98; John 100; John
 Wesley 103; Joseph
 Chamberlain; 103; Joshua
 100; M., Sr., 99; Mary 99,
 102, 103; Morgan 98-100;
 Morgan, second 98, 99;
 Morgan, Sr., 99; Mr. 144;
 Mrs. Agnes 37; Philip 103;
 Philip Reybold 103; Phillip
 Hicks 103; Rev. David 100;
 Rev. John 35; Robert T.
 144; Sarah 98; Sarah Ann
 103; Susanna 100, 102;
 Susannah 100; Thomas
 103, 155, 158; Wm. 103;
 Zachariah 98-100
JOSEPH
 Patience P. 97
JUDKINS
 Anna 91
KAVANAGH
 Morgan Joseph, Jr. 130
KEAN
 John 76, 77; Margaret
 Gottier 76
KEEN
 Hannah Holme 100
KELLEY
 Elizabeth Brinton 5;
 Margaret 33-35; Rebecca 35;
 Thomas 35
KENNARD
 Elbert E. 140; Rev. Edward
 84
KENNEDY
 Catherine DeHaven 37; James
 36, 38; Mary 38; Matilda 38
KENNON
 Wm. 71
KENON
 Albert 74; Elizabeth 74;
 Jane 74; Margaret 74;

KENON (Cont'd).
    Newell 74; Wm. 74
KENTMURE
    Viscount 68
KERR
    Alice Grace 20; Andrew 20,
    70, 71, 73, 142, 143;
    Andrew B. 73; Andrew W. 73;
    Charlotte 143 George 72;
    George G. 73; George
    Gillispie 20; Hannah 73;
    Hannah Gillispie 73; James
    B. 73; Mary 71, 143; Mr.
    18; Samuel 143; Samuel T.
    73
KEYES
    Clarence 56
KILPATRICK
    Margaret 50
KINCAID
    Jane 160, 162
KING
    Henrietta 93; Major 93
KINTY
    Mary 139
KIP
    Hendrick Hendricksen, Jr.
    98; Maritje 98;
KIRKPATRICK
    Margaret 47
KIRKWOOD
    Adaline 71, 72; Ann 71, 72;
    Capt. Joseph 70, 72;
    Catherine 71, 72; Elizabeth
    71, 72, 74; Hannah Maria
    71, 72; Josephine 71, 72;
    Major Robert 72; Margaret
    71, 72; Margaret Gillispie;
    Mary 72; Robert 72; Sarah
    71, 72
KITE
    Mary 86
KNAUSS
    Donald Lee 29; George E.
    28, 29; Oscar 28, 29;
    George Edwin, Jr. 29

KNIGHT
    Florence McKean 118
KOLLOCK
    Dr. H.G.M. 74, 75
LANDINGHAM
    Rev. J. L. 65
LARGE
    Joseph 71
LAROE
    Lydia 138; Pieter 138
LASHER
    Mary 30-32
LATTA
    Rev. J. 25
LAWS
    Porter 23
LAWSON
    Margaret 1, 3, 4
LEAK
    Abraham 104; Alice 104;
    Anna 104; Charles 103, 104;
    Charles Wesley 104; Delena
    104; Edward 104; Edward
    Elmer 104; Emma 104;
    Franklin 104; George Robert
    104; Helen 104; Henrietta
    104; Henry 104; Henry Clay
    104; Howard 103; Ida May
    104, 145; John 104; Mary
    Walker 104; Mathilda 104
    Robert 104; Roberta 104
    Sarah 104; Thomas 104;
    Violette 104; Walter 104;
    Wilmer Ernest 104
LEE
    Elizabeth M. 151, 152
LEETER
    Mary 90
LESLIE
    Charles Robert 112; Eliza
    112; Lydia Baker 112; Patty
    112; Thomas 112
LEWDEN
    Margaret   131-134
LEWIS
    Dr. Dorsey W. 23, 24;

Henry 79; James 79, 82;
Kate Adel 2; M. 23
LINDSAY
Elizabeth Craig 105; James
105
LINDSEY
Agnes E. 106
LINSEY
Agnes C. 102; Agnes
Elizabeth 99; Francina B. 99
George 102; George
Washington 99; James 101,
102, 106; James Sr., 99
LOCKWOOD
Margaret 23, 24; Martha E.
23, 24
LOINAN
John 155, 156, 158
LOMAX
Ernst S. 156
LONG
Charles 18
LORT
Joshua 111
LOWRY
John 47, 63; Mary 49, 63
LUNT
Nora M.(or W.) 15
LUTTON
Alice 28; Mary 103, 104
LYNAM
Adelaide S. 155, 157, 158;
Albert Jefferson 155, 156;
Alice 28; Andrew 156, 159;
Ann 155, 156, 158; Ann C.156
Anna Mary 159; Annie Maria
155, 157, 158; Catharina
156; Catherina 156;
Catherine 155; Christina
Ann 156; David 156; Eleanor
R. 155, 156; Eleanor
Robinson 156; Eliza 153,
156; Elizabeth McFarland
153; Ellen 159; Ellen B.
153; Ellen Bird 154, 155,
157; Hannah 155, 156; Jacob
155, 156; James K. 155,
156; John 155, 156, 158,
159; John R. 153, 155-159;
Joseph 155, 156, 158;
Lavina 155, 158; Lewis 156,
158; Lewis Harry 156;
Louetta 155, 157, 158; Mary
R. 155, 157, 158; Osburn W.
155, 157, 158; Penrose Bull
156; Robert F. 155, 156,
158; Robert Vincent 156;
Sarah E. 155, 156, 158;
Sarah McK. 155, 156 158;
Thomas 155, 156, 158, 159;
Thomas James 155, 156;
Thomas P. 155, 156, 158;
William Robinson 155, 156
MacDONOUGH
Maj. Thomas 140
MACE
Mrs. Guy 134
MACKEY
Catharine Evans 105; Hugh
Boyle 105; John Stewart
105; Mary 105, 106; Rachel
F. 65; Thomas 105, 106;
Thomas Lanson 105
MAHAFFEY
Elizabeth 141
MALCOLM
George Sawyer 133; George
Weir 133; John Baxter 133;
Kirk 133; Weir 133; Manlove
44; William 43
MANSFIELD
Piner 130
MANUEL
Amanda 28
MARTIN
Laura 54, 57; Rebecca 154
MARTINDELL
Phineas 9; Sarah Ann 6-9
MAST
Henry 79
MATHER
Rev. Cotton 69
MATHIAS
Annie P. 65

MATHIS
  Salome 30
MAULER
  Mary 118
MAXWELL
  Annie Bryan 16; Richard R. 15, 16
MAY
  Jane 112, 113
McALLEN
  Annie 27; Jane Eldred 26, 28; William A. 26, 27; Wm. A. 28
McALLISTER
  Edward 158
McAVANEY
  Catharine Ann 81; Philip 79-81; Philip D. 79, 81; Philip, Jr., 81; Sarah Elizabeth 80, 81; Warren 79, 81
McCALLA
  Mary 74
McCALLISTER
  Edward 155
McCARNS
  Anna 155
McCAULEY
  Absolom 107; Ann 106, 107; Barton Brook 85; Daniel 1, 82, 86, 106-108, 112, 113; Eliza Ann 107; Elizabeth 86, 106-108, 114; Elizabeth Baker 108; Elsie R. 8, 84, 114; Elsie Roberts 85, 120, 121; Ethlyn Gallaher 120; Frances 107, 108; Frances Baker 112; Hannah Louise 109 Harriet Selena 109; Harrieta 107; Helen Amanda 109; Henry 106-108; Henry Baker 108; James 1, 85, 86, 107-109, 114, 120, 121; James Albert 85; James J. 84, 86, 114, 120; James Jacob 109, 120, 121; Jethro 107, 108; John 86, 106-109, 114; John Hayes 84, 85; John Hayes, Jr. 85; John Henry 108; Lydia 82, 107; Lydia Ann 107; Lydia Moriah 108; Margaret Franc. 107; Mary Hughes 108; Mary Jane 107; Milicent Price 121; Milicent Roberts Price 108, 109; Nancy 106; Newell (Charles) 85; Rachel 109; Sarah 109
McCLELLAN
  Capt. Hugh 119
McCLISTER
  Mary 114
McCONAHEY
  Dr. James 71
McCORKLE
  Rev. 65
McCRACKEN
  Anna B. 17; Annie B. 16; James Henry 16; John 17; Kate Rebecka 16; Martha 17; Martha T. 17; Ruth Ann 7; Thomas C. 16; W. S. 16; Wm. S. 16
McCRERY
  Florence E. 84; Florence S. 85
McCULLOUGH
  Samuel 1
McCUNE
  James 71
McDONALD
  Alexander [II] 114; Alexander [I] 114; Ambrose 114; Charles 114; Elizabeth 114; George Weir 132; James W. 114; James Watkins 114; John 114; Louesa 114; Margaret 114; Mary 114; Mary McClister 114; Sally 114
McDONOUGH
  Commodore 140; Dr. Major Thomas 138;

McDONOUGH (Cont'd).
  James 138; Lydia 138
McDOWELL
  Jame 1; Julia 118
McFARLIN
  Eliza 155, 159
McINTIRE
  Ann 117; Anna 117; John
  117; John [II] 117; Lewis
  117; Mary 117; Mary [II]
  117; Robert 117; Sarah 117;
  Thomas 117; William 117
McKAIG
  Anna M. 62
McKEAN
  Allen 119; Andrew 118; Anna
  117; Benjamin 118; James
  118; Jane 118; John 118;
  Julia Miller 117; Martha
  118; Rebecca 118; Robert
  118; Samuel 118; Thomas
  117; William 117, 118;
  William Thomas 117
McKEE
  Ann 91
McKINLEY
  Caroline Amanda 116; Daniel
  116; Daniel Spencer 116;
  Harriet Ann Erwin 116; John
  116; Mary Jane 116; Samuel
  Erwin 116
McMULLIN
  James 10
McNIELL
  Mr. 18
McNIGHT
  Martha 61, 86
McSLATER
  Nell 56
McSORLEY
  Rev. F.C. 135
MEDILL
  Margaret; 155; Mary Jane 155
MENDENHALL
  Lydia 39, 40
MENTZ
  Malvina Kay 94;

Mifa Malvina Kay 93
MEREDITH
  Joseph 55, 57; Rebecca 58;
  Rebecca Ruth 54, 55
METEER
  Anna Chamberlain 18
  Mr. 18
METZ
  Malvina Kay 95
MILES
  Rebecca 101; Richard 101;
  Sarah 101
MILLER
  Anna Maria 87; Audrey E.
  102 Dr. Warrick 25, 26;
  Elizabeth Booth Aldridge
  77, 78; Francina 102;
  George 102; George P. 106;
  Helen W. 102; J. E. 26;
  James Edwin 25, 26; James
  Linsey 102; Jane 102; John
  102, 105, 106; John B. 102,
  106; Julia 117; Rebecca
  86, 89; Rev. M.(or N.) H.
  15; William 102; William C.
  25, 26
MINSTER
  John Davis 142; John Henry
  141, 144; William Davis 142
MITCHELL
  Abby F. 44, 45; Ellen H.
  155, 157; Emilie L. 156,
  157; Hannah R. 157; Henry
  C. 155, 157; Howard 153;
  Irwin J. 157, 158; J.
  Howard 153, 155, 157, 158
  Jane 32; Joseph 156, 157;
  Lizzie A. 153, 157; Lydia
  157; Martha Ann 44; Martha
  Elizabeth 160, 162; Martha
  W. 156, 157; Oliver 44, 45;
  Paul 156; Paul W. 157;
  Sarah 146, 148; Vincent 71
MOFFITT
  Thomas 16
MONTGOMERY
  Anna M. 116; Anna Margaret

MONTGOMERY (Cont'd).
115; Elizabeth K. 65, 115;
Emily 115; George Q. 115;
George Quincy 115; John
Henry 115; Mary Smith 115;
Robert 115, 138, 140; Sarah
Ann Smith 138; Saresa J.
115, 116; William Smith 115
MOODY
Elizabeth 1-4; James 1, 4;
John 1, 4; Mr. 160; William 1
MOOR
Bengaman 124; Bengaman [II] 124; Hester Ann 125; John M. 124; Mary 124, 125; Susan 124
MOORE
Alicia 78; Betsy 156; Elizabeth 51; Jean 47, 49; Rev. Francis H. 23; Sara 146, 148; Sara C. 147; Sarah 51; Thomas 51, 52
MORE
Hannah A. 86
MORGAN
Abel 100; Enoch 100; Enoch, Jr. 100; Jane 99, 100; Jane Rhydderch 99, 101; Rachel 100; Rev. Abel 100; Rev. Enoch 100; Rev. Samuel 100; Samuel 100; Thomas 100
MORRIS
Margaret 1, 4; Robert 37
MOTE
Henry 155; Mary Elden 141
MUHLENBERG
Rev. Peter 88
MURPHY
Dr. 25; Martha B. 26; Mary 134
MURRAY
Catherine 20, 68; Mable 156; Mary 131-133
NAGLEY
Elizabeth 88

NEILL
Col. 57; John S.M. 74
NESBIT
Wayne 156
NEWELL
Ann 124, 126; Henry 124, 126; John 123, 126
NEWTON
Rev. Dr. Richard 25
NORRIS
John K. 127
Mr. 124, 127
Richard 127
NORTONI
Mr. 134
OSBORNE
Susan 131, 134
OSWALD
Elizabeth Gillispie 68; James 68
PALMER
Emilie Wilson 147; Martha 18
PARKE
Francis G. 71; Mary Kerr 73
PARSONS
Martha 131, 133, 134
PASSAMORE
Jane Jones 100
PATRIDGE
Edith Emogene 117, 118
PATTEN
Francina 99; James 99, 101; Mary 98; William James 99
PATTER
Martha 91
PATTON
Francina 99; James 99, 102; Mary F. 98; Mary Francina 99; William James 99
PAXON
Mary 150
PAYNTER
Ann 18
PEEBLES
Jane 32

PENNINGTON
    Estelle 23
PENNOCK
    Minerva 149, 150; Mr. 149;
    Pusey 155; Sarah Wollaston
    150
PERKINS
    Mrs. Angie 12
PERRY
    Elizabeth 120; Joshua 102
PETERSON
    Mary 155
PHILLIPS
    Maggy 117
PIE
    Katherine 144
PIERSON
    Edward 156; Edward Coates,
    Jr. 153
PILLING
    Ann 151, 152; Isabel 2-5;
    John 2, 3, 5
PLUCK
    Mary Madeline 36, 37, 139
PLUMLY
    James 51, 52; Mary 52
POTTER
    General 126; Mary 126
POWELL
    John 101
PRALL
    John S. 93; Miss Sarah   93
PRATT
    Henry 128
PREDUX
    Mary 26
PREESON
    Wm. 111
PRETTYMAN
    Rev. C. W. 65
PRICE
    Andrew 120; Anna Margaret
    44; Bertha E. 151, 152;
    Caleb Newbold 144, 145;
    Clayton Vail 145; Edward T.
    122; Eliza Ann 122; Eliza
    Jane 122; Elizer A. 122;
    Frances Louise 130;
    George W. 122; Helen Maria
    122; Henry 120; Hugh F. 122
    Hugh T. 121, 122; Hyland
    120; Isaac 128, 131; J.
    Fletcher 23; Jacob 21, 63,
    120-122; John 120, 121;
    John Fletcher 144, 145;
    John H. 122; John Hyland
    122; John T. 121; Joseph
    120; Joseph Wilson 122;
    Josephine 122; Julian
    Cantwell Newbold 145;
    Lilbun 122; Lilbune 122;
    Margaret 120; Mary 120;
    Mary Louise 145; Mary
    Matilda 122; Milicent R.
    108, 114; Milicent Roberts
    120; Millicent 120;
    Millicent Hendrickson 122;
    Millicent R. 21, 86, 122;
    Millicent Roberts 121; Rev.
    65; Richard 120; Sarah
    Amelia 122; Teresa 63;
    Teresa T. 21; Teresha 120;
    Teresha Terry 120, 121;
    Tereshe T. 122; Toroshea
    121; Vachal T. 121; Vachel
    T. 122; Webster 160, 162;
    William 120, 122; William I
    119; William II 120;
    William III 120, 121;
    Wilmer 162, 163
PRITCHARD
    Mary 64; Susanne 64; Tobias
    64
PROBASCO
    Sarah Ann 93
PROUD
    Benjamin Franklin 2, 3;
    Isabel Wright 3
PROVOST
    Mary Jeanne 71-75
PURNER
    Edna 24; Emma 23
PYLE
    Ann 154; David 18;

PYLE (Cont'd).
    Ruth 81; Ruth A. 79, 80
QUARLL
    Lydia 82
QUICK
    Mary 93
QUIGG
    Rev. Howard T. 135
RAUB
    Mary 74
RAWLINGS
    Caroline 123; Elizabeth A. 123; Frederick 123; Mary Caroline 123; Richard Cromwell 123; Robert B. 123
RAWSON
    Ryron G. 47
RAY
    Lettice 18
REDGRAVE
    Agnes 60; Agnes Frazier 57, 59; Alzayda Frazier 57, 60; Isaac 60; James 60; Mary Elizabeth 60; Mildred 60 Mrs. John W. 57, 60
REED
    Albert 75; Albert Chrisman 125; Ann 125, 126; C.W. 125; Charles E. 75, 125-126 Charles Evans 126; Charles W. 75, 127; Chas. W. 74; Clayton M. 125; Elias S. 127; Elias Sipple 125; Elizabeth 124, 126; Elizabeth Ann 125, 126; Emma G. 75; Emma Gillespie 125; George G. 75; George Gillespie Evans 125; Henrietta 124; Henry Newell 28, 125, 127; Henry Newell, Jr. 125, 126; Henry Newell, Sr. 126; Isaack 124, 126; James 124-127; James H. 124, 127; James Henry 125, 126; James [II] 124; James H. 125; Jehu 124-127; Jehu P. 127; Joel 124, 126;
John 124, 125; Margaret 124, 125; Margarett 126; Margarett Sipple 126; Marietta 125; Mary 124, 126; Rev. 92; Thomas 124-126
REEVES
    Joseph Naglee 144, 145;
REYNOLDS
    Andrew C. 127-129; Andrew Cole 129-131; Andrew Cole, [Jr.] 130; Ann 127, 128; Ann M. 128-130; Annie Elmer Ellsworth 44, 45, 130; Elizabeth 127, 129; Helen 56; Irvin 56; James 127, 129, 131 James Price 130; James Ulysses Grant 130, 131; James [II] 127; James, Jr. 128; James, Sr. 128; John 128-131; Letisha 127, 129; Lillie May Price 130; Margaret Campbell 56; Martha 127-129; Mary A. 128; Mary Frances 130; Permelia 127-129; Sarah 127-129; Sarah C. 128, 129; Sarah Cathrin 128; Sarah P. 129; Sarah [II] 127; William 127, 129; William P. 128, 129; William Perrigrine 128; William R.127
RHYDDERCH
    Jane 101
RICE
    Albert D. 75
RICHARDS
    Alexander F. 157; Anna 157; Anna Mary 155, 157; Betty 158; Emilie M. 153, 157; Francis 158; Francis H. 155, 157; Grace 155, 157, 158; Irene 155, 157; John F. 153, 155, 157; John T. 158; John W. 155, 157; Laura Ann 158; Mildred B. 156, 157

RICHARDSON
    Sarah 41
RICKEY
    Ada Mae 65
RIDDELL
    Anna E. 38
ROBERTS
    Addie 128; Norma St. Clair 139; Sarah Griffith 101; Zacharias 139
ROBERTSON
    Fleta 2, 3
ROBESON
    Capt. 92
ROBINSON
    Eleanor 155, 156, 158; Vincent 155;
ROE
    Abner 60; Lucinda 60
ROGERS
    Helene Hester 130; Roseanna Jane 26, 27
ROMAINE
    Edward C. 95; Furman 95; James 95; Lydia 138; Margaret Keen 94, 95;
RONEY
    Sara 144; Sara Erma 141
ROOT
    Aurelia 11
ROTHWELL
    Mary 155
ROWLAND
    Isaac 53; John F. 53; Sarah 53
RUDULPH
    Tobias 85
RUNNELS
    Rev. Wm. 93
RUPERT
    Gideon 87
RUPP
    Ruth Elizabeth 47, 48
RUSKIN
    John 112
RUSTON
    Job 110

SABIN
    Rachel 146, 148
SALISBURY
    Ann Elizabeth 84
SAPPINGTON
    Dr. John R. 46; Rebecca N. 46
SAWYER
    Allen 134; Ann 132-134; Anna 133, 134; Annie 133; Caroline E. 132; Carrie 134; Carrie Eva 132, 133; Catherine 132; Charlie 133, 134; Clarentine 132; Ebby 131, 132; Edward R. 132 Elizabeth 132; Ella 134; Emma 134; Etta 133, 134; Eva 133, 134; Fannie 134; Fannie Isabella 133; G. M. 132, 134; George 132, 134; George B. 131; George M. 132, 134; George Meggeson 131; Hannah 132; Harriett 132; Helen 133, 134; Henrietta 132, 134; Jane 132, 134; James 133; Joseph 131-134; Joseph A. 133, 134; L. M. 134; Lewden 131, 132, 134; Lewden M. 132; Lewden McCullah 133, 134; Lizzie 134; Louis 134; Margaret 132-134; Mary 133, 134; Ogden 134; Rebecca 131, 132, 134; Rebecca Hanson Meggison 133; Robert 131, 132, 134; Robert Meggison 133, 134; Thomas 131-133; Thomas L. 132; Thomas Lewden 131, 132, 134; Virginia 132, 134; William 133, 134; William M. 132
SAXTON
    John 124, 127
SCARBOROUGH
    John 82

SCHOENBORN
    Edward Martin 34
SCHULTZ
    Elizabeth 160
SCHUNDER
    Catherine Ann 79, 81
SCOTT
    David 160, 162; Edith 162;
    Elizabeth 162; Ella 162;
    Frank 160, 162; James 118;
    Jane 118; Sarah 118;
    Virginia 32, 33
SCRIBNER
    Elizabeth 134
SCRIVEN
    Elizabeth 91
SEAVER
    Joseph 72
SEEMANS
    Lambert 128
SERGEANT
    Alling 149; Sarah 149
SHANER
    Emma Catherine 136
SHANNON
    Elizabeth 1
SHARP
    Margaret 102; Ruth 141,
    143; Sarah 63
SHARPLESS
    Amos 40; Suzanna 17
SHARPLEY
    Hannah 52, 54; Reverend
    John 84; William   52
SHAVER
    Elizabeth 87
SHIELDS
    Hannah Jones 100
SHIPLEY
    Agnes 75; Mary 75; Samuel
    R. 74, 75
SHONK
    Dorothy 79, 82
SHORT
    Clarence 2
SIDDELL
    Hen. 111; John 111

SIEBERT
    Sarah 90
SIMCO
    William 16
SIMONS
    Margaret 90
SIMPERS
    Richard 1
SIMPSON
    W. Percy 72
SIMSON
    Alexander 67, 68; Archibald
    67; Lilias 20, 67; Patrick
    67; Rev Andrew 20, 67, 68;
    Rev. Patrick 20, 67, 68;
    Richard 67; William 67
SIPPLE
    Ann 124, 125, 127; Ann
    Newell 124; Elias 124-126;
    Elijah 124; Elijah B. 126;
    Henry Newell 124; Lydia
    124, 127; Margaret 124;
    Margarett 126, 127; Tabitha
    124, 127; Waitman 124, 126
SKILLMAN
    Dora 136; John 93; Joseph
    135; Margaret 135, 136;
    Mary 93
SKINNER
    Elmer Elliott 11
SLACK
    Jon Wilson 145; Norman 145
    Sarah E. Wilson 145
SLEEPER
    Mary 91
SMITH
    Adah Clayton Frazer 136;
    Adam 137; Alice Anita 135,
    136; Annie 56; Annie
    Garrett 138; Annie H. 54
    Daniel 58; Dorothy 57
    Eliza Jane 137; Elizabeth
    137; Elsie Sylvester 135,
    136; Ethel 136; George 137;
    George I. 38, 137, 138,
    140; Isabella 59, 137;
    Jacob Reed 138;

SMITH (Cont'd).
James P. 137, 138; James
Reed 137; John 137; John D.
138; Mary 137; Mary Bomann
37, 38; Mary DeHaven 37;
Mary J. 38; Mary Jane 137;
Mary Louise 140; Mary
Rebecca 65; Samuel D. 137;
Samuel DeHaven, MD 138;
Sarah 91; Sarah A. 116;
Sarah Ann 38, 115, 137,
140; Sylvester 135, 136;
Thomas Alexander 135, 136;
Thomas Alexander, Jr. 135,
136; William 137, 140;
William H. 36, 137;
Winfield Scott 137
SMOOT
John 42
SNOW
Martha Ann 139
SOMES
Stella 32
SOMLINSON
Mr. 109
SPENCER
Myrtle 79, 81
SPICER
Mabel E. 44
SPRINGER
Ann 155, 156; Joseph 51,
52; Joseph W. 51; Levi 51;
Rebecka 51; Robert L. A.
51; Robert Louis 51; Sarah
51, 52; Thomas Evans 51-52
STAATS
J. Z. 44; Josephine 45;
Julia L. 45; Lena V. 45;
Martha V. 45
STAFFORD
Anna Mary 157; Edythe 157;
Frank 155, 157; Kathryn
157; Robert 156, 157
STANCAST
Joanna 155, 156
STAYTON
Jennie 56

STEAL
Allen 143
STEEL
Ada Laura 141, 144; Adeline
141; Allen 141, 142; Anna
Lucinda 141, 142; Caroline
141, 142; Catherine 144;
Dean 144; Dr. Walter H.
144; Elizabeth Garrett 141,
142; Emma 144; George W.
141, 142; Harriet Louisa
141; Harriett 143; Harriett
Louisa 141, 142; Hudson
141, 142; J. Edwin 15;
James 141-143; James H.
144; James, Jr. 143; John
Edwin 141, 142; John Thomas
141-143; Joseph 63; Justin
144; Louise 144; Lucinda
141, 142; Margaret Jean 63;
Mary Elizabeth 141, 142;
Mary Huggins 141, 142; Paul
144; Phoebe 144; Robert
143; Robert E. 141, 142;
Robert H. 142; Robert
Huggins 141; Rosalie 144;
Ruth 141; Thomas 141-143;
Walter 144; William T. 141,
142
STEELE
Jos. 69; Joseph 47; Mary
131, 134
STELZER
Laura 44
STEPHENS
John 134; John A. 134;
Virginia 131, 134; Virginia
C. 133; Will 134
STERLING
Adelaide 157; Alfred 157;
Alfred C. 153, 155, 159;
Anna Mary 157; Clara A.
153; Clara Adelaide 156
STERN
Louisa D. 115
STEVENS
Elizabeth 134; Virginia 134

STEVENS (Cont'd).
  Will 134
STEVENSON
  Arthur 134
STEWART
  Elis 67; Thomas 51
STIDHAM
  David 155; Mary 155, 158;
  Mary Jane 155
STIEGAL
  Alice 90; Baron Wm. 90;
  David 90; Jacob 90
STIMSON
  Comfort 41
STIRLING
  Alfred C. 154; Anna M. 153;
  Clara 154; Clara A. 153
STITLER
  William 28
STONE
  Eliza M. 132
STONER
  Sarah 90
STRAUGHAN
  Elizabeth 41-43; Henrietta
  42; Samuel   42
STREET
  Anna Gertrude 28, 29;
  Blanche Elma 28, 29; Ella
  Naomi 28, 29; James B. 28,
  29; Mary Irene 28, 29
STRICKLAND
  Cordelia 50; Cordelia
  Rayborn 48; Cordellia
  Rayburn 48; David Taylor
  48, 49; Isabella 48, 49;
  Margaret E. 48, 49; Martha
  A. 49; Martha Ann 63; Mary
  Scott 48, 49; Robert E. 49;
  Robert Evans 48; Sarah
  Rebecca 48, 49; William P.
  50; William Price 47-49;
  Wm. Price 63
STUDDIFORD
  Rev. Dr. P. A. 93; Rev. P.
  O. 93

SWITHENBANK
  Jeoffrey 79; Sarah
  Elizabeth 79, 80, 82
TAGGART
  Michael J. 44
TAYLOR
  George 40; Hannah 40
  Mary 40; Wm. S. 93
TERRY
  Eli 22; John F. 74
  Teresha 120; Theresa   121
THACKEY
  Hannah 110
THOMAS
  Eleanor 101; Elizabeth 6-8;
  Elizabeth Halwadt 7; Esther
  Jones 100; Joanna 98;
  Richard L. 7
THOMPSON
  Amy 149; Ezra 6, 7; Judge
  Daniel 7; Lizzie 6; Nancy
  33; Rev. H.S. 144; Rev.
  Howard E. 15; William 33,
  35
THOMSON
  George 161; Grace Ricketts
  18-20; Hannah (Evans) 18;
  Isabella 161; Jane 160,
  161; John 161; Rebecca 161;
  Samuel Young 161; Stephen
  161; William 160, 161;
  William Wilson 161, 162
THORPE
  John 79
TITUS
  Lewis J. 93-95
TOWNSEND
  John 79; Marian 124, 126
TRUMMAN
  Eliza ann 12; Hester 12;
  John 12
TUFT
  Ruth Ann 141
TURNER
  Mary 134; W. E. 74
TYSON
  Susan 83

UPDYKE
    Elizabeth 6
VAIL
    Agnes Pennington 144; Alice
    Smith 145; Clara Cantwell
    144; Martha C. 145; Martha
    Cantwell 145; Samuel C.
    144; Samuel Cleaver 145
VAN ARSDALE
    Abraham 135, 136; Elsy 135
VANCE
    Mary 138
VANSANT
    John C. 115
VEALE
    John D. 41
VINSINGER
    Cordelia R. 49; H. E. 47;
    Henry 47, 49, 50; Henry E.
    47, 49; Margaret S. 47;
    Margaret Strickland 48;
    Ruth Elizabeth 47, 49
    William T. 47
WAGGONER
    Elizabeth 83; John 83
WALKER
    David Washington 161;
    Elizabeth Ann 161; George
    160; Jerome 161; Josiah
    161; Margaret 160-162; Mary
    104; Mary Ann 161; Rebecca
    Jane 160, 161; Rebecca
    Wilson 161; Samuel Cochran
    161; William Wilson 161
WALLACE
    George 70; Joseph 69, 70;
    Mary Gillispie 70
WALMSLEY
    Robert 1
WALTER
    Ebe 34, 35; Tillie Crumpton
    34, 35; Tillie Crumpton 34
WARD
    Caleb 17; Christopher 91;
    Joseph 17; Justice John 78;
    Lucy Ann 17; Maria Louisa 16

WARDER
    Rachael 109
WARRALL
    Mary Ruth 65
WARREN
    Louisa 141
WATKINS
    Ada Carolyn 143; John III
    43; Joseph 43; Margaret
    41, 43; Roger Pennington
    141
WATKINSON
    Carrie Keen 95
WATSON
    Rev. Dr. B. 93
WEAVER
    James 28
WEBDELL
    C. W. 32
WEEKS
    Leon 11
WELLS
    Mary Melissa 146, 148;
    Melissa M. 11; Samuel B. 11
WEST
    Dr. Henry 71
WESTLAKE
    Evelyn 160-163; Willie 160
    Willis 161
WHATLEY
    Sarah 9
WHITE
    David 16; Miles, Jr. 113;
    Mrs. John R. 134; Rev. R.
    25
WHITEHALL
    Christine 18, 19
WILKINS
    Mary Caroline Rawlings 123
WILKINSON
    Carver 65; Hannah 67;
    Hannah J. 65; Hannah Jane
    65
WILLIAMS
    Anna 104; Benoni 5; Caleb
    B. 126; Colonel 119;

WILLIAMS
Dr. Thomas 23; Elizabeth 5;
Fannie Clayton 24;
Francis Clayton 24; Mary
Clayton 23, 24; Nathaniel
J. 23, 24; Rachel Jones 100

WILMER
Adelaide 160, 162, 163;
Isabelle 160; Samuel G.
160, 162, 163; William G.
161; William J. 160, 163

WILSON
Alexander 145; Alice 146,
147; Annie E. 146; Annie
Elizabeth 145; Annie Luisa
162; Barton 162; David
146-148, 161; David H. 147;
Edward 146, 148; Edward S.
147; Edwards S., Jr. 147;
Elija J. 145; Eliza 147;
Eliza R. 147; Elizabeth
160, 161; Emilie P. 147;
Ethel C. 147; George 123,
126, 160, 161; Hadley 147;
Henry P. 146-148; Henry
Palmer 147; Henry Palmer,
Jr. 147; James 14; James
Herbert 147; Jane 160-163;
Jessie 23; John 104; John
H. 145; John T. 104, 145,
146; Jonathan 146; Joseph
M. 147; Josiah 146; Lewis
160, 161; Lydia 146-148;
Lydia P. 147; Margaret
124, 161; Margaret Ann 161;
Margarett 126; Marian
Gilmore 147; Martha 93,
122, 161; Mary 160-162;
Mary Ann 160; Mary Evans
105; Patience 123, 126;
Phoebe H. 146, 147; Pusey
146, 147; Rebecca 160-162;
Samuel 160, 161; Samuel
Young 160, 161; Sara C.
147; Sarah 146; Sarah Etta
145; Sarah Hadley 147;
Sarah J. 146;
Sarah Mitchell 147; Stephen
146-148; Wilbur 162; Wilbur
Thomas 162; Willam 160;
Willard Springer 162;
William 160-162; William R.
145, 146; William V. 122

WILSON
Rachel 160

WINGATE
Edward 76-78; Margaret
76-78; Rebecca 76, 78

WITT
Isabella 148; John 148, 149

WOLLASTON
Amy 150; Ann 150; Charles
T. 157; Eleanor M. 157;
Eliza 149, 150; Ellen H.
157; Ellwood 150; Emma 150;
Frank 150; Hannah 149, 151;
Howard 155, 157; Isaac 150;
J. Paul 157; Jeremiah 149-
151; Joshua 150; Mary 149,
150; Minerva 150; Pusey
150; Sarah 149, 150; Thomas
149, 150; William P. 151

WOOD
Caroline 123; Enos 152;
Enos E. 151, 152; Enos
Evert 151; Francina 151
Herbert Franklin 151, 152;
John K. 151, 152; John
Nelson 152; John Wesley
151, 152; Martha Jane 151;
Mary Ann 151, 152; Mary
Flinn 152; Mary Pilling
152; Sarah Elizabeth 151;
Sylvester Alexander 152;
Willard F. 152; Willard
Franklin 151, 152

WOODWARD
Abner 154; Anna M. 153;
Anna Mary 154, 155, 157;
Ellen B. 153; Ellen Bird
Lynam 157; Emilie 155;
Emilie M. 153, 157, 158;
James 154; John 154; John
B. 159;

WOODWARD (Cont'd).
John H. 153, 155, 157, 158;
Lissie A. 153; Lizzie A.
153, 155, 157, 158;
Sarah 18, 19
WOOLSEY
Capt. George 8; Ephraim 8;
George 8; Jeremiah 8; Mary
Ann 6-8
WORTHINGTON
Ann 41
WRIGHT
Caroline Clark 2; Catherine
Brown 2; Elizabeth 102;
Elizabeth Kelley 2, 3;
Ernest Brinton 2-4; Ernest
Brinton, III 3; Ernest
Brinton, Jr. 2, 3; Eugenia
Isabel 3; Gypsy Prior 3;
Hugh Beard 2; J. P. 41;
John Pilling 2, 3, 42;
Martha 3; Mary Eliza 2, 3;
Mary Jervis 2; Norris
Nathan 2, 3; Samuel 5;
Samuel B. 2; Samuel Benoni
1, 2, 4, 5; Samuel John
2, 4, 5; Samuel John, II 3
YARDLEY
Joyce 110
YEATMAN
Marshall P. 40
YOUNG
Catherine Taylor 93; Dr. J.
Watson 93; Elizabeth 160;
Jane 160; Margaret 160;
Mrs. Henry S. 46; Rebecca
160, 162; Samuel 160, 162;
Sarah 160
ZEIGLER
Rev. 84
ZINBERG
Emma J. Armstrong 38
ZIRKLE
Lewis M. 87

www.ingramcontent.com/pod-product-compliance
Lightning Source LLC
Chambersburg PA
CBHW050633160426
43194CB00010B/1651